M[illegible]ial Money Mindset

If you want the fruits you need the roots

NEIL DOIG

Warning

Do not read this book unless you want a new way of living.

Forget the old concept of retirement and saving for the future.

This is Millennial Money Mindset

**This book contains financial guidance and not specific financial advice.
Please do your own research and seek professional financial advice if at all uncertain**

Investments can go down as well as up.

This book aims to empower you to make your own decisions about your money

Millennial Money Mindset:

If you want the Fruits you need the Roots

First published by Money Tipps 2019

MONEY TIPPS
Tax - Investments - Property - Pensions - Savings

Chapters

Prologue

'No snowflake ever falls in the wrong place'

Zen proverb

At 18, I lost half my savings investing in the internet bubble.

The dotcom boom had reached its pinnacle. My money vanished overnight, evaporating into thin air like the air from a bubble as the fragile skin is popped. Saving money from my wages each week working a summer job selling ice cream at a theme park. Back then, people were making their fortune speculating on internet companies. Buying any share of a company with a .com was easy money. Or so I was told.

In 1999 the potential of the internet was unbelievable. No one knew exactly what the internet did or could envision companies it would create like a Facebook, an Amazon or even what a Google was. Memories of the dot com boom returned looking at Bitcoin and blockchain technology today. Buying internet shares was my first taste of a bubble.

The internet shares I bought was called 'lastminute.com'. The irony of the name was lost on me then, along with the craze for Tamagotchi toys, the Y2K bug and the fashion for wearing double denim. I was going to be rich. What could go wrong?

Something was not going to plan. Turning on the evening news and seeing a sea of red from trading floors across the world beamed into our television sets. The words of the stock market crash popping in my ears from the reporters' lips. The pain in my gut was unbearable. Nobody told me this could happen. Thinking about how many hours I had worked for that money and how many ice creams I had to sell. The agony was too much to stomach.

Promising myself this would not happen again, I decided to understand and learn from this experience. I wanted to find a money coach, someone who has been successful in creating money previously. Taking the remaining money from my summer job and making another investment, turning out to be the greatest investment to date of my life. I bought a copy of 'Rich Dad Poor Dad' by Robert Kiyosaki costing £6.99. This book cost the equivalent of 90 minutes working that summer job. The upside of this investment was unlimited because it changed my money mindset. This book gave me patience, courage and a belief in better. I did what the book advised me to do and wrote down my dream goal. Setting my future goals by taking a piece of paper and wrote

'I will be a millionaire by age 35.'

All I needed to do was to think and I will grow rich and money will simply be manifested into my life. How wrong I was.....

Imagine putting on a pair of glasses. You can now see further than you ever thought possible. You can now see the leaves on the trees and can appreciate the smiles from people far in the distance as well as a car speeding towards you. This change of perspective gives you knowledge on how to act and live your life for the better.

Few modern inventions spread as fast as the thirteen-century invention of the eyeglass technology. The invention of eyeglasses has improved millions of people's lives throughout the years. The internet invention has spread even quicker. It now means we have instant access to thousands of books and millions of ideas. The ability to watch videos summarising writers from centuries ago on YouTube and access lectures from people who have long since died. Social Media allows communication with thousands (if not millions) of people. The internet has provided an abundance of goods and services at a click of a button.

The internet has changed everything! Today, the internet has created a flat world. It is just as easy to communicate with a publishing house in India as it is in Islington. Today knowledge is the number one factor of production, relegating capital, land, and labour. Today many jobs only need a laptop, the internet and a smartphone.

This book learns from the past, places you in the present and guides you to your ideal future. There are more opportunities than ever before. It is a wonderful time to be alive.

Today information alone is not enough. It is the skilful application of the right information at the right time that can change your life by giving you the knowledge to act

This book uses the latest cutting-edge research and knowledge on how to invest and grow your money. The best current business practises that wealth managers, financial advisers or financial planners use and can charge £100,000s to their clients for the same knowledge.

This book aims to change your perspective on how you see the world, giving you the technology to see further than you could ever imagine. This book aims to change your money mindset to reduce your stress and worry you may have with your money.

<u>Why should I read this book?</u>

Today everyone is an investor. If you have a pound coin in your back pocket then you are an investor. Choosing not to invest that money, will mean inflation (explained later) is eroding your hard earn money. Since 2018 if you started a job then you will be automatically enrolled into a pension and will now be in charge of how that is managed. In 2015 a change in the law (called pension freedom) means that you will have to understand and decide how to withdraw your pension when you stop working.

This is all massive change.

Looking after your money has moved from a want to a need.

You did not need to know about investing a couple of decades ago. You could manage perfectly well without paying any attention to the stock market and the over-excited reporters on your television as markets collapse and the world economy melts down as we saw in 2008.

Pensions were managed by your employer. You worked, and at the end of your career, you would get paid an income out of the percentage of your salary.

You could buy an affordable house by paying your mortgage payments every month from your job. At the end of the 25 years, you would own that house outright. You could save everything else in cash and feel alright about it as interest rates were around 5%. The current bank of England base rate is 0.1%.

Today everyone in one way or the other is now responsible for either keeping an eye on or creating a portfolio of investments that will pay for living costs and expenses for when you stop working. Today investing cannot be just a niche activity or a hobby for other people. It must be something that everyone is at least a little bit engaged with. Today investing is a life skill that everyone needs to know, as important as driving or cooking. Not understanding these life skills will make your life harder, more expensive and you will have less freedom and control over your life.

It is the individual (that means you) that needs to understand about our money. You make the decisions that will impact every aspect of yours and our family's future lives. This is great news. Today you are in charge!

Money worries have topped a poll of the biggest stress triggers in the UK amongst 25-40---year-olds according to a study that was conducted by the brand Garnier Pure Active in 2018 by Consultant Dr Justine Kluk.

In the UK 11.5 million people have less than £100 in savings or investments (Money Advice Service). Pension poverty is fast approaching where people don't have enough money for when they stop working. Today with rising living costs and housing a government pension will not be enough to live on in 2046 when the oldest Millennial collects their first state pension payment.

My mission is simple: To help people make better decisions with their money so you can live happier lives. This book guides you along the investment journey starting with a pound coin in your back pocket up to the lifestyle you choose. I also added a chapter that I was almost too scared to include that discusses the environmental crisis we are all facing.

This aims to do three things 1) Save you money from your pocket, 2) Save you time in your day and 3) Reduce stress and worry from your life

You will save £1000s from paying both expensive financial advice fees and fund manager fees. It will also help you avoid making costly investing errors to become financial independent quicker by following simple investing principles.

These advice fees may include initial fees, ongoing fees and even exit fees. It is industry standard to charge you an ongoing fee, which erodes your money every year investing (which could be decades), so it is the financial advisers who are becoming rich from your investments, not you.

You can also save £1000s from paying fund manager fees, who actively managing your money. You are paying for their expensive city offices, expensive suits, and expensive city lunches. Today it has never been cheaper or easier to invest your own money without having to pay for someone else manage your money.

1) This book aims to reduce your stress and worry around money. Giving you better peace of mind and improving your financial wellbeing. Meaning you can focus on the more important things in life, your friends, family or simply having more 'me' time.
   Money worries top a poll as the biggest stress and worry amongst 25-40-year-olds. This book aims to solve this problem by guiding you to a more secure future. Knowing where you are

heading financially will reduce your stress and worry. Being in control of your money and your future is a big relief.

2) This book aims to free up your time by automating your savings and investing. Time is our greatest asset. Freeing up your day so you can spend your time doing the things you love, maybe that is more time with friends, your family or simply having more 'me' time to do the things your love. The wealth of information from the internet has created a poverty of attention. We no longer have time to make the best decisions for a better life.

The strategies in this book use simple and proven investing strategies based on the latest evidence-based research, which is used by the best financial planners that will save you money from your pocket, time in your day and reduce stress from your life.

This book aims to accelerate your progress of becoming financially independent, where your investments can pay you're an income so you can choose how to spend your day. You can work for joy rather than necessity.

The youngest millennial retirement age is 68 for their state pension. Imagine stopping having to go to work and doing what you love 10 years or even 20 years earlier. Having 10 extra years to choose how to spend your time. Having enough money to choose to do the things you love. Where every day you wake up feels like the weekend, where you get to choose how to spend your time. Maybe that is spending time with your friends, family or deciding to do something more meaningful with your life than your current 9-5 job.

I aim to make financial guidance, simple, fun, and achievable.

You're never too old to set another goal or dream a new dream.

C.S Lewis (1898 –1963)

I want to give you this knowledge to help you make better decisions with your money. Today knowledge is the technology, it's the means of production. I want to give you money mindset so you can live a happier life free from stress and worry.

New discoveries, new technologies and new markets all spell opportunities. It's a wonderful time to be alive. We will be living longer than other generations. It will soon be common for people to live until they are 100.
There has never been a better time to set a new goal or dream a new dream.

'What's taking place is a revolution. Everything as you know it will change in the coming years. The nature of work, lifestyle and wealth is changing faster than ever before.

Daniel Priestly (Entrepreneurial Revolution 2018)

<u>Why Millennials have been screwed over.</u>

Today the Millennial can feel like a modern-day Cinderella. We seem to be working so hard and not getting any returns. The Baby Boomers keep telling us to stop buying lattes and eating avocado on toast and we will easily be able to afford a house.

The Boomers had the benefit of affordable housing, the golden age of pensions, no student debt and high-interest rates meant there was much more incentive to save and barely had to worry about investing for the future. Today it is so different.

Who Are the Millennials?

Millennials (also known as the snowflake generation) grew up at the turn of the century and were born between 1980 to 1996. The oldest Millennial will be 40 in the year 2020. Millennials do things very differently from their parents. In 1968 if you bumped into a 30-year-old, there was a 56% chance that person was married, had children, and had a full-time job and a mortgage. Today if you bumped into a 30-year-old today, there is less than a 23% that person would have all the same trademarks.

Baby Boomers (who were born just after world war two between 1946 and 1964) are now turning 70. The Boomers make up a lot of the population and because of this everything this generation touched became massively disrupted. From baby food in the 1950s to consumer electrics in 1980s and personal computers in the 1990s. Health care and medical expenses are set to rocket in the coming years as 70-year-olds require a greater amount of care as this generation age.

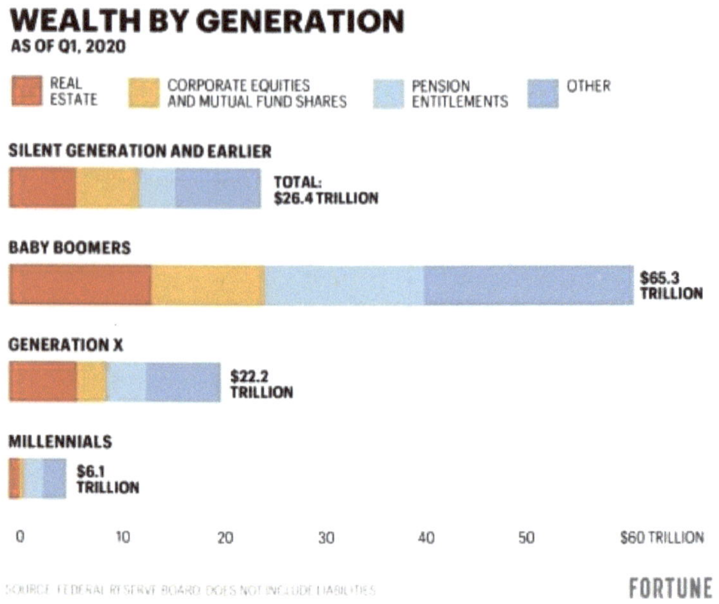

Why Millennials have been screwed over

Being among the majority has often meant that Boomers have got their way in terms of government policy due to the higher number of voters.

Average house prices in London have risen 518% since 1994 from £79,000 for an average house up to a price of £488,000 today (according to the office of national statistics). As a Millennial, it is hard not to feel envious of previous generations who take for granted of people having a home they can afford compared to average wages.

There have been three ways that millennials have been hard done by in terms of UK government policy.

1) Printing more money (£375 billion was created out of thin air called quantitative easing), 2) low-interest rates, 3) the help to buy scheme

1) Money printing means more money in the system and for every pound that is printed existing money is now valued less due to inflation. So the spending power of the pound coin in your back pocket has also been reduced. It also means that assets prices like the house you wanted to buy have now skyrocketed out of control. Excessive lending to people who could afford a house previously (subprime loans) caused the last financial crash. Rather than restricting lending to people who had been irresponsible, the government decided to print £375 billion of new money (quantitative easing).
2) Low-Interest rates mean getting next to no returns on any savings in the bank. The Bank of England (who are employed by the government) decided to reduce interest rates as an emergency measure and has now kept them low for 12 years. It was previously normal to get 5% interest rates so you would get £5 for every £100 you kept in the bank a year.

3) The Help to Buy scheme increased the demand for housing fuelling the already crazy London house prices. This scheme that was disguised to help first-time buyers actually hurt millennials The help to buy scheme was introduced in 2013 by the government to prop up a falling housing market and win an election to keep power. The Help to Buy (should be called the Help to Sell as it helps house buildings) means the government gives loans up to 40% of the property price to people in London. This increases a person's affordability who would not have the money to buy previously (there are echoes of the 2008 subprime financial crisis here).

   These schemes increased the supply of credit fuelling the house prices rising especially in London and other global cities.

   This has been great news for the Boomer generation all who own their properties and love to check their houses price rises on estate agents websites but bad news for Millennials who find buying their own home further and further out of reach.

The Good News

With Millennials now beginning to dominate the workforce, our habits, traits, and choices are now heavily influencing the market.

Today Millennials have never had so many options and choices available. Walk into any supermarket and decide from a vast selection of ingredients to make one of the hundreds of different recipes from around the world. Technology today is incredible, and it gives us access that our parents could only dream of. We can hail a taxi in minutes from our phones, we can order almost anything online, and have it delivered anywhere in the world the next day. You can fly around the world staying in someone's home for a fraction of the price and effort it would have cost a generation ago.

All this is massive change. However, the biggest change to our lives is today we now must manage our own money for our future self.

Imagine looking into a mirror and seeing the 60-year-old version of ourselves. Would your reflection be happy with the decision you are making today? Decisions made today transcend decades and will impact on the kind of life we will be living as our future self. Making small daily habits that affect our future self. We are much more likely to live up to 100 years old than ever before and need to have an income to pay for these later years.

The old rules do not apply anymore. Having good money mindset means you need to think differently.

Here in this book are the secrets about money that school, your job or your parents teach you.

We need to think of ourselves as a business. Where you grow and build assets that will look after you, so you don't need to work. Knowing the difference between an asset and a liability is key. An asset puts money into your pocket and a liability takes money out of your pocket.

Money mindset is much more important than tactics or picking individual stocks. To get money mindset. Follow the three laws of money.

1) Pay yourself First
2) Diversify
3) Re:balance

The balance sheet below shows income following assets (source: Rich Dad Poor Dad). The balance sheet on the left shows someone who has assets paying them an income so they can choose what to do with their time. The Balance sheet on the right shows someone in a job with more liabilities than assets meaning more money going out of their pocket than going in.

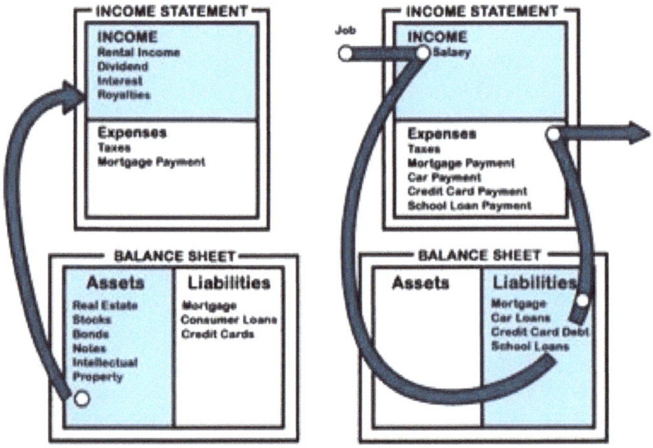

We have a choice to cling on to the old rules that are grounded more to old habits than sense or correct business practices that have been tested 1000s of time. We need to drag our finances into 2020 and craft a new approach to help our ourselves, our companies and the world to be a little better. it will not be easy it won't happen overnight so let's get started.

The only way things will change is only when you change. Work harder on yourself than on your job. Living pay check to pay check is not the solution. Doing the same thing and expecting a different result is the definition of insanity. You need to own yourself first. Become your own boss of your life.

There is a better path you can follow to achieve the lifestyle you desire. This book is the road map.

To get Millennial Money Mindset. Follow the three laws of money

1) Own yourself First
2) Diversify
3) Re:balance

Re: Balance. The Three Laws of Money Accumulation

Chapter 1

'Every generation needs a new revolution'

Thomas Jefferson (1743 – 1826)

The rules have changed.

The financial plan used to be easy: Baby Boomers would finish university debt-free, waltz into a job for life, buy an affordable house and finish the last day of work with a handshake, an engraved Rolex watch and a guaranteed income for life. Generation X's plan was also easy. It was easy buying a property because they were so cheap. Maybe buy two properties, maybe more, all at affordable prices. The astronomical rise in house prices has pulled up the property ladder making it unreachable for the next generation.

Today life is more complicated than ever. The world is moving faster, more connected and people have more complex lives than we have ever done before. Millennials need a new plan. Most importantly the risk of providing an income for your future has moved from the company and the government to the individual. This means understanding money has moved from a want to a need.

We don't just need a new plan. We need a new story. We need Millennial Money Mindset: If you want the fruits you need the roots. We need to own ourselves first.

Own yourself first

Imagine that you hold in your hand the winning lottery ticket. Money is now no object. You have enough money to live comfortably forever. How much money do you need for the rest of your life? Imagine you have more than enough money to last you the rest of your life. You don't need to stress about the ups and downs of the markets or worrying that you will one day run out of money. You could spend your life with family, friends, or doing things you love rather than stressing about money. This is what this book aims to teach you. Miss enough precious moments and you miss a lifetime. We want to work out how much is enough. This book aims to teach you everything you need to know and do with your money starting with a pound coin from your back pocket.

What is Wealth?

'Wealth is not the same as income' as said by Thomas Stanley in the *Millionaire Next Door*. Wealth is how long you can live your life without needing a job. Wealth means how many months of expenses you can live on without needing to work. You can make a good income and spend it all. Wealth is what you accumulate not what you spend.

Wealth is a result of a lifestyle of perseverance, hard work, and self- discipline, The longer your time frame the more successful your investment strategy is likely to be. This book aims to teach you how to be financially independent and retire early. Being self-reliant so that you are not dependent on anyone but yourself. This means you can choose to spend your time doing what you want to do rather than doing what you must do. This is having freedom. The choice of how to spend your time.

The investing tide has now turned and anyone who doesn't understand investing will be left not wearing any swimming trunks when the tide finally goes out. All this is a massive change.

Nowadays you need to own or be owed.

'Home life ceases to be free and beautiful as soon as it is founded on borrowing and debt'

Henrik Ibsen (1828 – 1906)

We are all tied to money, some by a loose thread and others by chains. Being in debt means you are chained to a credit card debt or a mortgage. To be financially free means you do not owe anyone anything or you are not owned by anyone. Modern-day slavery is being chained to credit card debt, receiving threatening letters demanding you work more to pay back what you owe. Today we need to own or be owned.

Changing your mindset from an employee to a business owner, where you are in charge is the first step to becoming financially independent. By becoming a business owner and building yourself a system with enough assets to replace your income over time, you want to think of yourself as the owner of your own company. You want to think of yourself as a business.

A Random Walk-Up The Escalator

Can you beat the market? Is it even possible? On today's morning commute, you may have used an escalator. Did you stand patiently on the right or walk up on the left in a hurry? It can be infuriating standing on the right holding on tight waiting for the right moment to join the other faster walkers coming up on the left-hand side of the escalator. It was proven by London Underground in 2017 that it would be 30% more efficient for everyone to stand two abreast on both the left and the right of the escalator. Like the markets, we have a choice of passively tracking the ups and down or actively take an interest. This change to the escalators was never a success because too many people continued to walk upon the left even after being shown evidence that staying still would be more efficient overall, we humans don't work like this.

We humans are not rational actors we are in fact, emotional creatures. The time when the efficient market theory ruled the day is over, the efficient market means that the price is always correct as it reflects all the available information. This book aims to prove that the efficient market hypothesis is redundant. Technology today has improved so that the average person on the street has access to techniques that fund managers use to beat the market and can use these strategies without needing to pay excessive fees. This book uses the latest cutting edge evidence-based research Today we need to be more effective with our investing. This means we need to use the market to help us achieve our own goals and objectives. Using the market more like a tool to get what we want from our lives and our purpose in life. Buying and selling when it's right for us rather right for the whole market.

Every day we are jostling with each other for position or status. We all want to out-compete and outdo each other. We, humans, love to compare ourselves with others. If we are a little better than we feel good about ourselves. We want to walk upon the left of the escalator. It feels good to overtake people, we feel like we are getting somewhere. The efficient market hypothesis states that all information in markets is reflected in current prices. The theory says that the price of a company is always correct and there is no point timing the market. However, while the market may be efficient, but we are not.

We are human beings and we are inefficient. The more we try to buy and sell to beat the market the more we pay in taxes, broker fees and the difference between the buy and sell price (the bid/offer spread). Even if we do beat the market (and it is possible using strategies in this book), then when or how do you take your money out and how much can you spend? We need to move from the efficient market and being effective with the market. We need to move away from the cold steel escalator of markets today and look to nature. If you want the fruits, you need the roots. Like growing a tree. You may not reap the rewards for many years to come. You require patience and courage and believe that there is a happier ever after. To get money mindset we must look to nature. The purpose of nature is the advancement and unfolding of life. Everyone naturally wants to be all they can be. We need to reconnect with nature from the smallest snowflake, the seed that grows into a tree, up the largest star in the sky.

A tree is like an asset. It takes many years to grow. Once grown it will provide shelter in the winter, shade in the summer and fruits to nourish our hunger. It takes patience, your courage and your belief that a small seed could grow into an asset that can give back to you.

Today we need to buy assets that will put money into our pocket. We need to build enough assets that will be able to pay us an income, so we don't need to work anymore. These assets will replace us needing to work for an income. Previous generations called this retirement. The aim is to be financially independent and retire early. This is being free. Being free because you don't have to answer to anyone. When you have enough money, you have more space and time to explore the world, to connect, to grow and to feel alive. Being financially free means you don't owe money. You are not owned by anyone. You don't owe money to a bank for a mortgage or a credit card. You own and are not owned.

You own assets that pay you money, for the rest of your life. You feel empowered and in control and less likely to have stress around money. This book aims to help you to be happier as seeking happiness is the very purpose of life.

You are an asset. An asset is something that puts money into your pocket. You can get a job or buy assets that increase in value over time. Everything comes back to demand and supply that Adam Smith made famous in his book Wealth of Nations. Every human has needs and wants, whether that want comes from the hunger in our stomach or from the desire for the latest toy, a pair of shiny shoes or a brand new gadget it makes no difference.

Let's Play a Game.

Investing is no different from any other game. Winning is much more fun than losing. Luck and skill both play their part. Having specialised knowledge is a way to increase your luck when investing. Firstly, education will increase your luck. For example, reading a book or watching an online course about investments and educating yourself is much luckier than not reading a book about investments. Secondly, know the rules of the game. Luck is when preparation meets opportunity. By understanding the rules of the game, you can help luck move in your favour.

Think of the game Monopoly, by having the experience you can take a few simple actions to improve your chances to win. This is like buying up the properties when you land on them rather than waiting until you have to pay rent to someone else after they have bought it. Investing is often not a science or an art but a practice. Like any life skill, you only learn how it works when you experience the gains and the pains that investing can bring. There are ways to become luckier. To influence your luck, you must start putting yourself in an environment where great ideas, great people and resources are flowing.

Today we are playing a different game than before. The Boomers and Generation X were born before us and like a real-life game of Monopoly have bought up all the properties. Leaving the Millennials to go around and around in a circle with just enough money to pay rent. Investing is like any other game; it has rules and ways to win quicker. Putting money into a tax-efficient wrapper like using your £20k ISA allowance or £40k annual pension allowance means your money will grow tax-free and therefore faster than if it was outside the tax shelter. Thirdly, knowing that switching from just investing in one company to investing in a fund of 50 or more companies (which can be done cheaply today) reduces by the risk you are taking by 60% due to reducing company risk*. Finally understanding asset allocation is the most powerful way to increase your luck. You can invest for your aims and objectives in life.

Different assets behave differently, and you can invest in different assets depending on what you want out of life. These four factors will help move you in the direction of travel that you would like and ultimately make you happier.

Adam Smith's Invisible Hand

Doing the right things at the right time for you is like an invisible hand on your back guiding you to your ideal future. Making little choices every day may seem insignificant at the time but they all add up over a lifetime. Every moment you take an active choice of the direction of your life it is a bit like a balancing scale that calculates your future life. This is by counting all the good and bad decisions you have made in your life. The outcome will be your future self.

Standing on the sidelines of the escalator may seem like the safest thing to do however you not only miss the opportunity cost of investing but also miss out on learning a life skill. The previous generation didn't need to understand investing because their company pensions would pay them an income for life after they stopped working. They would at least get a decent return on interest from the bank. Today we have to manage this ourselves and need to understand the seemingly complex world of investing.

You can't predict the future. It's too unpredictable and complex. Learn what you can control not what you can't control. Thrive no matter what happens in the economy. The only way things are going to change is when you change by making small choices every day between discipline and regret. Take that first step up the escalator of the market by educating yourself on how to invest effectively by reading, understanding and then applying the principles.

Farm Yard Finances

The pound coin in your back pocket is part of the same system that makes up every other business. Treat it well and it will look after you. Like nature, you can tame and train animals. Humans learnt this many years ago. Treat money like a pet. Tame the bull and bear and create a farm (discussed in chapter 9 called

Farm Yard Finances). This book will teach you about raising pension pigs, growing ISA chickens and creating cash cows and showing you how to grow money trees. To look to nature so that you produce more than you could ever consume, so that you never have to work again. Change your thinking to a business owner of your own farm, where nature provides for you effectively in spring, autumn, winter and summer rather than the cold steel escalator of the efficient market.

Imagine not needing to get up when that alarm goes off in the morning. You get the choice of whether to go to work or not. To work for joy rather than having to work for necessity. You will be free.

This book is not about investments. It is about the investor. It's about you. It's about using money as a tool to create the best life possible for you. We live in wonderful times. We have never had so much choice and opportunity to live the life we want.

From a small seed, great things can grow. If you want the fruits, you need the roots.

The three things that make a good investor are:

1) Education

2) Experience

3) Extra cash

Looking up at any mountain can seem impossible to climb, a cloud covers the peak. Not seeing the top gives you no point to aim for and you may even disbelieve that there is a peak. The summit does exist and I will show you the way.

Starting with a pound coin in your back pocket up to living the lifestyle that you choose. It is not just about money but improving your life so you can spend your time focusing on the important things, your friends, family and your experiences in life.

The first step is the three laws of money accumulation:

- Pay Yourself First
- Diversify
- Re:Balance

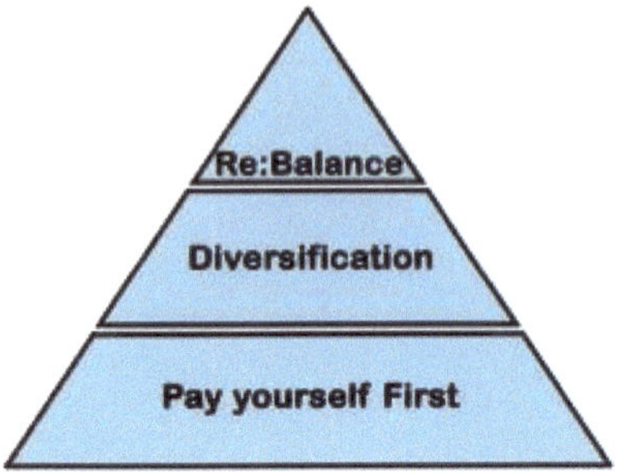

<u>Own yourself first</u>

Saving sucks! Do you ever feel you work hard all week and have nothing to show for it? Like you have more month at the end of the money rather than the other way around? Then you need to pay yourself first. Do you feel like you are going around in the payday circle of life? Without being able to save anything? Then you need to pay yourself first.

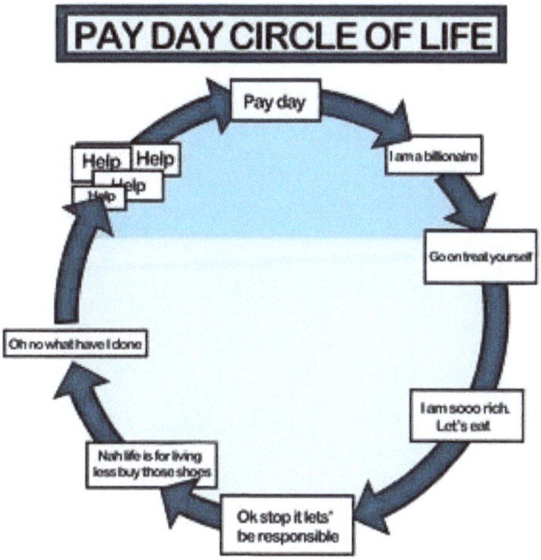

1) Pay Yourself First

Paying yourself first means paying yourself before anyone else. An investment plan that requires you to be disciplined and stick to a budget is too much work and time to manage. Learn to automate your finances to take the decision out of your hands. It's simple and obvious but many people aren't doing this. This means you can spend what you like, when you like, without the guilt of going over budget.

The problem is not how much we earn, it's how much we spend, ending up with nothing to show for it. When we spend everything we have it causes stress, worry and anxiety. We need to take responsibility.

We can make a choice and action in each moment. We need to be proactive. Take action. We need the belief that there is something better. We have a choice either to work all our lives pay check to pay check or learn to make money work for us. To create a life that will bring us the most happiness or at least be making progress towards achieving that aim. Enjoy life by owning yourself first.

Exercise

Work out at least 10% of your earnings and set up a standing order to move cash into a savings account or investment vehicle as soon as you get paid each month automatically.

Think of it like if you work 10 hours in a day then 1 hour of that time is paid directly to you as the owner of yourself.

Why are you working? You are working to give yourself and your family a better life in the future.

2) Diversify

Diversification is the only free lunch in investing. A mix of assets in your portfolio will mean that different assets complement each other and work together in synergy. It's like having an umbrella business for when it's raining and having an ice cream business for when the sun is shining.

The ice cream business is likely to do well when it's sunny and the umbrella company is more likely to sell more umbrellas when it's raining. This is known as asset allocation. Having a diversified portfolio will mean the sum of the total will be greater than the sum of all the individual parts. Different asset classes will reduce the risk you have in your portfolio whilst getting higher rewards.

Having money in land, businesses and some money in reserve give peace of mind that whatever happens in the markets, politics or economics you will be alright. This is a big relief. This means that it doesn't matter what happens in the markets. Up or down you still win. When you own the market, you will benefit from all your unique assets strengths and reduce their weaknesses.

3) Rebalance

Rebalancing is moving your assets back into the formation that best suits you. That may sound complicated and perhaps it is. It's the hardest step of the three laws of money to achieve, so isn't easy but it is simple (it is explained more in chapter 10).

Rebalancing your portfolio is like going to a party and forcing yourself to leave at the peak of the fun. Why would you leave at the height of the party? So you can catch the last train home, wake up early and do something productive that morning. You call your friend who stayed on at the party later. You find out they had a few more drinks, missed the last train and had to get a taxi home spending more money.

Rebalancing goes against our human instincts. We want to stay at the party whilst the going is good however to counteract our nature set up a system that will automatically rebalance your portfolio. By rebalancing your portfolio will give you mind space that you will benefit no matter what happens in the markets.

Don't sell out. Rebalance! The most common investing mistake is to buy on the up, with the assumption it will continue to go up and sell when it goes down on the assumption it will continue. Don't sell out, Re:Balance. Do this once a year to check that your asset allocation (or your Football Team in chapter 5) is still in line with your goals and aspirations.

To get money mindset. Follow the three laws of money.

1) Pay yourself First

2) Diversify
3) Re:balance

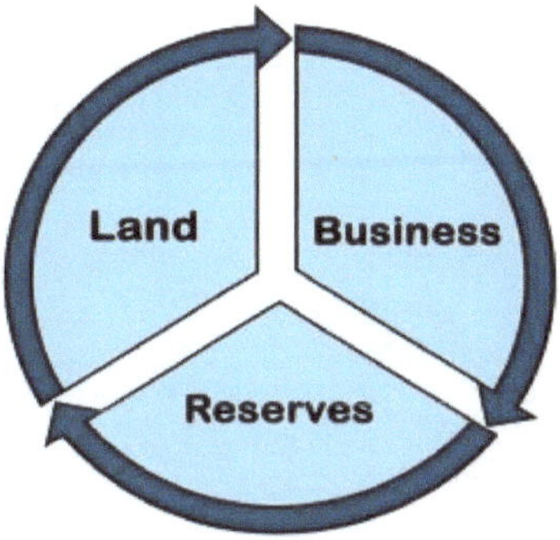

<u>Investing is a process, not an event.</u>

You hear about people getting rich instantly. Yes, this can happen, but these are the outliers and not the norm. Most of the wealth is patiently created over time. Similar to a baking recipe for bread following the steps in sequence can turn the raw materials into something completely different. If baked for too long the loaf splits and opens here and there, and these very cracks, in one way a failure of the baker's professionalism somehow catches the eye and give a better taste to our appetite. In isolation, these cracks look bad but consequence on the processes of nature enhances it and gives it the attractiveness.

When learning a new process, it may take time and you may not always be right however you can either figure it out by yourself or you can learn from someone who has successfully done it before and follow their process. You may be closer to figuring this out than you think. You may be missing a small element. Similar to yeast in bread without this small ingredient the bread will not rise as expected.

Follow the steps modelling the masters and learn from their experience. It will save you time, money and energy.

Millennial Money Mindset takes you from where you currently are to the lifestyle that you choose. The aim is to teach an automated investing system that once complete you can live off the rewards for the rest of your life. Previous generations called this retirement, building up large enough reserve of money to support you when you can no longer work.

A money tree grows from a pound coin 'seed', before you get the fruits you need the roots, your roots are your Money mindset. You must begin with the end in mind.

Like nature. Money is part of nature. Things are born, grow and then die.

The best formulas are the ones that have been tried and tested thousands if not millions of times before. We need a system that uses nature and is part of the natural system.

Investing is a natural system. The laws of supply and demand apply in markets just like that supply and demand in nature.

The three laws of money accumulation:

1) Pay yourself first
2) Diversify
3) Rebalance

If you want the fruits, you need the roots. Your roots are your money mindset. In Chapter 2.

Exercise 1)

Own yourself first.

Be responsible and proactive.

Pay yourself first. Pay 10% of your income into a separate bank account

Set up an automatic payment that transfers this money every month to another account as soon as you get paid. Meaning you don't need to think about saving every month ever again.

Chapter 2

Millennial Money Mindset

'What's your aspiration in Life?

My aspiration in life... would be.... to be happy'

Beyoncé Knowles (2013) from the album Beyoncé Knowles

Imagine a tree. A majestic money tree, and with this tree there are seeds. In life, our seeds are called our money and this money can be stored as value. Most importantly it's what's under the ground that creates what's above the ground. These roots are your money mindset and these roots affect what kind of fruits you receive in years to come. You can't have the fruits without the roots.

Everything in life is created twice, first in the mind and second in reality. Think of any house, an architect first thinks about the kind of house they want to create in their mind, they then draw up a plan on paper even before the first brick is laid. Before any tree has grown to maturity it began as a seed.

Picture the 60-year-old version of yourself in your mind. Where will you be living? How do you want to be living? What would the 60-year-old version of yourself say to you, especially about the choices and decisions that you make today? Our decisions and our actions taken today transcend decades and have a big impact on how our lives turn out in the future.

Start with the end in mind.

Reverse engineer your life, so start with the outcome you desire and then work on achieving that outcome until it happens. It's simple really when we think about it. Start with the end in mind, fast forward to the day you stop working - where do you want to be living? How do you want to be living? What do you want to be doing? When you look into the mirror, what you want to see reflecting at yourself? What is that version of yourself doing, feeling, thinking? Imagine the person you want to become, the future version of yourself. How you think, how you act, where you live. Imagine it and in your imagination, you become that person. Once you change your inner reality, then your outer reality starts to change with it. Like the mighty oak tree that grows from the humble acorn, anything of value takes time. You can't rush the oak tree out of the acorn, you can't rush the pounds coins out of the pennies, or the person you want to become from the person you are today. Patience, courage and a belief in better are required.

'The oak tree sleeps in the acorn. The chicken sleeps in an egg. The genius of your ideas that create wealth sleeps in your brain.'

Napoleon Hill (1883 –1970) Think and Grow Rich

A money tree is a business system that can survive on its own. Once fully grown this tree can provide fruit for you every harvest, they provide shelter from the rain and shade from the sun. The idea is to know how to survive and thrive in any market condition. Money is like a seed. The oak tree takes time to grow from the acorn. Anything of value takes time to grow. That's the laws of nature.

You may think money is scarce (there's not enough) or you may think money is abundant (there will always be enough). How you think and feel about money is important for your long-term wealth. What is your relationship with money? How did your parents treat and talk about money? Treat it well and look after it and it will look after you. Once you realise that money is abundant and it's only your time that is scarce then you'll understand how to build wealth.

A tree's root system is mostly underground and unseen. These roots are like your money mindset. What you think about the outside world is often reflected back to you. Your money mindset is your 'inner game', it's often unseen to the world. Your money mindset is your thoughts, habits, feeling and the relationship you have with money. Whereas your 'outer game' is the tactics, market information, how to analysis the price to the earnings of a company and technical knowledge. Your money mindset more important when building wealth. Investing can often be 80% psychology (money mindset or inner game) and 20% technical knowledge (outer game). A public victory with investing is often only won after you have a private internal victory. Money is often the crucial link between the internal and the external. If we have a poor relationship with money it may mean we have a poor relationship with our inner self. Having good money mindset is understanding yourself and what you want from life by beginning with the end in mind.

It's the thoughts that we have around money that trigger the emotion. These same emotions trigger our behaviour. Money can be a very emotive subject and this emotion you have towards money can impact the wealth you grow throughout your life. Having strong foundations (a root system) and understanding can provide a lifetime of wealth and value for you and your family. What is below is above and what is above is below. If you want the fruits, you need the roots. Let's grow a money tree.

'The outer conditions of a person's life will always be found to be harmoniously related to his inner state. A person's mind may be likened to a garden, which may be intelligently cultivated or allowed to run wild; but whether cultivated or neglected, it must, and will, bring forth. If no useful seeds are put into it, then an abundance of useless weed seeds will fall therein'

James Allen, As a man thinketh (1903)

Think of your most vivid memory of money? Maybe it was getting paid at your first job, winning on the roulette wheel or opening an overdue credit card bill and seeing a sea of red? Money isn't the most important goal. What we're after are the feelings, the emotions, we think money can create.
A money tree is a business system that can survive on its own. Once fully grown you'll enjoy fruits that it provides every harvest in autumn, shelter from the rain in winter and shade from the sun in summer.

A tree begins as a seed and once fully-grown bears fruit. You must focus on creating more seeds that you can eat and plant to re-invest. For any tree to grow it must first establish stable roots, a solid foundation and provide the food and water to grow. Your roots are your attitude to money or your money mindset.

Picture in your mind what happiness means to you. Imagine where you are. What are you doing? Perhaps you are eating and laughing with friends in your forever home, maybe you are playing with your grandson on your porch on a summer's evening, just as the sun is setting, many years from now. Or maybe you created the company from that idea you had in your mind helping solve millions of people's problem?

The purpose of nature is the advancement and unfoldment of life. Every human naturally wants to be all that we are capable of becoming. We cannot help wanting to be all that we can be, it's in our nature. At the core of our nature is an unconscious force or instinct that drives us forward. There is an inner nature of our being and a will for life that drives us forward and creates a better version of ourselves. The desire for money is the desire for a richer fuller life. The mind is like a garden, weeds will grow unless we proactively cultivate good thoughts. Our ideas are the beginning point of all fortunes. The computer, eyeglasses and the aeroplane, were all started as just an idea in someone's mind.

'You can't have the fruits without the roots'

Steven Covey (1932 – 2012)

Business is about solving meaningful problems, helping people and ultimately making the world a better place for everyone. A pound coin in your back pocket is the micro and the business world reflected in share prices is the macro world. Money is a measure that shows how much value a business has created in the world.

It's important to understand what money is. You see and touch money almost every day of your adult life. We may not use the physical pound coins in our back pocket as much these days The invention of money revolutionized human society. It meant new exchanges of giving and receiving could happen to create new relationships between people, increasing human capacity for freedom. We're now used to only seeing the numbers on a computer screen. Money could be said to be the original internet, creating a new limitless world with a sense of fairness and reciprocity.

Money is said to be three things:

1) First of all, it has a use-value. Meaning it is used for the means of exchanging one thing for another. You can use money to buy something that you want, and you gain money for something that you sell. This may be an object, or you can exchange your time for money and then you use that money to buy something.

2) Money is also a store of value. If you have £100 and keep it safe, then you will still have £100 that can be of use later (not taking into account inflation which we talk about later in the book).

3) The final property, which is the least understood but most exciting is that money is what is known as an emergence property. Once you understand this, great things can happen. Like the tiny insignificant bean that grows into the mighty stalk from Jack and the beanstalk. This is what gives money its magic. Emergence is the result of what is created from working in synergy. Synergy occurs everywhere in nature and will be discussed later in the book.

Money is Energy

Like the seed waiting patiently in the ground for the right conditions to grow, money has the potential energy to grow into great things. Energy is one of the primary forces: without it, nothing can be accomplished. It is the basic element in all forms of action. Energy is indeed life, and without it there would be no universe, no life. Energy is the working power in all achievement. Coal turns into fire, and water into heat into steam that drives the power station generating electricity to light our homes. The only permanent thing is energy as it can't be created or destroyed only changed or transformed from one state to another

Money is energy but we should not allow money to flow passively. We should cultivate our money, like a farmer tending their crops. A farmer is active and cultivates deliberately. They choose the right spot, waters, and provide nutrients. They pull up any weeds, make sure their crops get enough sunlight and harvest every year. The farmer builds fences to keep out wild animals like the bears. They know when to make changes and when to wait. Being active does not mean aggressively damming up flowing water. It means laying the groundwork to allow change to happen, taking advantage of the fact that water flows downhill and the different seasons of the year provide optimal conditions for your portfolio of assets to grow and provide when you choose.

What do we need in life?

Maslow's hierarchy of needs

Maslow talks about a hierarchy of needs. Meeting our basic needs like food, water, sex and shelter is the first foundation. After this, we possess higher needs of love and belonging finally getting to becoming self-actualisation.

He was original in his thinking as most psychologists before only studied the abnormal and the ill. Maslow looked at psychology with a different mindset, he looked at what constituted positive mental health. Looking at the process of what a person could become using their capabilities and creativity rather than what was wrong with them. This pyramid of needs shows the different stages of growth in humans. It illustrates from the bottom of the pyramid (or the roots of the tree) with basic needs moving up to the top of the pyramid, where you become who you truly are (self-actualization) This is where you get the fruits of your labour. If you want the fruits you need to first accomplish the roots

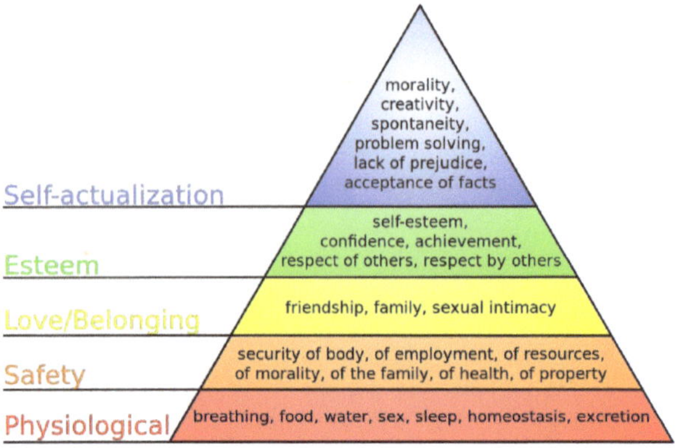

From Wikimedia Commons, the free media repository

Life is a Paradox

Humans have evolved to be constantly dissatisfied in some way. First of all, we need certainty in life, meaning meeting physiological needs, comfort and consistency. The second type of need is uncertainty which is the opposite of certainty. If we have too much certainty, we become bored and we need new challenges, surprise and adventure. Thirdly humans need to feel important or special and respected by others. Fourth, we need love and connection, approval and attraction to feel connected as a human. These two are also a paradox, because if you spend too much time gaining significant you may have trouble finding meaningful relationships. The fifth need is for fulfilment and growth giving you consistent, emotional, intellectual development. This is known as self-actualisation. The final need, where we go beyond ourselves, give, care and serve others (this final need is not included in Maslow's commonly understood diagram shown above and will be discussed in the epilogue). This final need is also a paradox of self-actualization as before you can give to others you must first give to yourself. Life is an endless serious of challenges. Once one challenge is solved another more complex challenge emerges. Suffering is an inescapable part of life. Once we understand this we can focus on progressing to the next step up the pyramid of needs towards happiness.

What is self-actualisation?

Your goal as a self-actualised person is to find yourself and live authentically according to your inner truth. We all know our truth; it's what we are at our very nature, our core, which can only be developed by looking inwards and not outwards. In other words, we are not just who we are but we can actively make ourselves better people all the time. Taoism is a Chinese philosophy and they call this the way or the Dao. Meaning the way is the path we forge continuously through our actions, choices and our everyday habits. We create a new path every moment of our lives. Happiness can be defined as the fruits of our desire and the ability to sacrifice. Happiness is knowing your purpose and making progress toward meeting this goal.

Purpose + Progress = Happiness

Self-actualization is about finding who you are and where you can make the greatest contribution. You must first meet your basic needs before you can move up the pyramid and meet the more complex needs. This is the same as investing.

Self-actualization means reaching your true potential or being who you truly are. Knowing who you truly are is the key, understanding your strengths and weaknesses and using this to your advantage by knowing where you will make the greatest contribution to others.

In addition to this sex is important to this pyramid too. Whether we admit it or not sex is a human instinct. We have evolved to reproduce. Humans evolved from living in small tribes. Our status in our group and where we are in the pecking order of our modern-day tribes can improve the chances of us having sex. Status symbols like fast cars or nice houses can make us feel like we have achieved something from our lives.

'Everything you and I do springs from two motives: the sex urge and the desire to be great. ... Both companies and people crave the feeling of importance'

Dale Carnegie, (1888 1955) *How to win friends and influence people*

Every person naturally wants to be all that they can become. We can't help wanting to be all that we can be. That is what it is to be successful in life. The desire for riches is the desire for a richer life. We have to understand ourselves and our fundamental nature as we are all as individual as a snowflake and have our gifts and genius that can contribute to the world in our own unique and special way.

Where can you make the greatest contribution?

Money is a technology

Money is just a technology invented by humans to make our lives easier. Once we understand how to use this technology everything starts to make sense. It is not money itself that we are after but the feelings, emotions that we think money can bring. We have a human tendency to compare ourself to others. We often determine our self-worth and how well we have done in life compared with others (known as the social comparison theory). We often compare ourselves with others to make us feel good. It has been said that money is the root of all evil, however, it is the love of money - or greed – that is the root of all evil. Money can be used for good or evil. It's the individual who gets to choose what they spend their money on.

Money is a technology taking us from where we currently are to where we want to be. Having a life plan helps us achieve that. We need to choose the best vehicles for our money with the time we have left (this is discussed in chapter 4).

Today certain technology has become a need for us humans. We often check our phones as the first thing that we do when we wake up and worry if we run out of battery whilst we are out. We get frustrated if we can't connect to the internet as we become disconnected to our friends and family. Money makes life easier. Money is just a tool or technology and like any tool used in the right way, it can help improve your life and move us further up the ladder on the hierarchy of needs. Technology has become so important that I have added it to my version of Maslow's Hierarchy of Needs, which includes electricity, money, transport, internet and in future perhaps blockchain will be part of our daily needs.

In the book *Be More Pirate* by Sam Conniff (see diagram) suggests that we should start off thinking about our self-actualisation or where we could make the greatest contribution even before moving up to the higher needs.

Beginning with your end goal in mind. Imagine you were happy; everything would be perfect. Where would you be? What would you be doing?

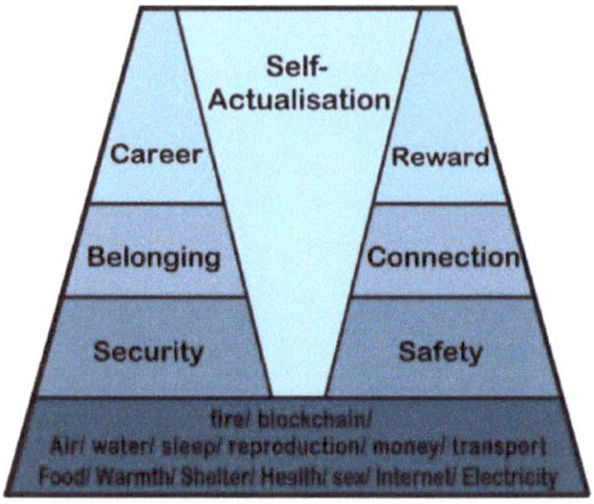

Peter Drucker said it best when he said that mathematicians are born, but everyone can learn trigonometry. He thought we are all born with an individual genius that could be used to create value for people. This value is not an art or a science, it's a practice. It's like learning a craft; we can all give a unique value to the world by having our specialist skill. You must learn how to manage yourself and your money like your own little business.

The good news is that new industries like blockchain, Artificial intelligence, the internet of things, new scientific breakthroughs, and expanding markets all spell opportunity. This is a wonderful time to be alive in. Progress is our most important product. Ask yourself: How could I do better? We must place ourselves where we can be effective and make the greatest contribution.

<u>What's the purpose of life?</u>

Is our purpose in life to seek happiness? We are all seeking something better in life. Like the motion of the earth around the sun, the motion of life is towards happiness. Just as a flower tends to lean towards the warmth of the sun and the honeybees and dragonflies head towards flowers, we humans tend to seek something better in life.

<u>Are you happy?</u>

Is happiness even a reasonable goal? Many other the great thinkers from history from Aristotle to the Dalai Lama have thought so.

Is it selfish to want happiness, as it can often seem selfish to want money? Unhappy people can be self-focused or socially withdrawn. Having money can make it easier to give to charity or have the time to help others. Having an abundance mentality means that there will always be enough, whereas a stoic philosophy means that the worst things in life can happen and you will still be alright.

> *'Today, flowers by the side of the road will only be preserved if we make a deliberate effort to preserve them. The world has become too complicated and the daily time pressures are too great and confusing.*
>
> *We often think that anything deliberate is ugly or mechanical. But art is deliberate and spontaneous. We can see the beauty of an English country garden in the spring and realise that deliberate attention can increase beauty and not destroy it.'*
>
> Edward De Bono *The Happiness Purpose*

Our feelings of contentment are strongly influenced by our tendency to compare. When we compare our current situation to our past and we feel like we are better off, we feel happy. Progress towards a meaningful goal can give us happiness. Like trying to capture an elusive butterfly, happiness is always moving, often frustratingly just out of reach. And if we are lucky enough to hold the butterfly in our hands and experience the joy of happiness, we look up and see there are bigger, more colourful, more beautiful butterflies. It is not until we realise that the butterfly was once a caterpillar and understand how far it has come how much it has changed that we can feel happiness. We may be chasing for meaning in our lives but what we are seeking is the experience of being alive, finding a purpose and experiencing the joy of being alive in each moment.

To be content in poverty is an honourable situation. If you are content, then it is not poverty at all. It's the person who craves and wants more that is poor. It doesn't matter how much someone has in the bank, how many houses they own or how much they are paid each month, if they want their neighbour's property then they are poor. If you do not value your past gains and are always hoping of gains to come or someone else's possessions, then you can never have a rich life.

Happiness is often not having what you want but wanting what you have. To appreciate and to be grateful for what you have and who you have become. Knowing what we want out of life can be the first step towards achieving happiness. Happiness comes from appreciating the progress we make with ourselves towards a meaningful goal rather than comparing ourselves with others.

Purpose + Progress = Happiness

What we are seeking is an experience of being alive. To experience happiness, we need a purpose and make progress towards it.

Having a life plan gives you a destination to head towards. Having what you want and wanting what you have.

Let's move to the investment journey.

Actions:

- Form a clear and definite picture of what you want from life. You can't create an idea unless you know what it is. Begin with the end in mind.
- Write down what happiness would mean for you.
- Where will you be?
- What will you be doing?
- Who would you become if you couldn't fail?

Chapter 3

The Hero's Journey

'There is no living thing that is not afraid when it faces danger. The true courage is in facing danger when you are afraid, and that kind of courage you have in plenty.'
L. Frank Baum, The Wonderful Wizard of Oz

Today we need a new story. The Millennial generation doesn't need just a new financial plan, we need a new financial story. The story that we are being told is no longer relevant. Stories are the way we navigate the world. They allow us to interpret the complex and contradictory signals. You can't take away someone's story until you give them a new one.

We need a story that learns from the past, places us in the present and guides our future. Every story like the Wizard of Oz follows a predictable pattern. It starts with the hero so frustrated with their current circumstances that it forces them on a journey to find a better life. Maybe you can relate?

Are you getting next to nothing from your savings due to low-interest rates? Scared to invest in the stock market after seeing the falls from the financial crisis on our television screens? Maybe you don't have the time to learn the seemingly complex world of the stock market? Perhaps you are worried about the retirement cliff edge fast approaching and the reality of people living in pension poverty.

So, what is this new story? This is often called the Hero's Journey. Like Dorothy from the Wizard of Oz waking up in a new world after the tornado, which is similar to where we are, waking up after the storm of the market crash. Every story follows a predictable pattern of moving from the known to the unknown. We, humans, move through a predictable learning cycle. We start in unconscious incompetence. Meaning that we don't know that we can't do a new task or new skill. We move to conscious incompetence. Meaning we now know we are bad at a task or skill. Then we move to conscious competence where if we focus on the task we can perform well, and finally, we reach unconscious competence. Where we no longer have to think about the task we, are still good and understand to apply the skill. This is having money mindset.

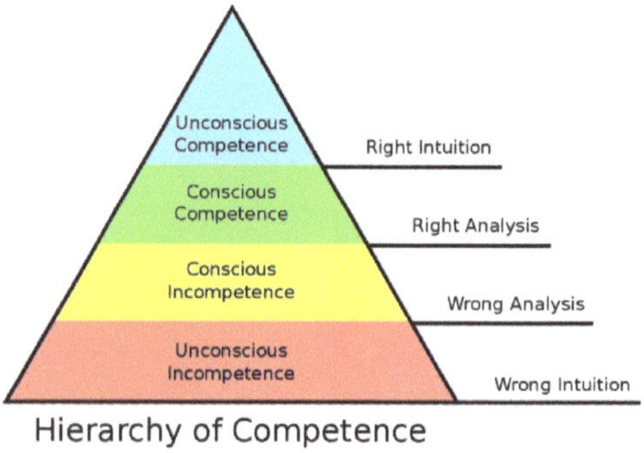

Competence Hierarchy adapted from Noel Burch by Igor Kokcharov

From Wikimedia Commons, the free media repository

The Hero's journey

Think about your favourite film from the past. The hero's journey takes the main character on an adventure from the world of the common day into a world of supernatural wonder. Fabulous forces are encountered along the way and a decisive victory is won. The hero then comes back from this mysterious adventure learning from this experience. The Wizard of Oz film starts with Dorothy lost and confused at what to do next after waking up after a tornado. She goes on an adventure to find a solution, a way to find home.

The hero - Dorothy - finds herself in the mythical land of Oz and goes on an adventure for a solution to find her goal of getting home to Kansas. This journey takes her along the yellow brick road, where she meets three mentors who help her along the way, the scarecrow who wanted a brain, the tin man who needed a heart and the lion who wanted courage.

At the start, her journey looks a long way maybe even impossible but each step along the bricks of the yellow brick road is a step closer to her goal of getting home. The first step on this Hero's Journey is often the hardest to take.

This 'hero's journey' takes you from where you currently are to where you want to be:

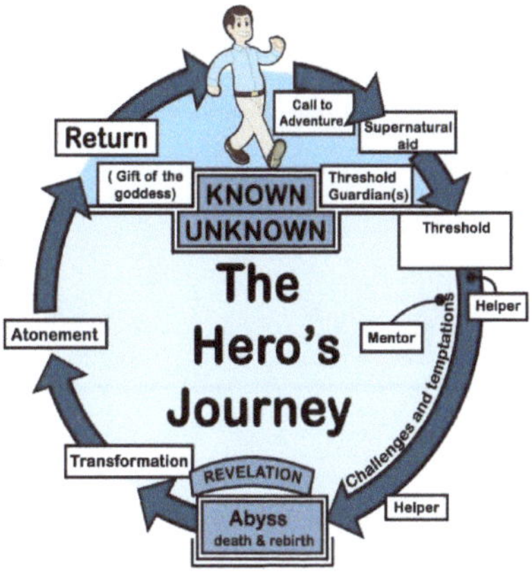

Joseph Campbell *The Hero's Journey*

<u>The Power of Three</u>

Pythagoras (the guy you studied in your maths class) taught that everything in nature was divisible into three parts and that no one could truly become wise who did not view every problem as being a triangle. He said 'Establish the triangle and the problem is two-thirds solved as all things consist of three.'

For Pythagoras, and for a lot of ancient philosophers, mathematics was the way something supernatural could be explained. Pythagoras taught that everything in the universe has a three-part structure; he also stated that every problem in the universe could be reduced diagrammatically to a triangle and the number three.

In his book *Nature's Law*, R.N Elliot explains how the number three is important in patterns of nature. There are three primary colours and blending these colours produces all other colours. This is like the scene in the Wizard of Oz where the film goes from black and white to colour as Dorothy enters the unknown Wonderful World of Oz. Paint a picture of your future life. Using the primary assets of land, business and reserves. You get to choose where you want to be. You get to draw your own adventure. Let's start your journey.

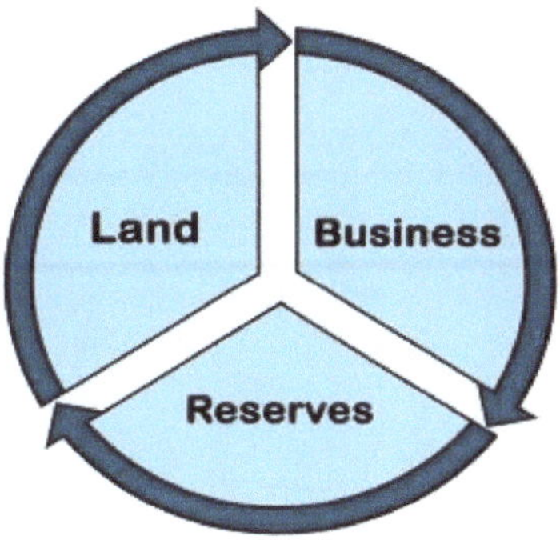

By picking up this book and getting this far then you have answered the call to adventure. You will take a step forward from the known to the unknown. There will be challenges and temptations along the journey. I will be your guide giving you financial guidance along the way. It's time for you to decide if you want to continue down the rabbit hole on your quest to find money mindset.

'This is your last chance. After this, there is no turning back. You take the blue pill—the story ends, you wake up in your bed and believe whatever you want to believe. You take the red pill—you stay in Wonderland, and I show you how deep the rabbit hole goes. Remember: all I'm offering is the truth. Nothing more.'

Morpheus (The Matrix 1999)

So, where are you going to acquire all this money? Here's the good news, you are your own asset. You can exchange your time for money. The average UK worker will earn more than 1.1 million pounds over an average 48-year career (according to a study in 2017). The more in demand your time is the more you can charge for it. Even if you are currently getting paid minimum wage pay yourself an hour of your day that you work to yourself. This may be hard and may not seem like much at first but as a snowball rolling in the snow it accumulates faster than you could ever imagine. You may think that you can't afford to pay yourself an hour of your time for each day you work but it's all the other stuff that you can't afford.

Why are you working? You are working to give yourself and your family a better life one day. To get this better life that you, not only hope for but deserve, you need to buy assets. These assets once grown will provide an income for you for the rest of your life. You will start to accumulate money on your money. Think of this like a snowball rolling in the snow. You snowball may start small but paying yourself every month your assets start to accumulate over time growing quicker and quicker the more assets you have.

'I packed my snowball very early, and if I had packed it ten years later, it would have been different than where it stands on the hill right now. So I recommend to students that if you start out a little ahead of the game. It doesn't have to be a lot, but it's so much better than starting out behind the game. And credit cards really get you behind the game.'

Warren Buffett The Snowball 2008 .

<u>What's an asset?</u>

An asset is something that puts money into your pocket and a liability is something that takes money out of your pocket. Income increases when you have assets working for you and when fewer liabilities are taking money from your pocket.

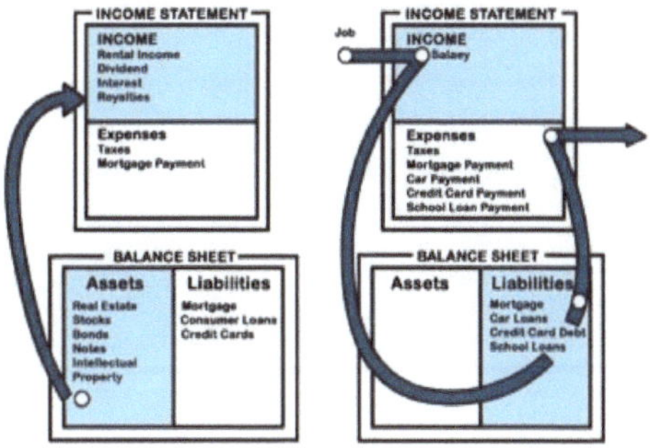

Income follows assets. The more assets you possess the more income you will have and the less income you will need from your job. Your net worth is how many assets you have in total minus any liabilities (debt from a mortgage, credit cards or loans). Think of your net worth like a small snowball. Every month you add more and more to your snowball. This snowball also grows using compound interest (explained later). The idea is to build up enough assets to pay an income for the rest of your life. In previous generations, they called this retirement. The three assets that you must understand are investing in land (Scarecrow), business (Tinman) or keep the money in reserves (The Lion)

<u>The rule of three for Money Mindset: Split your money between land business and reserves</u>

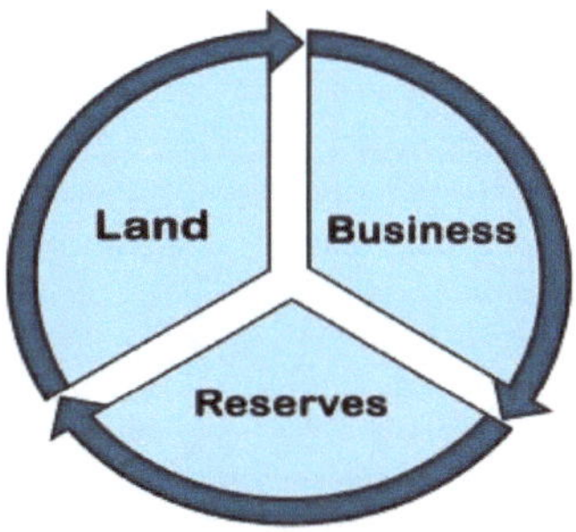

<u>We're not in Kansas anymore.</u>

In the Wizard of Oz film, Dorothy meets three mentors on her journey along the yellow brick road to get to her ideal life back in Kansas. A Scarecrow, a Tinman and a Lion. Each character has individual strengths and weaknesses and each of them working together become better than had they worked individually apart. The Scarecrow represents Land, the Tinman represents business and the Lion represents reserves (meaning cash, Bonds and insurance). Splitting your money between these three assets will mean you gain synergies that are greater than the sum of the individual parts. To get Money

Mindset means that you don't stress or worry about money. Diversifying between land, business and reserves mean that no matter what happens in the markets you will be alright.

"Let every person divide *their money* into *three parts, and invest* a *third in* land, a *third in* business *and* a *third let them keep in* reserves."

Talmud 1200 B.C

1) Land

There's no place like home

The first companion that Dorothy meets is the scarecrow (land). The scarecrow was looking for a brain. Land is simple to understand because the land is tangible. When you buy a house, you can touch the bricks that make up the house or you can feel the soil between your fingers. Land can be either residential, (where people live) or commercial, (where businesses are located.)

Everyone needs someone to live. Having your own home can give you comfort that you have somewhere secure to live and that you can create the environment you love. Shelter is one of our basic needs on the Maslow hierarchy so we as humans will always need a place to live. Owning your own place gives you freedom. It means that a landlord can't kick you out of your home at a moment's notice.

The scarecrow was looking for a brain. Land has often been said to be 'a no brainer investment'. Average house prices in London have risen 518% since 1994 from £79,000 for an average house up to a price of £488,000 today (according to the office of national statistics). However only investing in one asset is not a wise move long term. Property is still a market and can go down in price as well as up.

Many people think buying a house is always an asset and then spend a fortune paying for repairs and new kitchens not realising they have purchased a liability, meaning money flows out of their pocket rather than into their pockets.

<u>You can't eat your house.</u>

Many people think that their house will be their pension pot however you can't eat your house. Buying a house to rent out may provide an income for you however only relying on one asset class is not a smart move long term. You must use your brain.

<u>Land needs a brain.</u>

There is so much land, yet we make such poor use of it. Roughly half of England is owned by just 1% of the population. According to the book Who Owns England, which used data released through the freedom of information act in England. The author guy Shrubsole estimates that "the aristocracy and gentry still own around 30% of England" Most people remain unaware of quite how much land is owned by so few.

'Land ownership in England is astonishingly unequal, heavily concentrated in the hands of a tiny elite.' he writes, adding: 'A few thousand dukes, baronets and country squires own far more land than all of middle England put together.' Guy Shrubsole from the book who owns England continues 'The figures show that if the land were distributed evenly across England's population, each person would have just over half an acre – an area roughly half the size of Parliament Square in central London.'

The distribution of land is not shared using our brains as people are sleeping on the cold damp streets of big cities like London every night of the year, whilst many properties are left empty. Like the scarecrow from the wizard of Oz, we need to think of better solutions using our brains. (These solutions are discussed in chapter 11).

1) Business

The Tinman is the second person Dorothy meets on her hero's journey. The Tinman represents business and business needs a heart.

Buying businesses (or shares) are shares of a public company, which is listed on the stock market. By buying shares in a company you become an owner of that business and you have the right to vote on important decisions.

A business exists to provide goods or services and aims to make a profit. When buying businesses, you are not buying lines on a computer screen showing the ups and downs of the market on the evening news. What you are buying is an actual real business that is aiming to generate a profit. When we think of profit this may be associated with greed or exploitation because many of the early capitalists were only interested in what they could get away with. This cannot be denied. Nor can it be denied that profits come from exploiting the worker, the consumer or to generate profits at the expense of the environment. We can look at the profit as a source of reinvestment that can create new jobs or as a source for new ventures that may benefit workers, consumers or to create industries that may improve the environment or people's lives. Profit can be seen as a measure of the efficiency of how a company is run, as an incentive for businesses to save and invest in that business capable of raising the standard of living for all of society. These profits are given back to the shareholder who has invested in the companies in the form of dividends.

As these businesses grow, they become worth more money and people will be willing to pay more for these companies and you will gain an income or can sell the shares of a business at a profit. The Tinman doesn't have a heart and businesses are often portrayed as cold or not having a heart. Today businesses need a heart.

3) Reserves (Cash, bonds and insurance)

The final person of the three characters from the Wizard of Oz is the lion. The lion wanted courage. The lion represents reserves. Reserves can be three things 1) Cash, 2) Bonds or 3) Insurance.

Having cash in the bank for emergencies can give you tremendous peace of mind. Anything can happen in life and you will have enough cash to cover it. Perhaps your car breaks down or you lose your job. Having a minimum of £1000 or up to three months of expenses in a bank account for emergencies helps improve your money mindset. Having cash can also be great in market crashes. If share prices drop significantly you can buy these businesses at a discount, like having a winter sale. Having a large cash pile can make you feel safe, however, cash doesn't grow at a very large rate. Having money in a bank can give you interest. Interest rates are currently very low and won't generate enough returns for you to live on for the rest of your life. You can lose money over time by keeping your money in a bank due to inflation (talked about in chapter 7).

Bonds means lending money to companies or countries. With interest rates being so low the bite of the lion (of both keeping money in cash or bonds)has been removed.

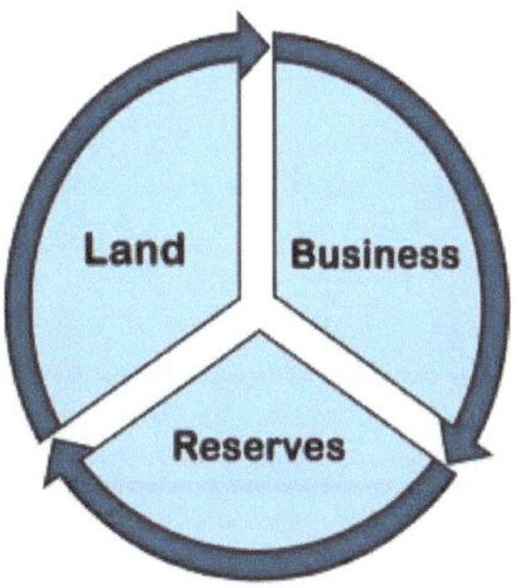

Becoming financially independent is to have enough assets that produce an income that you can live off for the rest of your life. To be self-reliant financially and not worry about when the next paycheck is coming in. The aim is to build a system to provide enough money for you and your family for the rest of your life. To not work for money and to have money work for you. In the past, this was called retirement. Where you worked and saved up enough money to change that money for a guaranteed income for life.

Today the rules have changed. Retirement is not the goal. The goal is to be able to choose what you want to do with your time. This is achieved by having enough assets that pay you an income for life. You can then concentrate on more important, productive aspects of your life.
Where you have more time, freedom and control so you can enjoy life to its true potential.
Be this more time with loved ones, more holidays and experiences, or whatever else. The point of wealth is to get the life you want, whilst feeling secure and in control.

The oldest Millennial current state retirement age is 68 in UK (in the year 2048). This book aims to question the old concept of retirement and offer you a new way of living. By doing simple things today that will give you a better tomorrow. The goal is to be Financial Independent and Retire Early (FIRE).

Get Fire'd.

Most people see financial independence as someone who has an abundance of material possessions like a big TV, lots of cars and the latest gadget. Often people who display a high consumption lifestyle have no or little investments. Someone who is financially independent gets pleasure out of owning assets that will increase in value over time and pay them an income, replacing the need for them to have to work, or perhaps to work for joy rather than necessity.

This wealth will give you the freedom of how to spend your time. Allowing you to pursue your dreams or to pursue happiness. You are not going to create a vacuum in your life by trying to remove all the bad things from it. The goal is to create a business system that will eventually replace you. So you have enough assets working for you that will replace your income. Removing the need for you to go to work each morning, to give you time to pursue all the things that bring you closer to happiness. To be Financially Independent and Retiring Early (FIRE) you only choose to work because you want to. Perhaps because you enjoy the work, the community or perhaps as it does well for the world. To wake up each morning feeling like it is the weekend.

The Age of Mass Consumption

Imagine you are eating a chocolate bar. The first bite is amazing, the second bit is still good and so is the third bite. Once you get to the second chocolate bar you don't want it as much and the third chocolate bar is less satisfying still.
More consumption doesn't always equal more fulfilment in our lives. Having more doesn't always make us happier. In economics, this is called marginal utility. Being conscious in your spending and asking yourself why you are buying this item. Understanding your needs versus your wants can help understand your spending. More money doesn't necessarily mean more happiness. Once we meet our survival needs and reach a level of comfort. More doesn't always mean better.

Once we understand how much enough is getting more doesn't always fulfil our lives as much as before. More consumption may make us less fulfilled. Like eating too much chocolate. More extravagance does not make us more fulfilled (As shown by the graph below).

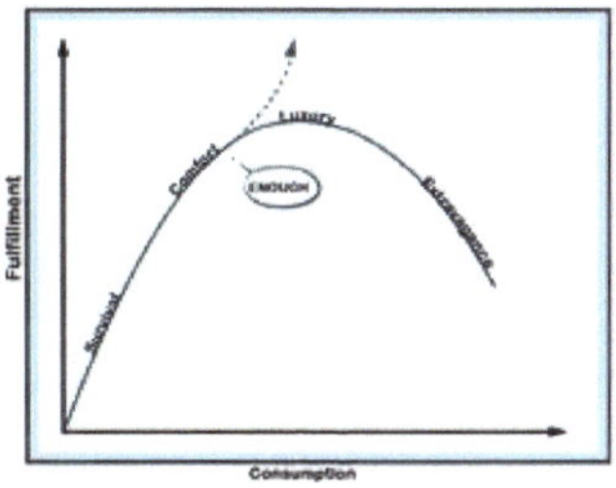

Spend less than you Earn

Spending less than you earn means playing great defence. Being conscious in your spending and asking yourself why you need this item. Understanding your needs versus your wants can help you understand and manage your spending. More money doesn't necessarily mean more happiness as the graph demonstrates.

More money doesn't equal the same proportion of happiness. There is a limit once our basic needs are met and that's why more money doesn't equal more happiness. Friendship, love and belonging are things that can't be bought with more money.

Assets produce income. Having enough assets will create income that you can live on for the rest of your life. Income follows assets.

Income gives you cash flow moving in the right direction. The flow either positive or negative is called cash flow.

Credit Cards

Credit cards can often feel like free money however they are one of the most damaging things to your long-term wealth.

Credit cards take up valuable mind space. Meaning you're constantly thinking and worrying about the debt you have accumulated. There is increased stress of remembering to pay bills on time. Or the time in your day wasted by calling credit card company asking not to be charged a fee, this valuable time could be enjoying themselves and living life. We humans can only think of a few tasks at the same time. It is much more productive to focus on building wealth rather than stressing about getting out of debt.

Delayed gratification

Delayed gratification is being patient and the ability to be able to wait for what you want. Not needing to have the shiny object right away as soon as you see the advert but actively putting off the need until another day. Being frugal is not sexy but it is the cornerstone to wealth building. Apply the two-day rule, if you want to buy something wait two days before you purchase it. This allows you to decide if you need it or if it's just instant gratification pretending that you want it.

It's a bit like when you go food shopping hungry you get home and realise you have purchased a whole load of crap that you don't need. By delaying gratification, you will only get what you need. This applies when buying investments too. The longer your time frame the more successful your investment strategy is likely to be. To build wealth we must control spending and budget.

How to Budget?

Budgeting is proactively telling your money where to go. If you don't take the time to plan your spending, you are playing rubbish defence. The hour spent doing this could save you much more than you would earn that hour. Set up your budget automatically. Have a main account that your income gets paid into. Work out how much you want to spend and get this amount sent to your bank account each month. You will soon get used to spending this money. This may seem like a pain to set up, but it will take no more than an hour. This hour's work will save you hundreds if not thousands of pounds over your lifetime. Knowing what you want to spend your money on creates artificial scarcity and pushes you not to go over that budget. The whole meaning of life has become where to store our things. The things you own end up owning you. All this stuff we work so hard to buy, can't live with but inevitably can't bear to part with.

'You are not the clothes you wear. You are not the contents of your wallet. You are not the grande latte or you are not the car you drive.'

Brad Pitt *Fight Club (1999)*

Today's culture depends upon teasing our wants but not satisfying them. We work hard to acquire more stuff but often never feel fulfilled because there is always something faster, newer or better available. The distance between what we have and what we want is called the margin of discontent. Today's world has taught to desire things from a young age. 'What do you want for Christmas? What do you want for your birthday? We often understand the amount of time and mind space most of us give to consumption. Not only do the things we own to fill up cupboards space but also space in our mind too.

Today the average person is bombarded by adverts selling us things and has created 'Hyper consumption'. We can often see thousands of advert messages per day. It's not surprising that we have become seduced by the pull of the new and the desire for more that has been created. Ask yourself: Do you work for things or possessions? Are you needlessly buying crap you don't need and rarely use, mainly to impress others? If you earn money just to spend it all, then when you spend more you will need to earn even more. This takes up more of your time you could be better spent enjoying yourself with friends and family rather than just buying more stuff, which ultimately won't bring you more happiness. As the graph below demonstrates from a survey (from the University of Michigan in 2013) that shows our happiness levels don't rise higher the more we earn once we reach a certain level.

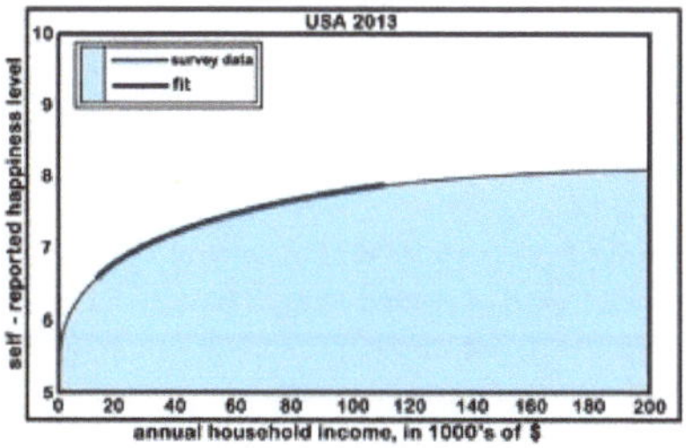

Credit cards are damaging for your long-term wealth

Never buy on credit cards. Get into the disciplined habit of saving up for it rather than buying it on credit. Every day we are bombarded by adverts, urging us to buy things we don't need. This makes it difficult at first especially as there is so much temptation from the advertiser, but they are getting rich off you buying and consuming stuff not you

Credit cards alter our perception of the value of a product. When cash tangibly leaves our hands, we are more conscious that we are spending money than when we use a card. Credit cards make the transaction seem less real and therefore are more likely to spend more. The trouble with easy credit is that people can't afford it when they are working let alone when they stop working.

With credit cards we can often get caught up in the trap of three things 1) Accelerated spending, 2) mindless spending and 3) latest and greatest spending. It's often common for people to get trapped in all three situations. Consumers spend more than they can afford and buy new stuff faster, more easily and more often.

Mindless spending

Mindless spending is where you don't know or can't work out what your money has been spent on. It's like when you go shopping hungry and end up buy loads of stuff that you weren't planning on buying. Or popping out to wander around the shopping centre in your lunch break and come back with stuff you didn't plan to buy. Being more intentional with our money is important. Being mindful rather than mindless with our money. Being in control rather than being out of control

Latest and greatest spending is keeping up with the neighbours, who we don't even like. Feeling like we have to buy the latest and greatest gadget just because it's the new edition.

We tend to value whatever is new and original over what is old and durable. The more our houses bloat with stuff, the heavier and more trapped we feel. As Neal Lawson wrote in the book 'All-consuming' 'The more we consume the less space we have to be anything other than consumers'. Our drive to be seen by others that we are successful by having more material wealth can often exclude our most basic needs like family and community. We thought we could fill these needs through shopping and buying and accumulating more and more stuff.

We have a choice between discipline or regret. We can either have discipline in our spending today or regret our spending tomorrow. The discipline to buy assets rather than the regret of having liabilities.

Picture the 60-year-old version of yourself. When you look back what do you want to have achieved in life? Do we want to be known for what we have achieved, what we have done or what we have given back to society? More money doesn't necessarily mean more happiness. More things don't make you happy. It's moments in time that make us happy.

We are human and we are social creatures. We buy things for several different reasons, sometimes because it feels good, we get a small chemical high every time we buy something, it can make us feel more attractive to find a partner or it can improve our status. Having a nice new car increases our status. Where are we now on the pecking order and more importantly who am I now above in the group? Status symbols are a way of showing to others that we have been successful in the past and confident we will continue to be so. We will also be attractive to others. However, buying more stuff doesn't always make us happier. It can often be buying things to impress people we don't like.

Credit card bills take up valuable mind space as you're constantly thinking and worrying about the debt you have accumulated. Most people's brains are not wired to do the buy now pay later calculation as we struggle to understand the principles of exponential growth. We humans can only think of a few tasks at the same time. Focus on building wealth rather than getting into debt. When spending money by credit cards, the transaction often seems less real as it's not money you earn. This way, it increases the amount you spend and your debt. Compound interest creates momentum.

Disposable Income

Many people today live paycheck to paycheck. Once a month you get paid and then after you pay your fixed costs like rent, transport and food there is usually some leftover. This is called disposable income. Most people are going to spend all their earnings until it's gone. They might spend it on movies or ice cream or to travel. These are all short-term pleasures that are gone in an instant. The great thing is when you work, money replenishes. Every month there is another £1000 or whatever into your account of disposable income you can spend. You get to choose how to spend that. If you choose to set up an automated system that pays yourself 10% that will grow.

The journey of a thousand miles begins with one step.

Lao Tzu 4th century BC

Compound interest:

The secret within the secret to building wealth is to pay yourself first and then begin to compound this money by reinvesting the gains from your investment. Compound interest is the interest on your interest.

Albert Einstein said that Compound interest was the eighth wonder of the world due to its power to increase wealth over time. It is the interest on your interest. Invest £100 at 5% interest and you will receive £105 at the end of the year. You then can invest £105 in the second year and you will have £110.25. This grows quickly over time.

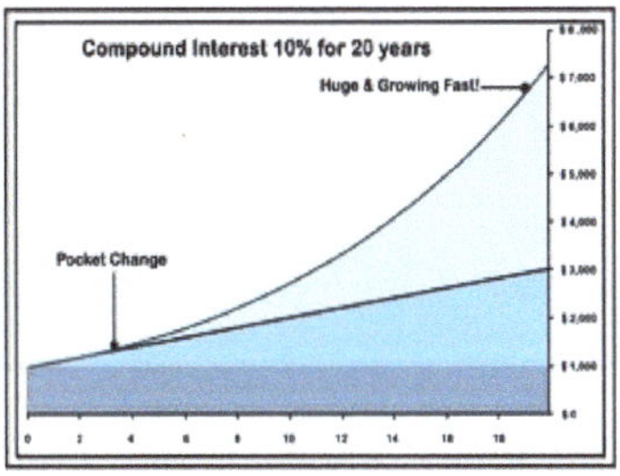

The Rule of 72

To calculate how quickly your money can double

Would you prefer to have £1 million today or one penny that will double every day for 30 days? If you chose the million pounds, you would lose millions. If you chose the penny, on the second day your penny would be worth two pence, on day three it would be four pence, on the fourth day it would be 8 pence. By day 18 the penny will have grown to £1,310.72. By day 28 it will be worth over a million pounds: £1,342,177. On the 30th day, it would be worth an astronomical £5,368,709! If the penny were to be allowed to double for another 30 days, the penny would grow to over £5 quadrillion (five thousand trillion!) pounds. Sometimes, less is more...

The easiest way to calculate compound interest is the rule of 72

Compound interest sounds complicated, but it is just the interest on your interest. It can show you how quickly your money can grow. To understand it just use the rule of 72. The rule of 72 works out how quickly your money will double using compound interest.

To know how quickly your money can double use the rule of 72

Divide the number 72 by the rate of growth that you get with your money and this will give you how long the amount of money invested will double.

72/8% (growth rate) = 9 years for your money to double

72/5 % (growth rate) =14.4 years to double

With current interest rates close to 0% in a bank, it is difficult to grow your money. This is why investing is so important. Today everyone needs education and the experience with handling money and investing.

When you pay yourself first (the first rule of money) every month and then also compound the money. The power of growth rapidly increases.

When using credit cards, the power of compound interest works in reverse.

The interest on credit cards can wipe out any momentum you gain, charges on credit cards, overdraft payments, broker fees from buying and selling shares too often. The high rate of return your credit card companies charge means that your money is working against you. It's a massive headwind blowing in your face as your set out on your adventure.

Money is just energy and flows towards value. Nothing rests, everything moves, everything vibrates.

Where do you spend your time? What do you think about most of the time?

Look at your expenses, where is your money going to? Where is your cash flowing?

My challenge is for every Millennial 25-40-year-old to have a £1000 cash buffer emergency fund. Emergencies happen. Bad things happen. Having an emergency fund of even £1000 frees up our mind to think clearly and choose the action that would benefit us the most in both the present moment and the future present moment.

Let's not judge people for what they have, the possessions they own, the watch they wear, the car they drive. Let's instead value people for who they are, what they have created, who they have become and what they have given back.

Exercise 3

Build an emergency fund.

Having £1000 in a separate account that is not instantly accessible and cancelling credit cards will do wonders for your money mindset freeing up mental capacity to focus on the more important things in life.

Chapter 4

The Road Trip

"Fix your course to a star and you can navigate through any storm"

Leonardo da Vinci (1452-1519)

Think of Investing like planning a road trip. It's a long-term process rather than one single event. You first need to know your final destination, have a plan for the best route that can get you there in the time you have with the amount of risk you are comfortable with. Finally, pick a vehicle for the trip.

A clear image of your destination will get you further than heading off in any direction. It's better to be pulled by your dreams than being pushed by your fears. Having a dream or vision with actionable daily habits will drive you even faster in achieving what you want. You will be pulled by your purpose, vision or mission in life rather than being pushed by a 'to-do list' of chores.

Technology Changes

Today investing has never been easier. Technology today has meant that we can do things that people would only dream of a few years ago. We can invest in hundreds of different companies, large and small in each corner of the globe, which reduces the risk we need to take and improves the rewards we gain.

A similar thing happened to the car industry in 1900. Think back to 1900, a time when the automobile car industry only provided luxury cars to the very rich. It was a young Henry Ford who decided to build a car that was mass-produced and could be driven and repaired by the owner making car ownership accessible for the masses. Previously it was only for the rich requiring a chauffeur.

Nowadays we have the technology to invest and manage our money cheaper, easier and more conveniently than ever before. These investment vehicles are like turning a key in the motor car, investing for our future can now be done by the touch of a button. These investment vehicles not only enable us to get where we want but also like the motor cars of the past give us freedom, mobility, power and romance of designing our ideal life in the future.

There are opportunities now to be financially independent and not have the drudgery in the morning of commuting to work for a 9-5 job that you hate for the next 20 years until you can retire at 67. Today you can put money into an investment vehicle knowing the number you need to get to live on for the rest of your life. This will give you the ultimate freedom that Henry Ford's generation had stepping into their very own motor car for the first time, turning the key, deciding their destination and then feeling the wind in their hair as they started moving.

Imagine Henry Ford trying to explain how this new horse-less carriages work to someone who has never heard of a motor car before let alone been behind the wheel or put their foot onto the accelerator. Looking under the bonnet at the car engine looks complex, with many moving parts, and can seem daunting.

We are in the same situation with investing. We have these amazing investment vehicles provided by the Financial Technology (FinTech) industry which can allow you to design your ideal life through your life plan and choose how fast you want to go depending on how much you put in and your risk profile.

Today, we need education on how we use these vehicles. Simple steps and processes can massively reduce the amount of risk you are taking like putting on a seat belt or driving slower in icy condition.

We are not taught how to use these new vehicles at school or in the workplace.

Living without clear goals is like driving through thick fog. No matter how powerful or well-engineered your car is, you will drive slowly, making little progress. Having clear goals will clear the fog immediately. Clearly defined, written goals enable you to put your foot on the accelerator. Having set clear goals will clear the fog immediately by focusing on your future and where you are going and what to do to get there. Dr Edward Banfield of Harvard University said that long-time perspective was the most important determinant of financial and personal success in life. It's so important that this study from Harvard in 1953 showed that having written goals can double the amount of money you can make in a lifetime. It enhances the ability to think several years into the future whilst making decisions in the present. Saving every month for 30 years, you can become a millionaire by the time you retire using the power of compound interest.

'We greatly overestimate what we can achieve in a year and greatly underestimate what we can achieve in 5 years.'

Peter Drucker. *Effective executive.* (1909 –2005)

Here are three questions to ask yourself based on ideas from the Financial Planner George Kinder.

1) Imagine you hold in your hand the winning lottery ticket. You now have more money to last you for the rest of your life. Financially everything is perfect. You can live the lifestyle you want and will never run out of money. How would you spend your time?

2) The doctor tells you that you only have 5 years to live. What would you do with your time left to live? How would you change your life?

3) Finally, imagine a doctor tells you that you have 24 hours left to live. What did you miss? What do you regret not doing? Who did you not get to be?

Any plan is better than no plan but what is it you want from life? Investing is like a plan, although often a boring plan. It's like having a map to your destination. You start with an amount of fuel in your car (like the cash in your bank) when you are running low on fuel you need to go and top up your tank to enable you to keep heading towards your goals. Following a map and directions in a set order over a defined period to get the results you want. Most people will never know what they want. What if what you want is too imprecise to produce a meaningful and actionable answer? You must take control to get the results you want.

<u>Cash flow</u>

Think of cash flow like the petrol in your car. The more cash reserves you have the longer your investment journey can last. Cash flow tells the story of how a person handles money. What is missing in most people's education is not how to make money but how to handle money. The cash flow to live the life you want to live. Cash flow is the total amount of money being transferred into and out of your bank account or business (you are now your own business). It's the flow of money around a system. Cash flow is like the petrol of any business providing income in and expenses out. The aim is to have more money coming in than going out. Having assets that pay you an income, will mean that cash is flowing into your business. Having liabilities (like credit card payments) will mean cash is flowing out of your business. Paying yourself first means you make sure you get paid first.

To have enough income you first need to build assets.

'Imagine Your Life Is Perfect In Every Respect; What Would It Look Like?"

Brian Tracy (motivational public speaker and self-development author)

Design your future, today. 'What are your goals?' To replace the question, take a step back and look at the big picture. As Tim Ferris says 'What is the opposite of happiness? Sadness? No. Love and hate are two sides of the same coin. The opposite of love is indifference. The opposite of happiness is boredom. Excitement is a better definition of happiness and precisely what you should strive to achieve. When people say follow your passion or bliss, it's the same concept as excitement. It isn't what do I want or what are my goals but what excites me. Remember boredom is the enemy, not an absolute failure.'

Practice ideal thinking in everything you do. Create a 5-year fantasy by thinking about what you would do if you couldn't fail. What would your life look like if everything was perfect? Imagine no limitation. Practice 'blue-sky thinking' says Charles Garfield from the book *Studies of blue-sky thinking and peak performance.* What would have to happen to me to create my perfect future? Dream big and always begin with the end in mind.

'Happiness is the progressive reality of a worthy idea.'

Tim Ferris, The Four-Hour Work Week *(2007)*

Happiness emerges after taking steps or making progress toward getting your goal in life. Some people call this having a purpose. Where you have clear exciting goals and ideas you will feel happier about yourself and the world. You will feel internally motivated to get up every morning and work on your dreams. The future is going to be better than anything that has ever happened to you in the past. There are no limits. Having a purpose and having progress towards that purpose equals happiness.

'We all have a plan until we get punched in the face'

Mike Tyson (born June 30, 1966) is an American former professional boxer

It's not the desire alone that will make you rich. Desire is important; although far more important is design. As Daniel Priestley says, 'We live in a world where successful outcomes are designed to occur far more than they are desired into existence.' The Ferrari accelerates up to 70 mph because of the engineering. The passenger seat isn't put there for a guru to sit and read motivational quotes to stir up the driver's emotions. The Ferrari goes fast because it was designed to go fast and built that way after testing and improving over many years not because of a well-constructed life plan. It wasn't wished up by thinking positive thoughts and that morning's goal-setting session. These are amazing feats of human innovation had something to do with desire but mostly it was the design that got the job done.

The Volvo in the slow lane can comfortably reach speeds of 70 mph even if it's driven by your old aunty Deirdre just by putting her foot on the accelerator. This is because the car has been designed successfully to achieve those speeds. If that same car wanted to travel at 300mph no amount of training, goal setting and dream boards will make that car travel that fast, it's just not designed to drive at that speed.

Successful investing succeeds because it was designed to succeed. It is an ecosystem of assets (different types of investments) that have been brought together so the sum of all the parts is greater than the individual assets.

Investing is different from speculating. Investing is buying assets that generate an income so over time statistically will go up in value. These tend to be profitable businesses that you own a share in that business. This is by lending money to people and business and charging them for that service rather than borrowing money from other people. Speculating is buying lines on the screen in the hope someone else will pay more for it. The problem with speculating is that you are trying to take and not give; ultimately you are going against the forces of nature. It's like wanted to reach your destination before actually driving the car. Anything of value takes time. Making money from speculating is possible but only if you are adding value. Trading is something different. Generally, trading is moving somewhere from point A to B. There may be a way to make a profit on the difference in price called arbitrage. An example could be Uber taxis. A business created from not just moving from point A to B but then picking up an additional fare at C before going back to the start (this is known as backhaul in logistics). This is using technology to utilise previously dead time, making the whole process more efficient (and therefore more profitable).

Like driving a car, you steer the investment vehicle in the direction of travel. You make the decision now, with your hands on the steering wheel and your eyes watching the road in front of you. No one can guarantee that the decisions you'll make will be the right one. You can only make a decision you think is best in the moment using all the possible information you have available.

Decisions are essentially bets. There are no right or wrong answers, only the best decision with the information you have at that moment. The winner of the Nobel Prize in 1978 Herbert Simon said it's impossible to have perfect and complete information in any given time to decide. We can only think about a few things in a day. What information consumes is the attention of its recipients. Hence a wealth of information creates a poverty of attention. The internet has meant we have so much information available, we just don't have the time to consume and process it all.

Time is our most precious asset. We have a limited amount of time each day, to do all the things we have promised ourselves. Today we are living busier and more complex lives, with more options than ever before. It can often feel we have an unlimited 'to-do list' of tasks that need to be completed and a limited amount of time to finish them. Our will power is often like a car battery, we start the day off at full charge and as we do each task our will power is depleted. The more we get stressed the closer our batteries get to being empty each day.

Our problems with money are often the last thing to be tackled during the day as our daily problems from life always seem more urgent and important. Therefore, it's often not done at all. We need to allocate that attention effectively

A driver may have the best vehicle available to them but if they don't have the knowledge, skill and experience to masterfully use this car then the driver won't get anywhere.

"All events of wealth are precluded by a process, a backstory of trial, risk, hard work, and sacrifice. If you try to skip the process, you'll never experience events."

M.J. DeMarco, *The Millionaire Fastlane (2011)*

Experience and education give you the confidence to make decisions. However, you can't make a perfect decision, because you never have full access to all the information in the market and you can't know what other people are thinking all the time.

With your investment decision, you can take the slow winding route, which is safer but will take you longer to get to where you want or the take the faster path with more ups and downs, similar to going the mountainous route, which has more peaks and troughs and you are more likely to crash. However, with this riskier route, you may be more likely to crash you may be more likely to arrive at your destination quicker. You can also have a balance between the two. Go the third route, the path that is ideal for your goals, aims and aspirations. Rather than continuously struggle knowing the path that is right for you will give you confidence in your investing decisions. Have balance. It's using the balance of diversification, where the easy road turns hard and the hard road turns easy. It's hard to start, as you need to make the decision that is right for you. This will depend on several factors like your age, your risk tolerance and your capacity for loss (how much you can afford to lose). It is making these decisions initially and having the courage to stick with them that is the hard part.

Think of the steering wheel you need a combination of factors to have balance on the road of your life. There are several key decisions you need to weigh up and some of them are not as obvious as they initially seem, as over time the difference between risk and reward change over time and between individuals. Having not enough balance means you will fall faster from the highs and land with a bump off the road. You need to decide between inflation and volatility, between security and flexibility and time versus money and how well you want to eat versus how soundly you want to sleep.

Starting the journey is often the hardest part. It's called inertia, (from Newton's law of motion) meaning that it's easier to stay where you are than to start moving.

Newton's three laws of motion

1) Inertia: Things at rest will stay at rest until there is a greater force that is acted upon it. Think of pushing a car. It's much harder to get it going before it has moved. This is inertia. Paying yourself first creates a force. When you take action and start paying yourself first then compound interest will start working in your favour, it gets things moving and investing gets easier.

2) Momentum: Once things are moving, thinks will continue until a greater force is acted upon it. It is much easier to accelerate when there is a rolling start or you haven't fully stopped. Different size of companies moves at different rates. If you apply the same force to a small company and a large company, the small company will move quicker. Think of applying the same force to a pushing large car and a small light buggy. The smaller buggy will travel further even when you apply the same force. Diversification keeps this momentum using the Football Formation Asset Allocation. This will be discussed in the next chapter.

3) Every action has an equal and opposite reaction: When forces are applied with investing you will get an equal and opposite reaction in your life. Rebalancing will mean you get a balance from your life from the security that you are heading in the right direction financially. This means there's a flow happening that automatically and continuously balances and rebalances these energies. This is living in harmony.

Any action causes an equal and opposite reaction. We have the choice of what actions we take daily. When we finish a day of work and our head hits the pillow we can look back and either has been a good day and has gotten you closer to your purpose or a bad day, which has not.

Choose your investment vehicle wisely and the route that will get you there. Money is just a vehicle to get you from where you are currently to where you want to be in the future and then decide how fast you want to get there.

Remember low risk and high risk are just poles of the same thing, just like light and dark and hot and cold are all poles of the same thing. They are not good or bad just different. Although we may think one end of the scale is good and the other end bad. Having a low-risk portfolio is not good and having a high-risk portfolio is not bad. It just depends on what you want to achieve in life. Risk and reward are intrinsically linked, meaning that the more risk you are willing to take with your investments over the long term you are more likely to get a greater reward. Having Money Mindset means you can adapt to the matters of degree depending on what you want out of life.

You can take the slow, safer route and it may take you longer to get there or the riskier road has more ups and downs, more hairy turns and you're more likely to crash but you get there in a faster time.

If you're willing to accept these risks, then this is the path for you. There are different vehicles for different adventures.

The easy road turns hard and the hard road turns easy.

Exercise 4) Answer these questions. Then fill out your life plan template for the short, medium and long term writing down where you see yourself for each of the four categories.

1) Where would you be in 5 years? What would you do if you couldn't fail?
2) Imagine the day that you stop working. Describe a picture of what you are doing? Tell me about what your happiness would look like? What would you do if you couldn't fail? Where would you make the greatest contribution? What do you enjoy talking about on a Saturday night? What would you do on a Saturday morning if the choice was yours? What excites you and lights you up when you talk?
3) Imagine a doctor now tells you that you have one day to live. What are you feeling? What do you regret not doing with your life?
4) Where do you want to be living? How do you want to be living? Who do you want to become? What does a perfect life look like for you?

LifePlan

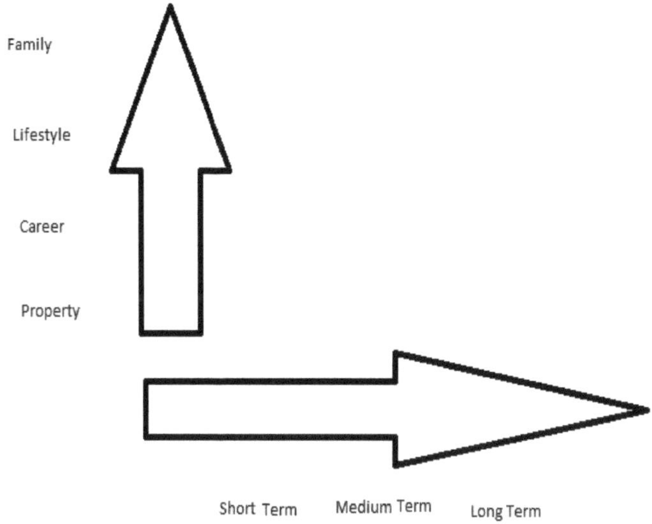
Family
Lifestyle
Career
Property
Short Term
Medium Term
Long Term

Chapter 5

Football Formation Asset Allocation™

"I'm going to tell you the story about the geese which fly 5,000 miles from Canada to France. They fly in V-formation, but the second ones don't fly. They're the subs for the first ones. And then the second ones take over – so it's teamwork."

Sir Alex Ferguson Football Player and Manager

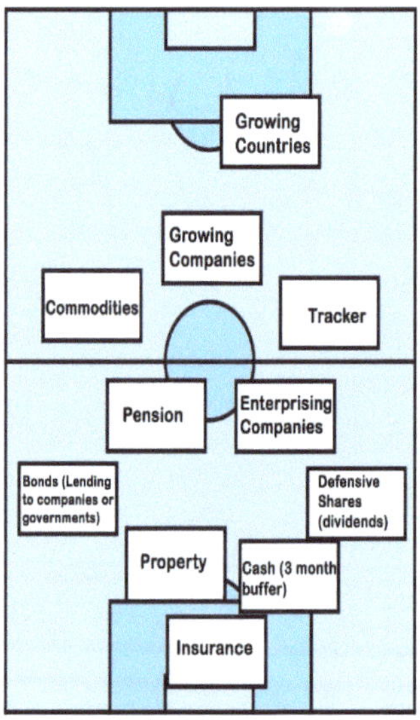

Any world-class football team has great individual players. It is the team and the combination of the individual players that make teams so great, the right balance of defenders, attackers and a goalkeeper. Imagine having a team of only goalkeepers, you'd end up scoring very few goals. The most important investment decision you make is the long-term mix of assets you hold. These assets also need great individual performers that work together as a team. Combining individual talents of each asset you will have a world-class performing portfolio.

A football game aims to score more goals than you concede. To score a goal is like money going into your pocket and to concede a goal is like money leaving your pocket. If you live a good life, you get to live to 90 years old. Like 90 minutes on the pitch. When you score goals money goes into your pocket and when you concede a goal then money leaves your pocket.

The game aims are to score more goals than you concede and to build up your team of assets. Each asset is like a football player, with different personality types depending on the position in the team that they play.

When an asset increases it's like scoring a goal and money goes into your pocket. When a liability increases it's like conceding a goal and money leaves your pocket. The main aim of the game is to score more goals than you concede in the time you have to play. If you live a good life, you may live to 90 years old. Like 90 minutes on the pitch. We all have a limited time on the pitch of life.

Investing is like managing a good football team. You pick the formation of your players or assets depending on their strengths and abilities. You need many different qualities that work together to form one cohesive team that is greater than the individual parts. Investment management is simple but it's not easy. It's simple because the principles of successful investing are relatively simple in number and easy to understand. You face risks in managing your money and the two most important ones are inflation and volatility. Inflation is the reduction of the spending power in your pocket and volatility is how much zigs and zags or ups and down that the asset historically moves. Investing is easy with a firm commitment to a long-term plan and strategic asset allocation framework.

The most important investment decision is your long-term mix of assets. An asset puts money into your pocket and a liability takes money from your pocket. In terms of football an asset is scoring a goal and a liability is conceding a goal.

Having a solid defence to prevent you from letting in goals (or losing money) and a vibrant attack that will score goals for you and put you in the lead (or gaining money). Rebalancing your team every year like you would a real football team. The old buy and hold investing model is as outdated as the 1970 Brazilian players today. Imagine if you still had an 80-year-old Pele playing for your team, you probably wouldn't score many goals as if he was playing in his prime. Companies like football players also have a lifecycle. They are born, reach their peak and then die. Think Kodak or Polaroid, these once great businesses were the start-ups of their day. Like a rising sun, everything has their time and the sun has set on many once-great companies.

<u>The Modern Portfolio Theory</u>

'Diversification is the only free lunch in finance.'

Harry Markowitz (Nobel prize winner in Economics 1990).

Having a mix of assets in your portfolio will mean different assets complement each other and work together. Diversify within each asset class and between asset classes. Bad things happen. Be patient and persistent. Good things happen too and usually when you least expect it. Success emerges from what seems like nowhere.

Football Formation Asset Allocation™ is based on several Nobel prize-winning economic theories. One of these is the modern portfolio theory. Harry Markowitz won a Nobel Prize for his work in 1990. He wrote having a diversified portfolio could reduce risk and increase returns for investors. Meaning a team of imperfectly correlated assets provided higher returns with a reduced amount of volatility. This system uses the most up to date industry practises and evidence-based research.

The modern portfolio is the way that a portfolio (or team of investments) is picked to maximise returns and to minimise losses. According to this theory, we can't just look at how well an individual investment performs but we must look at how each investment changes in price concerning other investments in your portfolio. Similar to a football team

Risk and reward are correlated. This was the finding of William Sharpe who won a Nobel Prize for his work. There is no way anyone would pick an investment that is riskier than another unless we were rewarded for taking that risk. Every person then is risk-averse and wants to build a team that maximises returns and minimises risk (risk is discussed in chapter 7).

An investor should be rewarded for the risks taken If you are offered two identical returns, one of which takes more risk than the other, then the investor would always choose the less risky option. Investors should only take the risks necessary to achieve their required level of growth.

Imagine an 85-year-old has more than enough money to last for the rest of their life. Let's say you are 10-0 up and it's the 85 minutes of the game, then there is no reason to have a team of attackers investing in smaller companies. For your peace of mind, that 85-year-old person should have a defensive portfolio by replacing strikers with defenders and have a team made up of cash, bonds property and perhaps a small number of defensive companies. However, a 25-year-old should take a different tactic. They have much more time on the pitch of life and can take more risks by having more strikers on the pitch like growing companies and growing countries as they may not be taking that money out for another 35 years and by that time your team would have scored lots of goals

Think of this as a football team. Each player has unique strengths and weaknesses. A team only made up of attacking players is much more likely to score goals than a team of only defenders, however, this team of attackers will also more likely to concede more goals as they are taking higher risks.

A team of only defenders will be more likely concede fewer goals (as they take fewer risks), they will be less likely to score fewer goals as they don't take the risk necessary to score these goals.

The different assets (or players) work differently in different stages of the economic cycle (discussed in the next chapter). The idea is to build your team depending on your risk profile or your age profile. The younger you are the more time you have on the pitch of life to influence the game and the score.

You should have a defence, midfield and attack. If you want to score goals then smaller growing companies is your first striker.

Defence

Goal Keeper

You are the first asset. Your money mindset is important here. The way you think, feel and behave with money is important to concede fewer goals. You can increase the value of this asset through education and experience. The more value you offer to people and the bigger problems you solve for more people, the more people will pay for your services. If you are a qualified doctor in a specialised area with high demand and a low supply of other doctors in this area, then you will be paid more for your knowledge and ability to treat patients. As an asset, you can take out insurance to protect yourself if you die, get injured or you can get income protection to cover you for redundancy.

Centre back

The next defender is cash. Having cash in the bank can give you confidence that no matter what happens in life, you will be alright. Having an emergency fund starting at £1000 rising to 3-6 months of expenses gives you tremendous peace of mind, reducing your stress and worry.

Centre Back

Property forms part of your defence. This is the roof over your head. Property is currently unaffordable for many people (especially in large cities around the world). The aim should be to have your own property for the long term. Property is a market like any other asset and although currently property prices are unaffordable that may not always be the case. By owning a property you build up your own asset rather than needing to pay a landlord. There is also potential to own a buy to let properties (in a cheaper part of the country or the world) where someone else lives in your house and the tenant pays you rent.

Left Back

Bonds is a stable steady asset to have in any team. Bonds is where you are lending your money to governments or companies. This money is used for investments maybe it is building a new factory or transport link Rather than owning the company like buying shares you are only lending money, which you will get back after an agreed time. You will get paid interest (known as a coupon) for lending this money. If the company or government you lend your money to goes bankrupt bondholder will be ahead in the queue of shareholders to get your money back. This is one of the reasons why bonds are such a good defensive asset to have in your team.

Right Back

Dividends from companies.

The ups and downs of the market is only half the story of companies. Businesses aim to make a profit when selling their goods or services. These profits get returned to the shareholder in the form of dividends. Companies that pay a large dividend tend to do well in all market conditions for example medicine (people still get sick during recessions), utilities like water, electricity, internet companies.

Midfield

Pension

Pension is another midfielder. Often seen as boring and little understood. This asset keeps you safe as a defensive midfielder. Pensions are often the unsung hero as they are tax-efficient. There are three different types of pension, (pensions will be explained further in chapter 9). Today if you work at a job your employer has to auto-enrol you into a pension scheme. This means you don't need to think or worry about building this asset (although check what fees you are paying and you can choose the asset allocation of your pension).

Tracker

This midfielder tracks the market up and down with the run of play. A tracker follows an index of leading shares as the price rise and fall. The good point about a tracker is that it looks for the avoidance of serious mistakes or losses because whatever the market is doing that is what the tracker does. The downside is that they are boring. You can't go to a party and tell everyone how clever you are by buying the latest tech stock. The tracker refuses to be active by tracking the market up and down removing the human emotion from the investing decision.

Commodities

Imagine you sit down for your evening meal tonight. What will you be eating and where did all those things come from? These commodities are shipped from all around the world to make up your dinner. Even the chair you sit on and the knife and fork you use will be made from commodities. Commodities are raw materials that make up our day to day life. Commodities are very supply and demand-driven and move up and down very quickly.

Enterprising Companies

This asset is being active and looking for opportunities to outperform the market. This is looking for an edge over the broad market by spotting an opportunity that the rest of the market doesn't yet appreciate. There are several strategies to do this including looking for value in a business by studying the fundamentals of a company (the price of the shares compared with the earning of the business), technical analysis, which is looking at trend lines and graphs, behaviour pattern looking at human behaviour and spotting opportunities and also looking for 'castles in the sky', which is a top-down approach where you look for opportunities on how a sector will perform in the future taking into account population demographics, new technology and future demand

Attack

Strikers

Smaller growing companies will grow faster than larger companies. It is much easier for a small company to double in size than a FTSE 100 company (which is the 100 largest companies in the UK). Small dynamic growth companies are also riskier than established businesses as the risk of the small company going bust is higher due to it being in an untested market. Fama and French won a Nobel prize in economics on their work on the performance of smaller stocks versus larger stock

Growing countries (or developing countries) is the next striker in your team. Investing in growing countries will lead to greater growth over the long term. A pound coin invested will go further than a more mature market. You are taking a greater short term risk for a lower long term risk looking at the evidence. The BRICS (Brazil, Russia, India, China and South Africa) have grown faster compared to more developed markets. Walt Rostow's work suggested that developed countries have tended to pass through 5 stages to reach their current degree of economic development. Today African nations, Vietnam, Turkey and Cuba are the frontier markets. This means they will more likely to get you goals at the risk of losing goals.

Synergy: 1+1 =3

Working as a team creates synergies, which create something better than what would have been created otherwise. 1+1 really can add up to 3. Despite what we have been told our whole schooling and work lives.

Harry Markowitz, who won a Nobel prize for creating his modern portfolio theory said that the only free lunch with investing is diversification. This means that your team of players (or an investment portfolio) working together as a unit will create natural synergies and the whole of the team will be greater than the sum of the individual parts (or players).

Synergy happens when a few different things work together and create something better. "The whole is greater than the sum of the parts," meaning the whole has properties its parts do not have. You may see this in a business where perhaps a work colleague in marketing has completely different skills to someone great with numbers and accounts. By cooperating and working together you get the best skills from both workmates. By offsetting some of your weaknesses so you can focus on your strengths. This is working in synergy.

Similar to your investment portfolio unexpected things and wonderful things emergence through synergy.

This happens with money, and when a pound coin is put into a system that works together it will be greater than if you took each pound coin working on its own. This comes about because of interactions among the individual pound coins.

Things get exciting when the individual parts have different qualities that work complementarily to the other parts as they benefit from the unique difference and thrive in different conditions and become better by working together. Using a stock market example one company say a sun cream producer will do well in sunny conditions and a rain jacket company does well in rainy conditions. Having both companies in your portfolio or ecosystem will be better than just holding either individual company.

Synergy means working together or co-operating, and when we do this the whole is greater than the individual parts. Synergy is everywhere in nature. The essence of synergy is to value each other's differences. To respect them and build on our strengths to compensate for our weaknesses. Synergy means a higher better way like a team playing together so they can focus on what they are good at. To specialise on our best self.

Working as a team creates synergies which create something better than what would have been created otherwise. 1+1 =3.

<u>Specialization</u>

Do you have more assets or liabilities? Is your portfolio scoring or is your team conceding? Is money going into your pocket or is money leaving your pocket? The Football Formation is Asset Allocation™ is the best way to build your portfolio with different complementary assets. Like an ecosystem, each player has unique strengths and weaknesses that working together has a total that is greater than the sum of the individual parts. The beauty of this system is that you can tailor it to your needs yourself without the need of a financial advisor. Getting educated in financial guidance is one of the best ways to reduce your risk without paying excessive fees for advice you don't necessarily need. If you are younger or have a higher risk tolerance then you can play a more attacking and aggressive formation. If you are reaching the twilight of your life or have a cautious risk tolerance you can play a much more defensive strategy. The system aims to help you learn what you can control and what can't so you can thrive no matter what happens.

You can pick the team depending on your risk profile or the time you have left on the pitch of life. The younger you are the more ups and downs of the markets you can ride out. You can choose to be more defensive or more attacking. Each player (or asset class) has their personality type and perform differently depending on each stage of the economic cycle. For example, the commodity gold does better during a recession and small growing companies do better in a recovery of the business cycle (explained in the next chapter).

If you are younger you can afford to take more risks as you have the time on the clock of life to see more ups and downs of the market. If 11 assets are too overwhelming, then start with a five a side formation, meaning pick five assets.

The second of the three laws of money is to diversify.

Football Formation Asset Allocation

Goalkeeper = Protection or insurance

Centre back = Cash

Centre Back = Property

Left Back = Lending money

Right back= Defensive companies that provide dividends

Centre Midfield = Pension

Centre Midfield = Enterprising companies

Left Wing =Commodities

Right Wing = Tracker of an index

Striker = Growing Companies

Striker = Growing Countries

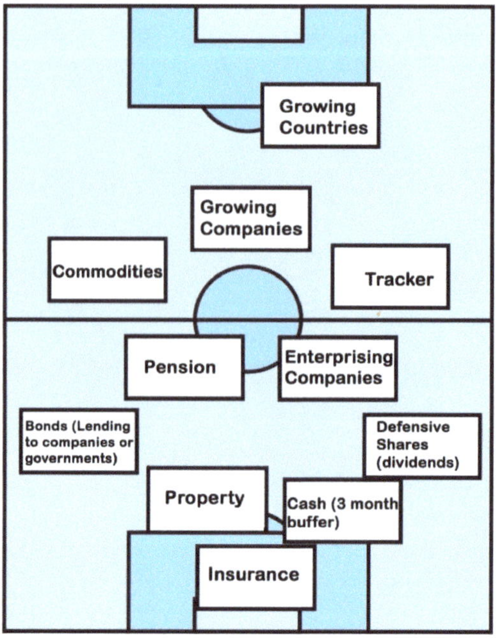

Based on the Modern portfolio theory by Harry Markowitz.

Here is the learning experience Football Formation Asset Allocation™, which contains a card game, an online course and face to face lessons, a life plan and cash flow forecast. This five-step method for money mindset is a step by step learning experience where at the end of the course you will have the knowledge, experience and confidence to implement your own investing plan. You will be empowered to make your own decisions and will be automated and set to your own risk profile. We explain in even more details about each player and gives you different formations depending on your risk profile.

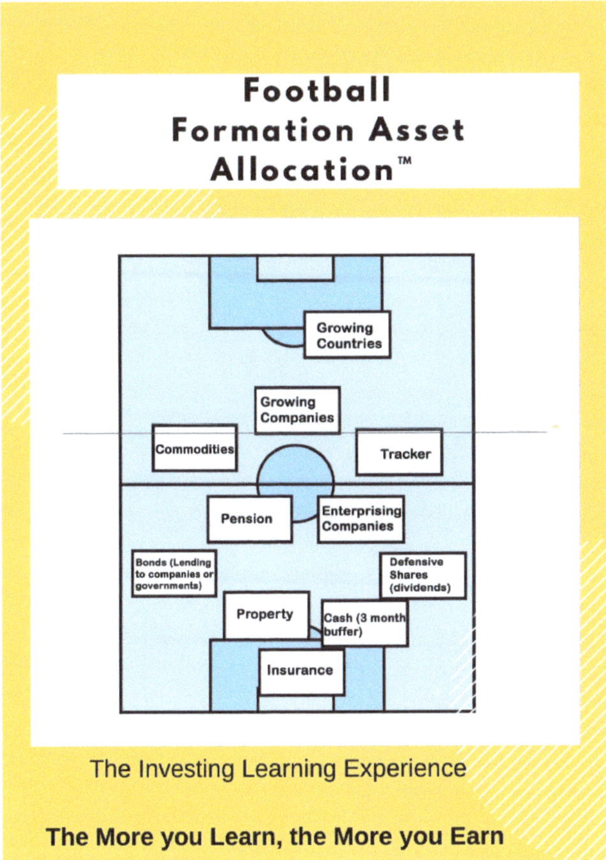

Exercise 5

Start your team off by picking five players who you want on your team?

The good news is that you may already have some of these assets. If you are employed, then you will automatically be enrolled into a pension. If you have savings or an emergency pot (from chapter 3) then you will have another player. The aim is to have a portfolio that is right for you.

Football Formation Asset Allocation card game is now available in shops. Pick your own investing team and learn how to invest.

The Football Formation Asset Allocation online learning experience is also now available

Chapter 6. The Seasons

Everything flows out and in everything has its tides: all things rise and fall: the pendulum swing is in everything; the measure of the swing to the right is the measure of the swing to the left, rhythm compensates.

The Kybalion Hermetic Philosophy

The seasons are beautiful. The sound of the birds singing in spring, the smell of freshly cut grass in summer, the sight of the changing colours of the leaves in autumn, the feeling of the snow crunching beneath your feet as you walk in winter.

Each season of the year has its own beauty and it has its role to play.

Each season of the year is unique in its own way. Each season has its gifts and has both its limitations and its opportunities. The seasons are both segments of time and states of mind.

With markets, just like the seasons, there are distinct cycles. This is called the business cycle. This cycle has patterns that mean it's more probable that the economic winds will be colder in the winter of recession than it will be in the summer of expansion. Knowing these patterns can mean the difference between planting the right seed or investment that will flourish in these conditions or planting a seed that will not.

Millennial Money Mindset aims to 'season proof' your portfolio so that you can thrive in any condition. This gives you tremendous peace of mind that no matter what happens in the markets you will have an asset class that will do well. This means that it doesn't matter what is going on in the economy. You don't need to sit and watch boring business news or read the financial newspapers every morning because the ups and downs of the markets become irrelevant to you. This will free up your time to do what you choose to do with your time, rather than watching lines on a computer screen go up and down. When the next financial crash happens (and it will come) and everyone else panics and is stressed. You sit back and relax, safe in the knowledge that part of your portfolio is going up as the rest of the market is collapsing (you can actually make money when the market goes down, which is called shorting the market).

Nature is its own free market and just like the economy the laws of supply and demand also apply. The economy is a more efficient allocation of resources than any design could achieve. A more efficient economy is created to the benefit of a whole society. Adam Smith used the analogy of an invisible hand of the markets, this hand moving resources to where they would be the most productive, the balance of this supply and demand would be reflected in the price. There is always an action and a reaction, an advance and a retreat, and a rising and a sinking. Everything happens according to law.

Weather

In this seeming order of the seasons, there is also chaos and unpredictability in nature just as there are chaos and unpredictability in the markets. No one can predict what the weather will be accurately a year from today, there are too many variables and random events. In markets, no one knows for sure whether the daily stock price will rise or fall a year from today, there is no perfect information.

The daily market fluctuations are like a stream that is in constant motion. It doesn't start, stop or wait even when the market is shut, prices are still in motion.

Markets move up over time as human innovation beats market fears. New problems are solved and ways to do things become more efficient, as technology improves. The market is not just a line on a screen. Each dot represents a piece of data or information flow. The market is made up of actual real-life businesses that produce earnings and profit. The market flows like a river that follows patterns of nature, although unpredictable. They form channels and deltas of information. Like a river the markets doesn't stop, even when the markets are closed, prices still move.

The market is just showing what value is perceived by the market at that moment, things can change in an instant. To bet against the market (to short a stock) is to bet against its fundamental nature, however, if taken at the change of tide can lead to great fortunes as markets often move faster on the way down.

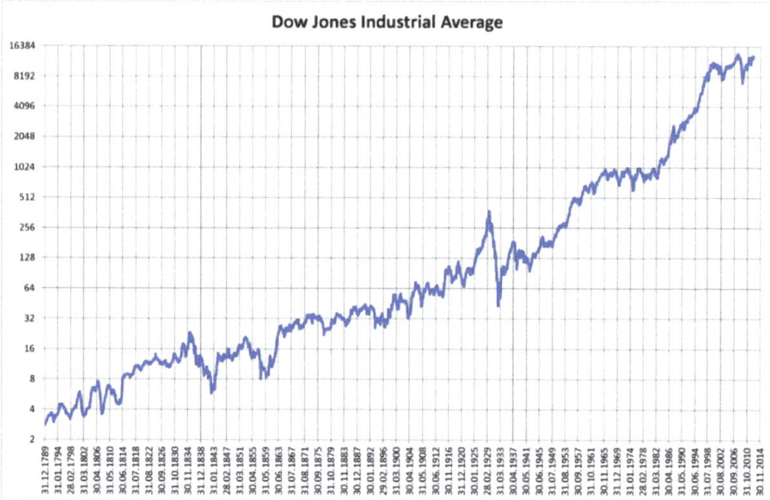

This graph shows the Dow Jones Industrial Average from December 1789 to August 2014 (monthly closings). The Dow Jones Index measures the 30 largest companies in the United States of America. The Dow Jones all-time high of 29,551.42 was reached on February. 12, 2020, a result of the longest bull market in history. The biggest cumulative loss suffered by the Dow Jones was during the Great Depression, when it lost nearly 90% of its value between 1929 and 1932.

<u>The Business Cycle</u>

The business cycle, also known as the economic cycle or trade cycle, is the downward and upward movement of gross domestic product (GDP) around its long-term growth trend. GDP is the total value of goods produced and services provided in a country during one year.

In 1860 French economist Clement Juglar first identified economic cycles 7 to 11 years long, although he did not claim that these patterns were regular or could be predicted. The economist Joseph Schumpeter (1883–1950) added that a business cycle has four stages:

1. expansion (increase in production and prices, low interest-rates) (Summer)
2. crisis (stock exchanges crash and multiple bankruptcies of firms occur) (Autumn)
3. recession (drops in prices and in output, high interest-rates) (Winter)
4. recovery (stocks recover because of the fall in prices and incomes (spring)

Looking at these patterns you can see that they are like the patterns of the seasons of the year in nature. The four seasons are Spring (recovery or revival), Summer (expansion or prosperity), Autumn/ Fall (Crisis or liquidation) and Winter (recession or depression).

The forces of the business cycles were expanded on by Malcolm Rorty. The business cycle and the four stages are illustrated below (although he called each stage something different the principle remains the same)

This illustration paints a picture of business changes covering several years. The picture is like a river curve that flows up and down across an imaginary normal line, with mountain peaks representing good times and the river valleys representing hard times.

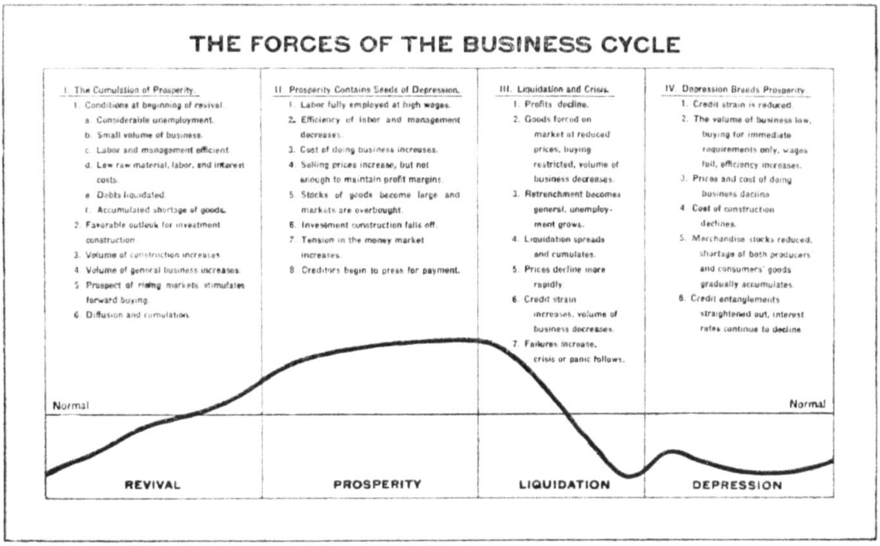

The Forces of the Business Cycle, 1922

Author: Malcolm Churchill Rorty,

From Wikimedia Commons, the free media repository

Spring (Recovery in the economic cycle)

Nothing gold can stay,

Nature's first green is gold,

Her hardest hue to hold.

Her early leaf's a flower;

But only so an hour.

Then leaf subsides to leaf.

So Eden sank to grief,

So dawn goes down to stay

Nothing gold can stay

Robert Frost (1923)

Green shoots of growth or recovery start to appear. The Stock market recovers from low prices. There is considerable unemployment, and only a small volume of surviving business, which starts to increase. The unproductive companies have died out during the cold winter months and this allows new companies to become established and start to grow. New technology and invention create new products and new opportunity.

Innovation and entrepreneurship create new business niches by offering goods and services where there is a market need where there previously wasn't before. Often it doesn't need to be new technology or invention. It is taking one or two ideas and creating a newer, fresher product by combining the best of both products. This convergence of many different technologies is creating synergies that can improve efficiencies. For example, the iPhone uses the telephone, computer and satellite tracking to be able to host a new app like Uber, which offers ride-sharing around a city, where perhaps the public transport wasn't very good or offers a reduction the price of a taxi due to these new efficiencies. Uber was started in 2009 during the green shoots of the 2008 financial crisis.

Summer (expansion in the economic cycle)

On the Grasshopper and the Cricket

The poetry of earth is never dead.

When all the birds are faint with the hot sun,

And hide in the cooling trees, a voice will run

From hedge to hedge about the new-mown mead;

That is the Grasshopper's he takes the lead

In summer luxury, he is never done

With his delights; for when tired out with fun.

John Keats (1795 – 1821)

Prosperity, expansion and increase in production and prices. Labour is fully employed and the cost of doing business increases. The selling price increases and markets become large and overbought. Too much stability can be a bad thing for the markets. Stability can bring instability. When the good times in the economy continue for too long A 'Minsky moment' (named after the economist Hyman Minsky) can occur due to increased confidence that asset prices will continue to rise. This is a sudden major collapse of asset values, which is part of the credit cycle or business cycle. People take on too much debt and are too confident in a bull market, which causes people to speculate as their memories of any previous downturn are lost in a haze of amnesia. This causes prices to rise and to be higher than the intrinsic or actual value of the business. Eventually, this, in turn, causes prices to fall.

Autumn (Crisis in the economic cycle)

Fall, Leaves, Fall

Fall, leaves, fall: die, flowers, away;

Lengthen night and shorten day;

Every leaf speaks bliss to me

Fluttering from the autumn tree.

I shall smile when wreaths of snow

Blossom where the roses should grow;

I shall sing when night's decay

Ushers in a drearier day.

Emile Bronte (1818 – 1848)

The Autumn, (also known as the fall), is where market crashes happen. Prices decline as goods are forced on the market, the volume of business decreases, prices decline rapidly and failure increases. This brings crisis and markets crash and bankruptcies of firms occur. There is widespread panic in the markets as prices fall. It is possible to make money in a falling market. This is to short the market, which means bet against the rise in prices and you make more money the further the prices fall.

Markets generally move up over time, human innovation beats market fears. To bet against the market is to bet against its fundamental nature. Part of a 'season proof' portfolio maybe be to have a short position, this means you will make money even when the market goes down. This can bring tremendous peace of mind that even in the darkest days of winter and no matter what happens in the market you will still be alright.

Winter (Recession in the economic cycle)

The First Snow Fall

The snow had begun in the gloaming,

And busily all the night

Had been heaping field and highway

With a silence deep and white.

Again, I looked at the snow-fall,

And thought of the leaden sky

That arched over our first great sorrow,

When that mound was heaped so high.

James Russell Lowell (1819 – 1891)

Recession breeds prosperity. The volume of business is low, cost and price of businesses decrease. Like the winter of the seasons, anything that is unproductive dies, giving space for new green shoots of revival. Having cash reserves in your portfolio can mean you can buy shares on the cheap below the fundamental value of the business. This is like buying something in the 'winter sale'.

When buying a business, you are purchasing something of value. Assets will provide goods or services that will be valuable and in demand in the future. The world is changing and what people find valuable today may not be the same as what someone will find useful tomorrow. A Kodak camera was the height of technology at one time. To be able to take a photo and have that instantly transformed into a picture that you can keep. Today we have digital cameras and Instagram instead. Recessions (or winter) can reduce a companies market share or may even kill off any unproductive companies. This is like a winter frost that kills off anything unproductive in the garden. This gives room for new green shoots to grow and new life to flourish.

The Investor is like a Gardener

The experienced investor is like an expert gardener who has witnessed many seasons and knows when a business is ripe for rebalancing or when it's still growing. Like an apple that's been left on the branch too long in the autumn, without being harvested, a company that has not been harvested by rebalancing your portfolio can rot.

> *'All bull markets are the same. They are born on pessimism, grown on scepticism, mature on optimism and die on euphoria. The time of maximum pessimism is the best time to buy and the time of maximum optimism is the best time to sell.*
>
> Sir John Marks Templeton (1912 –2008)

Different asset classes behave differently in different seasons (or times of the business cycle). The aim is to build a portfolio with different asset classes that will perform differently in each part of the business cycle. The aim is to season proof your portfolio so that you can thrive in any condition.

Today we have never had access to so much information. This mass of information and the power and ease of the internet allows us to buy or sell a share within seconds.

There is a big difference between information and knowledge and a greater difference between knowledge and wisdom. Turn on any business news channel and you will receive a wave of information. The daily fluctuations of the markets just as the daily weather temperatures are almost irrelevant looking back over the history of the human species. Herbert Simon described this as Bounded rationality (and won a Nobel prize for this work). Meaning that no one has access to perfect information, we don't and can't possibly know everything in the markets and can only make decisions with the available information. This means that it's impossible to know with 100% certainty of any event even for the most intelligent person. We as humans can only process a certain amount of information because the human mind has a limited capacity to process all the information and limited time to make the decision. Therefore, even individuals who want to make rational choices are bound to make satisfying rather than maximising choices in complex situations.

However, the natural state of the market is to move upwards. This is due to new inventions. Innovation creates new industries and employment such as medicine and technology that improve and add value to people's lives

We are subject to the laws of supply and demand every day. The things we buy in a shop are priced by how much it costs and how much someone is willing to pay for it. As well as the price of a company or a commodity is due to supply and demand and how much someone is willing to pay for it. Can these daily movements be predicted? The chartists who study technical analysis seems to think so.

Technical analysis

Technical analysis (also called Chartists) is looking at charts or lines of market prices and trying to spot patterns to predict and profit from what the price will do next. Many chartists believe that the market is 10% logical and 90% psychological. Crowd behaviour creates trends and as the price rise, more and more people want to profit from the increased price. These trends tend to continue until something happens to change the demand and supply balance. The trend will be your friend until the bend in the end.

Technical analysis is often seen as a 'dark art' as it is mostly used by traders trying to predict accurately the price of something in the future. The price of the market is ultimately down to the supply and demand balance. There are so many variables involved in that pricing it becomes impossible for technical analysis to be accurate every time. Technical analysis can be used as supporting evidence of the fundamental value of a market. With investments timing is important, what to buy is important but when to buy is more important.

At its core, technical analysis follows the laws of physics and Newton's three laws of motion. Newton's first law of inertia says that something at rest will continue at rest until a force greater than itself acts upon it. The second law of motion says that once moving this momentum will continue until it meets a greater force and finally, Newton's third law of motion states that every action has an equal and opposite reaction. Markets move in waves as suggested by R Elliot in his book Nature's law. Each rise and fall has predictable patterns as it follows the mathematics that exists in nature. These waves get their patterns from the mathematics that are commonly seen in nature. Simply put, the stock market is a human creation and believe it or not, we humans are emotional creatures, therefore, reflects human's natural behaviour.

These patterns are seen in nature from the smallest seashell on a beach and the patterns in sunflower seeds to patterns in hurricanes and up to the vast Milky Way galaxy. They all follow a mathematical pattern which was first written about by the Italian mathematician Fibonacci in 1202 AD. Fibonacci discovered these numbers after observing the breeding patterns of rabbits. He wrote that the proportions of many natural structures followed a predictable sequence when measured. He discovered that any two adjoining numbers equal the next highest number and create what is known as a summation series. This series of numbers follows 1 2 3 5 8 13 21 34 55 89 144... For example; 1+2 = 3, 3+5=8, 13+21=34 etc.

R. Elliot goes on to say that this law of nature is seen in human bodies too. Each hand has five fingers and each foot has five toes. Each arm and leg is subdivided into 3 sections. From the torso, there are 5 projections - 1 head, 2 arms and 2 legs (these are Fibonacci numbers). When we measure the proportions of our arms, our hands and down to the patterns of our DNA it shows this golden ratio of 1.618

The Golden Ratio.

The golden ratio is a simple mathematical pattern that has fascinated biologists, architects, mathematicians, musicians and naturalists since the start of history. This pattern is seen in not only in nature but also to the design of the Great Pyramids of Giza, to Leonardo Da Vinci's painting of the Vitruvian Man, (which has gone on to symbolise the renaissance period*)*. Dividing any Fibonacci number by the one before it and you get the same number 1.618. This is what is called the golden ratio. In nature, so many things flourish when they meet the golden ratio design.

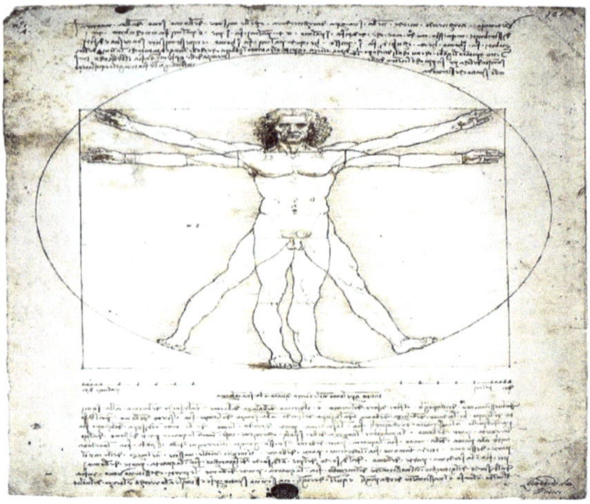

Author: Wikimedia Commons contributors

Why is this important?

This pattern of nature shows one of the most efficient ways of doing something. Nature is the most efficient allocation of resources than any design could make. The golden ratio pattern in plant leaves allows the most efficient amount of rain down to the roots of many plants. With investing the three things to look at before you decide to buy anything are: 1) Why are you investing (this is discovered when creating your life plan), 2)Consider what to buy (what Football Formation you decide to create will help you decide what you want to invest in), and 3)When to invest (which is the most advanced element to consider). Technical analysis will help you here. Timing is an essential element.

'The Golden Ratio supports the notion that there is more order in nature than we think, as in the symmetry of leaves and the geometric perfection of a snowflake.'

Simon Sinek, *Start with Why*

World-class traders use Fibonacci patterns and the golden ratio to spot patterns changes in price charts and try to predict where prices will go next. Fibonacci patterns have been said to be the code of trading as it demonstrates exponential growth given optimal conditions (like the breeding rabbits Fibonacci was studying). This pattern is said to be pleasing to the eye and provide a mathematical pattern for proportion and even beauty. Repetitive patterns in markets mixed with the psychology of masses and long-time frames show there are waves of similarities. Trends and corrections lead to market cycles. R. Elliot suggests after researching 75 years of chart patterns that there are predictable patterns of five waves that move up and 3 that move down. This may work in theory, however, to achieve this, in reality, is much harder than it sounds. This replies on trying to work out which season of the economic cycle we are currently experiencing.

There are many different size waves to consider, from daily patterns to regular economic cycles of 7-11 years, to larger waves from new technology which are known as Kondratieff waves. The Russian economist called Nikolai Kondratieff who discovered these patterns of the waves was executed under

Stalin's regime because his economic model predicted accurately that there would be a sharp decline in farm production.

WAVES OF CHANGE

These waves suggest that there are larger waves in the economy. They rise and falls ever 50 years.

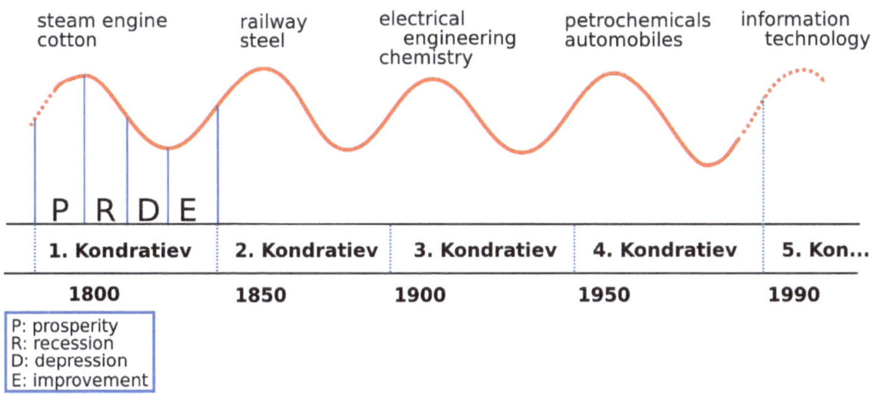

From Wikimedia Commons, the free media repository

These waves happen when new technology disrupts old existing technology. This new technology can create new jobs and improvements in the quality of lives of millions of people. This was shown in 1800 with the introduction of the steam train in 1850 with steel and railways, improvements in engineering, chemistry and electricity in 1900 in 1950 automobiles and petrochemicals and finally in 2000 the internet. Will Blockchain technology be the technology that causes the new wave of innovation? These developments enable bursts of disruptive product or services. This technology makes it easier to solve peoples' problems or give massive pleasure. The latest Kondratieff wave we have seen is the internet. Today people can communicate instantly across the globe as easily as having a face to face chat or moving vast amounts of money across the globe instantly. The internet or the information age has enabled bursts of disruptive product or service innovations, fuelling a sharp increase in industrial, and therefore economic, growth. These waves of change also carry with them the seeds of the next wave, so the cycles repeat, with periods of approximately 40 to 60 years.

SIXTH WAVE: THE PRESENT

The world is entering a "Sixth Wave of innovation" of Kondratieff cycles. The technological drivers have been built on technologies from the previous wave, such as computers, the internet digitization and computing power, plus newer areas:

- Environmental technologies
- Biotechnology (including genetic engineering)
- Nanotechnology
- Robotics
- Health technologies
- Blockchain
- Internet of things

Business Evolution

Business evolves becoming more and more complex over time. An economy is a natural thing, evolved and not designed. It responds to billions of inputs, past present and future. Any market has far too many inputs to predict. These inputs are too numerous, ambiguous and subtle for any person, group or computer algorithm to master. Humans are complex beings and we are bounded by our rationality. Meaning we don't know what we don't know.

Businesses occupy market niches.

Humans did not invent supply and demand. It has existed in nature for millions of years. Nature always grows what is ultimately best for the greater whole. Both species and companies that no longer abide by the law of supply and demand will soon be extinct.

With companies, like with species, it is often not the fastest or strongest company that survives, grows and evolves but the company that can adapt the fastest to the needs and wants of the customer. Often a customer may not realise that they need or want a product and it's a company's role to change the perception of the problem and offer a solution through effective marketing. Niches are found in both nature and business. This is where a species (or company) fits into its environmental conditions, where it has abundant resources and limited competitors to thrive in its environment.

It has been said that in business there is a continuous gale of creative destruction, whereby new products and processes displace old ones, is far more important than price competition among existing firms and products. The problem has been not how capitalism administers existing structures but how it creates and destroys them. Replacing the old with the new. Constantly changing to customers wants and needs.

The economy has been described as a circular flow which is the flow of money, goods and services around the economy. However, the circular flow excludes any innovations and improvements, which leads to a stationary state. Schumpeter described the hero of his story as an entrepreneur. As they look for value in the circular flow and create something new and original.

The Entrepreneur's Revolution

An entrepreneur is someone who connects, builds and combines things to create something better. An entrepreneur is someone who starts and builds a business, which innovatively creates value for customers. Entrepreneurs also take a calculated risk as their idea or concepts have not yet been tested or proven by the market. An entrepreneur creates profitable businesses to solve a problem for someone.

Today we need to own ourselves first and be our own business. We need to be entrepreneurs. Think of one of the richest people in the world today: Warren Buffet. He is not just an investor, but he is an entrepreneur. He looks for value and gives his money to companies in exchange for a share in that business. An entrepreneur is like an investor that shifts economic resources out of a lower and into higher production and a higher yield. Right now, we are on a cusp of history. It's a revolutionary time. Technology since the 2000s has been building like a giant wave. This has grown in size and speed thanks to convergence. This is where several unrelated ideas bump into each other and create massive, unpredictable results. iPhone meets Google maps and there is the development of a mobile application; you now have a new efficient transport grid-like Uber just from an idea in a human's brain.

The game we often play unconsciously and compulsively is to avoid loss. It is natural as humans. Money that we need in the future seems smaller or not as important as it looks far away and therefore smaller than the money, we hold in our hand today. It's often hard to picture and believe that planting a seed today will create fruit in years to come.

'The entrepreneur disturbs this equilibrium and is the prime cause of economic development, which proceeds cyclically along with several time scales.'

Joseph Schumpeter (1883 – 1950)

The business should be an ecosystem growing and evolving. Gone are the days of machinery and peak efficiency. The business should be more like the seasons growing in spring and reaping the rewards in autumn.

Business cycles are like the season which have predictable patterns of economic cycles over the long term but paradoxically unpredictable in the short term like the weather. New ideas, new technology and new hope encourage a new exciting age. New technology or a combination of new technologies like the renaissance age, or the age of enlightenment.

If money can be used to create new technology or employ more people it could create natural synergies that add value to everyone. These can be times of great prosperity

Although you can't control nature it is possible to work with the laws of nature. Like a farmer who cultivates their crops. A farmer is active and deliberate. By choosing the best location, pulling up any unproductive weeds and fertilising the soil and sowing the correct crop for the conditions. Knowing what will flourish in that climate.

Spontaneous order is what happens when entrepreneurs see the needs and desires of people and then go out to create a product that solves their problems. These innovations are usually introduced by new people rather than by existing businesses and by new firms rather than by those who already occupied prominent niches in the circular flow.

'It is the entrepreneur who innovates and applies new combinations of factors of production'

(Heertje, 2008).

A good investor knows when to make changes and when to wait by understanding the patterns of the season. The farmer is proactive, looking for better ways to be more productive, using new technology to their advantage.

The seasons are in balance. Have reserves (cash and bonds) for the fall (Autumn) and to last you through the winter. Summer may go on longer than expected. Like the day to day change in weather, the day to day fluctuations of the markets can't be predicted. Like the seasons the markets follow a set pattern a similar spring, summer, winter and fall.

In the summer think of winter and in the winter think of summer.

Follow the three Laws of money accumulation

1) Pay yourself first every month.
2) Diversify and
3) Re:Balance.

Chapter 7

The Risks: Play to Win or Play not to lose

'A ship is safe in the harbour but that's not what it was designed for'

John A Shedd (1928)

Are you Taking Enough Risks? Why is Risk so Important to Understand When Investing?

Imagine owning a sailing ship in the 17th Century. Aiming to move cargo from point A to point B getting the most profits whilst taking the least risk. You wanted the largest income from your ship without it bothering your day to day life too much. It's very similar to investing today. Every pound coin you invest is like a small ship working for you, every minute of every day. The more risk you are willing to take the greater your reward over the long term. Risk is paid for taking chances.

Taking risks could be doing business with an unknown market or going a little further afield than was previously thought possible. Now imagine stepping foot on board with your cargo vessel. You feel the wind on your cheek as you look out to sea, your footing is a little uneasy as the deck rolls up and down with the waves of the sea. There are many risks to consider and like any human you want to maximise your returns, whilst taking as little risk as possible.

Why should we invest?

There's always the option of leaving your ship in the harbour, to choose not to harm your ship battling against the elements of nature, or risk meeting pirates along the way or to take the chance of getting lost and not making it to a safe port without losing your supplies. It seems an easy option, but being in harbour is not what your ship was designed for. If your ship didn't make the perilous voyages then there would be no tea for your morning cuppa, no wine to drink with friends and no clothes to wear to work that day. Investing, like shipping is a balance between risk and reward. Taking no action can seem like the easy option. Not investing and keeping your money safe in the bank can be viewed similarly - this is not what money was designed for. Taking risks is part of life. If we stop taking any risks, then global trade would stop, and the economy would grind to a halt. We would not be able to exchange our goods and services with someone else who wants or needs this and both parties would be better to exchange their specialist knowledge and benefit from their strengths making it a win/win/win.

What is Risk?

Risk is a slippery and elusive concept which is little understood especially with investing, however, the dictionary definition of risk is 'the situation involving exposure to danger or harm'. With investing the aim is to get the most rewards, taking the correct level of risk for their situation. Every day we encounter risk. Even undertaking a simple task like just going to work we are taking risk.

The world is an unpredictable and unknown environment which can never be risk-free. Even if you never leave the safety of the harbour walls you are missing opportunities that you may have received by applying for that job, asking your future wife on your first date or putting your money into the stock market. Risk is an unavoidable part of the investment process. Although there are many different types of risks when investing, the two main types that will affect your portfolio are market risk (the volatility in the market price) and inflation (the erosion of the pound in your pocket).

The main risk you will face is volatility, which is mainly considered as the ups and downs of the market. Volatility is what most of us fear. It makes the headline news when the markets take a tumble and cause fear among us that we may lose the money that we've invested. Think of these ups and downs of volatility like the waves in the ocean. The more risk you take the bigger the waves. If you are closer to shore in a sheltered bay, then the waves will be less a boat anchored in that bay will less likely to sink or be capsized by the waves in this less risky area. The further out into the deep ocean you sail, the bigger the wave then the greater the risk; however, with this greater risk comes greater reward.

Risk is measured by the volatility of returns called standard deviation. This measures how wildly the investment moves up and down. The greater the standard deviation, the greater the volatility and therefore the associated risk. An example of an investment of this type, with returns fluctuating, wildly would be cryptocurrencies in 2015-2018. Investments with returns staying close to its expected returns are said to be low risk and therefore low standard deviation.

A good investor is someone who gets both a return and their original money back. The aim is to get the desired reward by taking the least amount of risk available. The best investors think differently from the rest. Learning to identify an opportunity to buy or sell does not mean that you have learnt to think like an investor. The aim of investing is to get the most rewards whilst taking the correct level of risk for your situation. With investing often people want to be risk-free so that they don't lose their hard-earned money. Keeping money in a bank for many people seems to be a way to be risk-free however this is not true. There is inflation risk and opportunity risk of not taking your chances.

Inflation

Inflation is the increase in the price of goods and services over time. This affects the buying power of the pound coin in your pocket. It is the silent killer as it slowly erodes your wealth over time. Think about the spending power of cash compared with a basket of shopping. The pound coin (or other currency) in your back pocket could buy much less today than in the 1980s. If you are going to generate enough income from your assets for when you stop working, then you need the courage to invest. Many people only think about investing as the ups and downs of the market. However, inflation can be just as damaging to your wealth over the long term.

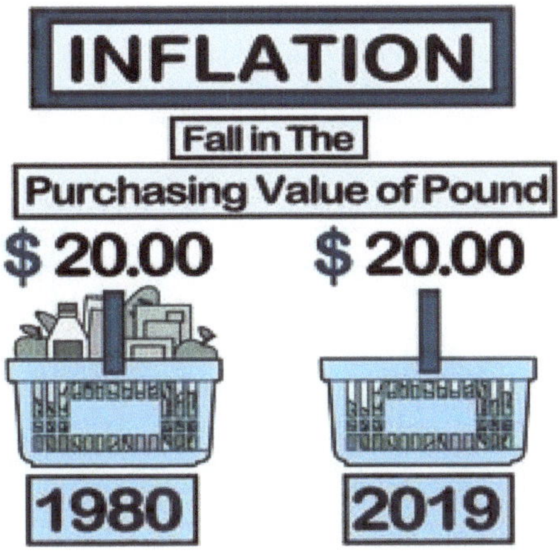

Inflation risk is rising prices that reduce the real value of your money. It's the rising prices of everyday goods that you buy in your weekly shop.

Think of inflation as the wind against your cheek. Often you don't take any notice of the breeze but over time there is a huge difference in how far you get between sailing with the wind in your face or blowing at your back. Inflation is measured in the UK using the retail price index (RPI). It takes several everyday items from your shopping basket that are bought in a weekly shop. It measures these items to see how much prices have risen or fallen (a falling price is called deflation).

World Inflation rate 2019. From Wikimedia Commons, the free media repository

Here is a World map showing inflation. As you can see inflation can reach 25% in some parts of the world.

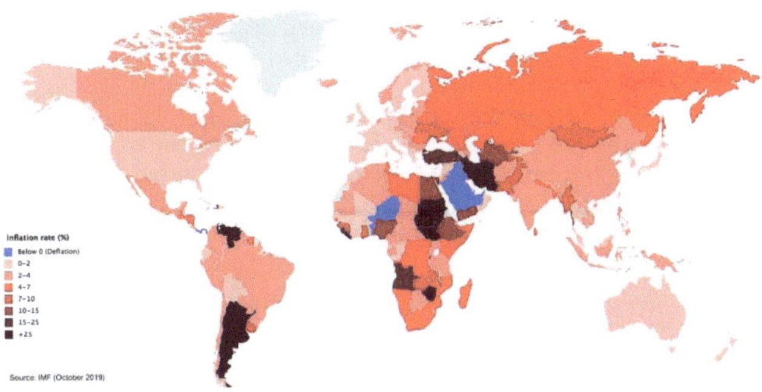

World Inflation rate 2019. From Wikimedia Commons, the free media repository

Here is a World map showing inflation. As you can see inflation can reach 25% in some parts of the world in 2019.

The hard route often turns easy and the easy route can turn hard. There is a cause for every effect an effect for every cause.

Three Ways to Reduce the Risk you Take with your Money.

Sailing a ship in the 17th Century included many dangers: treacherous seas, bad weather, piracy, and even mutiny. These hazards mean that a merchant's fortune could literary disappear overnight. Like investing today there were three ways you could reduce the risk. Reducing your risk means that you are more likely to make a profit, it will also give you peace of mind that you will not lose all your precious cargo and your life's savings overnight. This will give you a better night's sleep.

1) The first way to reduce your risk is through diversification. Having different asset classes in your portfolio (like shares of a business, bonds, property, commodities and cash) and diversifying within that asset. By having different shares of a business that provide different types of goods and services that business will perform better or worse in different environments.

Investors can reduce the risk of their portfolio by holding a range of different types of assets. Different types of investment perform differently under certain market conditions, and therefore by having a diverse range of asset classes the fluctuations caused by most economical events can be smoothed. This is opposed to investing in only one asset class, which increases the volatility and therefore the risk. The downside of one asset class will be counterbalanced by the upside potential of another investment. This offsetting would not occur if both investments had the same characteristic. Diversification is effective where an individual asset moves in different directions. You should diversify within asset classes too meaning different types of the same assets class like large or small companies or different types of commodities. Different sectors and different sizes of a company can behave differently and reduce your risk by holding a variety of assets.

2) The second way to reduce your risk is through insurance. Owners of ships would pool their ships with other ship owners. So rather than putting all your cargo on one ship (or all your eggs in one basket to use the common phrase), you split the risk between not just one ship but hundreds of ships. If one ship sank all owners would suffer a small loss however this would be much better than risking it all on one ship. Today you can insure yourself for any loss by insuring yourself against loss of life, and injury as well as many other things.

3) A third way to reduce risk is to have enough reserves to cover any fluctuations. By reserves, I mean cash or bonds, which tend to be more defensive. It could be possible to invest your reserves when the market is down to take advantage of the lower prices. Having a three-month cash buffer means you don't need to sell any assets in an emergency when perhaps the market is at a low price.

The risks and rewards. Often called the risk versus reward, like it was the fight between two competing teams making a difficult choice. You have options, you actually have many and that's often the problem. You can either choose one way or the other but there is a third way. A combination of both. There is a sweet spot. Just like there is a sweet spot in sailing. This is when you get the most force out of the wind before it gets too dangerous and you have to 'tack' or turn back into the wind. You learn this only with experience, from several hours out at sea with the wind blowing against your cheek and the waves rolling beneath you. You cannot know which way the wind will blow or have ferocious it will be. You can only choose how you set your sail. Improving your knowledge, decisions you make and your money mindset.

The concept of risk is little understood especially with investing, as often you need the courage to take a risk. It feels safer not to make a bold decision, but you must understand that by not making that decision and acting on that choice you are still making a decision. It's the decision not to move forward and generally, if you are not moving forward you are going backwards particularly with investing.

<u>It's Balancing Act</u>

The two main types of risk that will affect your portfolio are market risk (volatility or the ups and downs of the market) and inflation, which is the reduction of the pound coin in your pocket over time as other prices rise.

Volatility is like waves in the ocean, whereas the wind is like inflation or deflation. You often don't feel the wind of inflation on your cheek in your day to day life and only notice when there is a storm blowing. By then it's too late

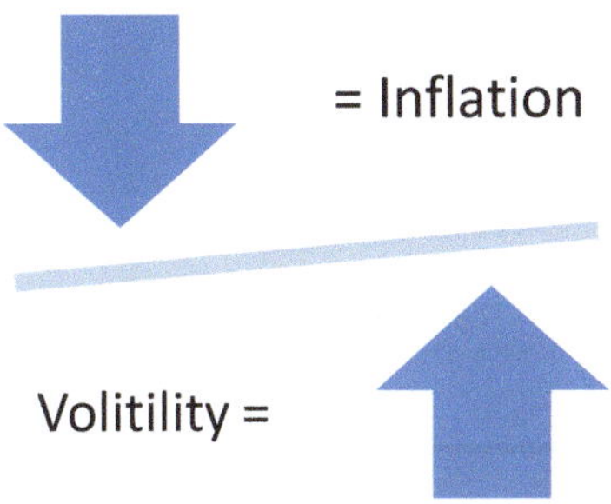

<u>How well you want to eat versus how well you want to sleep at night.</u>

The amount of risk you should take all boils down to how well you want to eat versus how well you want to sleep. By this, I mean that taking more risks over the long term will lead to better returns and therefore you'll have more money to eat at fancy restaurants. This would be compared to sleeping well at night as taking higher risks can often cause more stress of losing your money.

Having a low-risk portfolio may mean you sleep better however often won't get you the gains you need to eat well later in life. Taking too many risks can mean you don't sleep soundly at night.

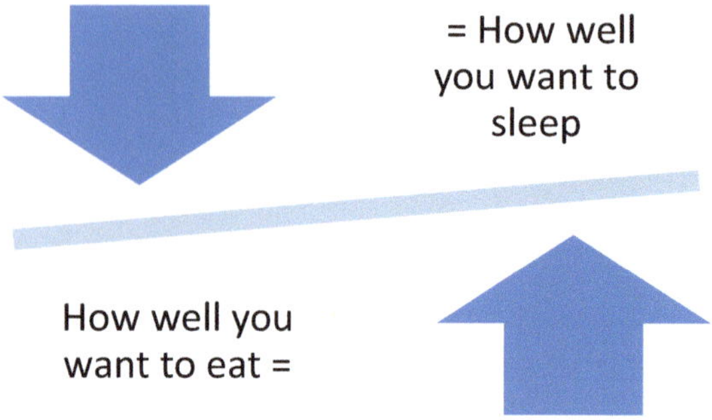

Choosing your investment vehicle should depend on your aims and objectives based on you. This is by understanding yourself, your knowledge and expertise, your risk profile, your age, how long you are investing for, and your capacity for loss

Capacity for loss

Capacity for loss means your ability to withstand the losses. This may sound complicated but it's really important when understanding your risk profile.

Imagine two people. One person has £100 to invest, the other person only has £1 to invest. Both people invest £1 into cryptocurrency (an asset much higher on the risk scale). If cryptocurrency drops by 50% the person with £100 still has £99.50 yet the person with only £1 is down to 50p.

The person with £100 can afford to invest in much higher risk assets. That person has a higher capacity for loss than the person with only £1 if the first person invested the £99 in safer assets.

How much do I need to live on for the rest of my life?

Goals drive financial plans. Once we understand our goals from our life plan (in chapter 4) we can then calculate how many resources we require to meet these goals and we can implement an investing strategy.

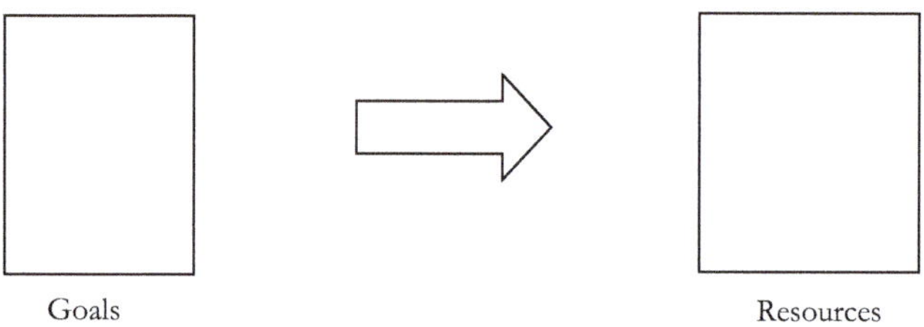

How Much Risk Do I Need To Take to Reach My Financial Plan?

The most common questions asked with investing is 'How much will I get from my money?' Or 'how much risks do I need to take?' Or 'When can I retire?'. Whilst this is impossible to know for certain as there are way too many variables, this is a simple way to give you an indication.

Remember Pythagoras from chapter two. Pythagoras said any problem starts with a triangle. To understand how much money, you want to receive you first need to understand your time and your risk.

1) Time (how long until you need to use the money)
2) Risk (How Much Risk are you willing to take)
3) Reward (How much will you get back from your investment)

With investing the answer most people want to know is what returns or reward they will receive.

First look at the time you are looking to invest (number of years), The more time you invest the longer that investment must grow. Then look at how much risk you are willing to take. The greater the risk you take the higher the returns (in general). The greater the risks you take the luckier you will be. This leads to more value created and the rewards you will receive.

Time + Risk = Returns

Three pieces of information you need are time, risk and return (or your rewards) for giving that money.

Risk taken^2 + Time^2 = Rate of return^2

$A^2 + B^2 = C^2$

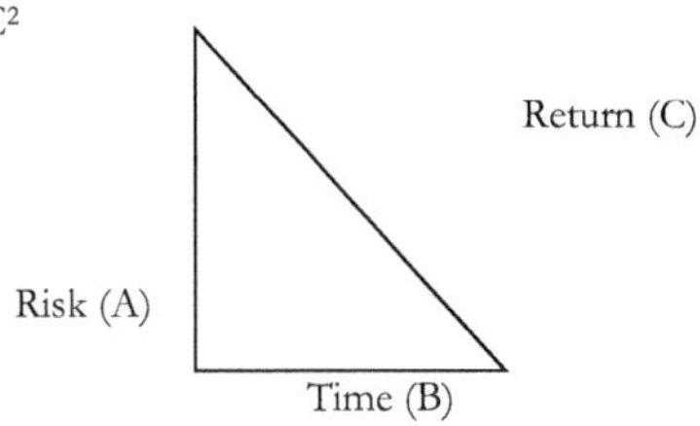

Time is the other major factor with investing than risk. A 25-year-old can afford to take more risks than a 65-year-old because if they are both investing today, the 25-year-old will be invested for a longer time if they both want to sell those assets aged 70 (the 65 year old will be invested for 5 years and the 25 year old will be invested for 45 years old).

Risk is simply the degree of uncertainty attached to an expected rate of return. Increased risk increases volatility. Small stocks and emerging markets can get much greater returns in the long term compared with 'safer' assets like cash, but they also experience more price volitilty. When creating a financial plan, it's important to understand our relationship to risk as it is to determine goals and resources. We need to be clear with how much risk we are willing to take and understand how many ups and down our path is likely to take. Especially when understanding that we humans are emotional creatures (explained in the next chapter).

Inflation risk and volatility risk are the two main forms of risks when investing. However, there are other types of risks.

Counterparty risk

This increases massively when you only invest in one company. Mathematicians have worked out that the risk you take reduces by 60%, whilst getting similar returns by investing in several companies rather than only investing in a single company. The more companies that you own the more the risk drops (up to about 50 companies). The ideal amount is between 30 and 50 companies in your portfolio. The good news is that with technology it's never been easier to spread your risk by investing in investment funds or index trackers where you invest in many companies rather than buying only one company.

Inertia risk

This is the risk of not getting started. This is the risk of missing out by doing nothing. Many people don't invest as they think they will get it wrong or the market will crash as soon as they put their money in. The length of time you invest is one of the most important factors with investing. Starting today is one of the most powerful things you can choose to do.

Behaviour risk

Humans have evolved to be terrible investors. As we will learn in the next chapter, humans are often our own worst enemy when it comes to investing. We have evolved to want instant gratification, to want to eat the tasty treat straight away rather than investing money to get a return in 20 years. Investing often doesn't feel right. Doing the right thing long term can feel like the wrong thing short term. Especially in a market crash where many people fear and panic in the market.

Currency risk

This means having all your money in one currency. This is another reason why just holding cash is so dangerous because the government of the currency you hold could default on their loans and the money that they owe. This would make the value of the cash in your bank account be worth much less. This happened in Germany in 1930s and Argentina in 2001.

Operational Risk

This is the risk that arises during the investment process. This may be you doing something wrong. Perhaps you press the wrong button and you sell rather than buy or maybe you buy too much or not enough. Operational risk also includes the platform you are investing into. Meaning staff errors or a counterparty failing to settle the money you invested or even systems failures. Another operational risk is fraud.

Political Risks

Political risk is the markets reacting to a political result of an unfavourable political party. Perhaps the potential for a country to become communist rather than a capitalist regime. South Korea is priced lower than other similar countries due to its proximity to unstable North Korea. Brexit is another example of political risk when there is an unexpected political result, which is seen by the markets to be unfavourable to the economy.

Event Risk

This is a risk of something happening unexpectedly. This may be a natural disaster. Japan had a tsunami in 2011, which caused major damage and flooding. This also had a detrimental effect on their economy and stock market costing $360 billion (according to Wikipedia).

How much risk should I take?

So how do we manage risk to get the most return, whilst taking the least amount of risk possible? We need a tried and tested method that has been used for thousands of years. The best way is to look at nature.

How do you find the easiest way to do anything? Use the path of least resistance. Use The 80/20 principle.

The 80/20 Principle

An economist in 1896 found that 80% of the resources in Italy were held by 20% of the population. This is known as the 80/20 Principle and is named after the person who discovered it the Pareto Principle. Vilfredo Pareto found that this ratio not only worked in the economy but also in nature. 20% of the pea pods in his garden produced 80% of the peas. This means that this is the optimal way of allocating any resource or the easiest way to do anything. This also relates to money.

This 80/20 principle can be applied to everything in nature including humans. Knowing this can be applied to the markets and your wealth. 20% of your efforts will produce 80% of your results. Having 80% in relatively safer assets and investing 20% in higher-risk assets is a great way to reduce your risk and increasing potential rewards, without risking all your money rather than having all your money in high-risk assets.

The Pareto Principle

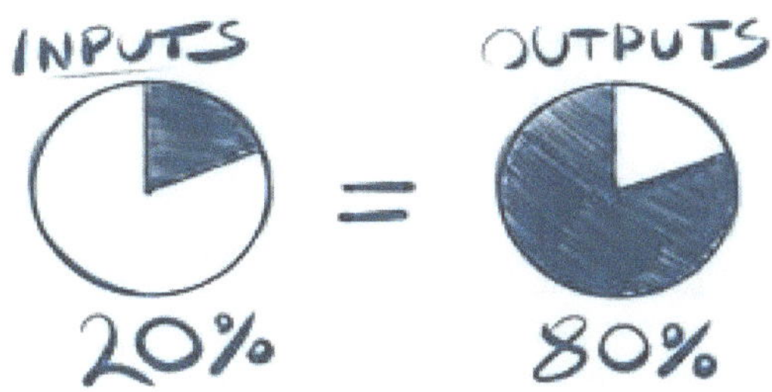

Using the 80/20 principle is a great way to build your wealth as 80% of your outcome will come from 20% of your efforts.
Imagine 20% of the money you earn will create 80% of your outcomes.

Sow, Grow, Dough Model

This is a simple 'rule of thumb' model you can use as a guide if you don't know how much to allocate between your pension and your government ISA allowance, both are tax-efficient investment vehicles. (These are discussed in chapter 9).

Sow, Grow, Dough Model

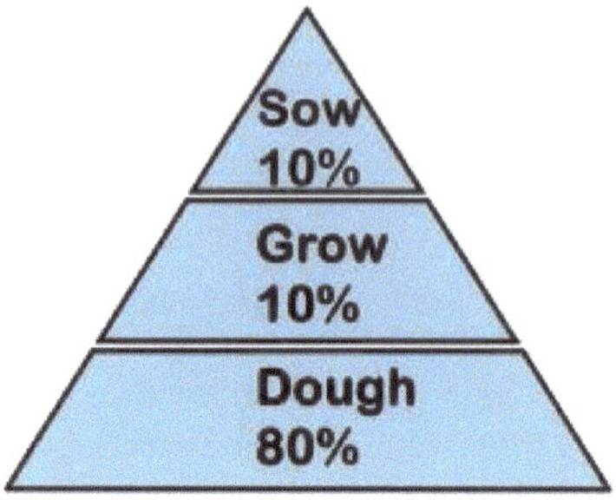

10% in pensions to sow for the future
10% to grow in ISAs
80% of your dough to spend on what you like

This means 10% of your money you earn into to sow for your retirement. The other 10% of the money grows for the future. You can spend 80% of your income (after tax) on living your life

These two combines to make up the Pareto Principle of 20%. The other 80% of the money you earn is your dough (money you can spend to live your life). You can spend it however you like. The good news is if you are in the UK and employed your employer now must by law to contribute to your pension automatically.

Think of it like for every ten coins you receive from your income; you can spend eight coins for your DOUGH and then invest two of these coins. One coin you SOW into your pension and the other coin you GROW by investing into your ISA allowance.
Life is for living and this will give you massive peace of mind that you are looking after yourself for the future.

Where do I Invest?

There are several low-cost investment platforms or online brokers which you can invest at very little cost to you. These multi-asset portfolios will invest cheaply into 100s of companies listed on the stock market of different sizes and sectors from around the world, they will invest into several different government bonds and corporate bonds globally as well as investing into a range of commodities, they will invest into both residential and commercial property globally and keeping money in cash of different currencies.

Depending on the risk profile you choose the portfolio will be allocated a different amount in each asset class.

This spreads the risk you take meaning you will get a better return in the long run and will smooth out the ups and downs of your investments. Reducing the stress and worry you feel when investing.

All you need to do is to work out your risk profile from a menu of risk profiles (usually about five) from low risk to high risk.

In Money Tipps interactive workshops, we guide you through implementing your investment strategy and help you understand which risk profile would be right for you you depending on your circumstances.

Money Tipps use the latest technology to help you simplify your finances and plan for the future. Once you understand the principles you can use cash flow tools to get an accurate picture of your circumstances to help you improve your investing, whilst reducing stress and worry and aiming to retire earlier or only working because you want to not because you have to. So you can live your life as you choose.

Picking your investment vehicle and understanding your Risk Profile

Kayak: Cautious Investor

Invested mainly in cash

The winds are calm, and the sea is like a mirror with little or no waves.

You feel safe in your canoe paddling and splashing about. It seems like summer will never end and you have all the time in the world.

The waves are tiny and even the biggest wave gently lulls at the side of the boat which feels like being gently rocked to sleep. Being lulled into a false sense of security. The problem with these conditions is that without any wind or force you are not getting where you want or need to be going.

This is a very cautious investor who is unwilling to accept large fluctuations in the value of your money. This risk profile is keeping most of your money in cash. The problem with taking little risk is that it fine in the short term but time is ticking away. The forces of inflation are slowly eroding your hard-earned money. You may not want to leave your money all in cash for more than five years. You understand that in times of low-interest rates the returns that you get back will be relatively low.

You must understand you are vulnerable to the effects of inflation. Cash is easy to access as it is liquid. You can sleep well as you don't worry about the ups and downs of the market. However, the returns provided will mean you will not eat well in the future.

The wind may not seem much on a warm summers day however taking low risk today turns out to be more risky long term.

<u>Canal boat. Lower Medium Risk</u>

<u>Invested in cash, bonds, property and some money in the stock market (about 40% in the stock market)</u>

A canal boat is more risk than a kayak. Has a small engine to combat weather (market conditions). It does not move very fast compared to a speed boat but is quicker than a kayak. You can still sleep much well as the canal boat is protected from storms

You are a cautious investor and want the value of your money to keep up with inflation. You will be investing for three to five years. You want the opportunity of getting better growth over the long term. You investing will mainly be kept in bonds, property and cash

You are comfortable investing a small amount of your money into equity, which are shares of a business in both the UK and abroad. The price of these companies may fall in price. You also accept that if you take your money out that it may be possible for that to be lower than the money you put into this investment.

A cautious investor will be invested in safer asset classes like bonds, property and more stable equity-like dividend stocks from more developed markets. Both government Bonds and company bonds will make up a proportion of the total. Cash will also make up some of this portfolio

Speed Boat: Medium Risk

Invested in the stock market (about 60%), bonds, property, cash and some gold

You are willing to put more of your money into higher-risk assets, which has the potential for higher returns.

You are looking to invest for 5 to 10 years or longer. You understand that the price you pay for these investments may drop in value significantly. You want your money to keep up with inflation. You must realise that there could be significant falls in the value of your investments

You are in much deeper water than the small boat with a motor you don't need to notice the small currents in the water (currency) as you have diversified your portfolio internationally. Tide (market conditions) is still a factor but having a larger engine means you can power through this.

Waves (volatility)do have an effect but less so now you're in a larger boat and you can power over the smaller ones. Taking more risk venturing away from the coast may seem scary however this portfolio will have bonds (both government and companies) for safety (perhaps 30-40%) so you can motor into a harbour for safety if there is a storm coming. There will be a higher proportion of equities and some small companies. There may be a small portion of emerging markets.

You realise that there may be some falls in your investment, understanding this risk gives you a higher potential to achieve better long term returns.

Upper medium: Sailboat

Invested about 80% into the stock market (including smaller companies and emerging markets), bonds, cash, property, some commodities (like gold)

You can either use forces for or against you. The two main forces are volatility and inflation. The sail boat uses wind and currents to its advantage, which saves on fuel. Forces like compound interest and rebalancing mean that you are using nature to your advantage. Saying that markets are similar to the weather, you can often see the current trends

If an experienced sailor is in charge of the boat then this wind speed or risk can be used as an advance. The power of the wind can power a boat without the need for an engine, which uses petrol (your income).

This risk of being out in higher wind is paid off with the reward of moving faster, getting to where you want to be quicker. It may be true that this strength of wind may turn into a hurricane and in nature, there are hurricanes every few years but this risk (as long as you are experienced and have the correct equipment) is worth taking that chance.

However, weather is just as unpredictable as the markets. You could be out for a nice sunny day sail and the weather forecast look good all the experts say there is nothing to worry about and out of nowhere the pressure drops and you feel the breeze on your cheek pick up. An experienced sailor could trim the sails so not to be blown off course. An inexperienced sailor maybe entered danger. Benjamin Graham Intelligent Investor recommends having only 75% invested in stocks and having 25% invested in bonds. Bonds are like you safe harbour where you can ride out the storm. There may be some emerging market bonds as they offer a better return.

There will be a higher proportion of smaller companies, growing companies and emerging markets. There may be a small number of frontier markets and some commodities. There will be higher risk sectors like, technology and commodities.

You are investing for 5 – 10 years or longer and understand there there is a potential for significant falls in your investment.

Jetski: High Risk and High Reward

Invested into the stock market (100%), including smaller companies and emerging markets. There is no bonds or little cash reserves in this portfolio

Increasing risk. This is a much more aggressive strategy. You are not able to have a cup of tea on board. This vechicle can be loads of fun as it has lots of ups and downs.Are you prepared for the ride?

If you are young and have the stomach for some risk then this is for you.

You are looking to get exceptional returns from your investment. You understand that this will be at a high risk to your money. To invest in this level of risk you need to have considerable experience with investing and can invest for the long term. Your portfolio will be made up of lots of higher-risk assets. You accept that there may be sharp falls in the value of your investments.

There is nowhere to hide on a jet ski. This portfolio is likely to be 100% equity and no bonds to get a better return. If you get caught in the tide or the weather turns bad there is no shelter.

This is investing in smaller nimble companies with very little in reserves like cash and bonds.

If the weather turns cold you may wish you had chosen some less volatile assets

To invest into this vechicle you must accept potential for sharpe falls in the value of your assets. This higher risk gives a better potential for higher returns especially if you are investing for the very long term..

Rocket ship: Speculation

Speculating on high-risk assets or trading trying to buy and sell to time the market

Going to the moon. The moon looks so close, you feel like you could reach out and touch it. Remember only a few people have landed on the moon successfully. Most people who have tried have either used up all their money or blown up in the process. From our perspective on earth, the moon is visible every night and it seems like you could just reach out and touch it. If going to the moon represents consistent success as a trader we can say that getting to the moon is possible. However, the journey is extremely difficult and only a handful of people have made it. Speculating is similar.

There is a difference between investing and speculating. Investing is buying an actual living breathing business that over the long term will generate profits from selling their goods and services and you also expect to get your money back from this venture.

Speculating is much more short term where the aim is to get in and out of the market at profit-taking the value from the market. Speculating is trying to predict the moving of the share price.

Trading (speculating) looks so easy from afar but when we start doing it we realise it's not as easy as it looks. The odds are actually agains you and it may be more beneficial to diversify your portfolio.

Examples of speculation are Bitcoin, foreign exchange trading and penny stocks. These assets can be used as part of an overall balanced portfolio.

There is no guarantee of any returns at all and there is a potential to lose all your money when speculating. This is for the experienced investor only. The best strategy is to trade or speculate as part of an overall strategy which includes some safer assets. The more assets you have the more risk you can take due to having a higher capacity for loss. Speculating should always come with a warning.

Human Behaviour and our 3 Different Brains

Chapter 8

'Be fearful when others are greedy and greedy when others are fearful.'

Warren Buffet

Are you investing or just speculating, and how to spot the differences in today's market?

Humans are not always rational and are more driven by emotion than we realise. Think of some of your colleagues or family members.

Do they always act rationally?

Have you ever acted irrationally?

Have you ever visited the supermarket hungry and ended up buying a whole load of food that you were not planning to? Most of the food being junk food. Perhaps you have been so hungry that you have devoured a whole chocolate cake, which was not in your best long-term interests? Our behaviour is driven by different parts of the brain due to our evolution. When investing we need to understand which part of the brain is making the decisions. This is particularly important during a market crash when people panic and we make silly decisions which is not in our best long term interest.

Think of the market like it is a person. An emotional person. Every day this person offers you a price on a business which depends on how they feel that day, rather than the actual worth of the business due to its fundamentals of earnings and assets. If is it being greedy, it will charge more one day and if it is scared, he will want to get rid of his businesses and will sell for much less.

How many of your colleagues, family members or even your partner would you call rational all the time? As humans, we are not rational. We do things for bizarre reasons, we have emotions. This is the same as markets. The stock market is made up of lots of people making individual decisions. We can act very differently in practice than we should in theory due to our emotions.

We are emotional creatures. We have not evolved to be good investors. Our emotions often make us do the exact opposite of what would suit us long term. A falling stock market may cause us to panic and sell at a time when it would be better to buy. We may greedily buy into the latest fad or trend trying to make our riches only to realise that we have only bought nothing but hot air. Our brains are not wired to be good investors. We have evolved over thousands of years and our brains lead us to do things that don't always benefit us in our modern world.

Most good investment decisions go against what you think would be a good decision. Investing can be counter-intuitive. Often, the right thing to do doesn't feel right at the time. We have evolved from a time when we didn't need to invest for our future self. In the past if we found a tasty treat there were no refrigerator to store the food for later, we would have to eat it then and there or the food would go bad. Our ancient brains don't understand the concept of investing. The concept of investing a pound coin today that you will get your pound back with a little bit extra 20 years later often doesn't make evolutionary sense to our ancient brains.

Mr Market's Split Personality

Mr Market is the best metaphor explaining how stocks become overpriced, from Benjamin Graham's book *The Intelligent Investor.* Graham uses the image of the market like a person, who is grumpy some days and euphoric other days. When Mr market is feeling grumpy, he thinks the world is going to end and therefore the rational person can pick up a bargain. Grumpy Mr Market does not price something as a rational person would. When Mr Market is euphoric he never imagines the market could ever fall again. This means the price you pay for something is going to be much more expensive than the underlying price of that company. Is Mr Market still around today?? You bet he is.

Would you be willing to let a person into your house once a day to tell you how they were feeling and you'd have to agree to the price they were selling their goods, depending on if they were euphoric or grumpy? This is exactly what the news reports do. The price of the company you buy is priced only on how the market is feeling that day. It may be euphoric and you pay more or the market may be grumpy and therefore that day you get a bargain

To win in finances you should not ignore Mr Market, but do business with him but only to the extent that it suits your interests. Mr Market's job is to provide you with a price and your job is to decide whether it's in your interest to act on it. You do not need to trade with him because he begs you to. By refusing to let Mr Market be your master, you transform him into your worker, someone you do business with. An investor who allows themselves to get worried by a market move downwards is turning his greatest strength into his greatest weakness.

Thinking Fast and Thinking slow

Imagine the different personality differences between Homer Simpson from 'The Simpsons' cartoon and Sheldon from 'The Big Bang Theory'. Both represent different ways to go about a problem. Sheldon is the human part of the brain, very logical. He is very rational and doesn't do anything without a good reason for doing it. He wants to have all the information before making the best logical decision. Unfortunately, the markets don't work like this. No one can have access to all the market information and the market often behaves in an irrational emotional manner.

Homer Simpson on the other hand makes decisions because he feels like it. He often doesn't think before he acts and ends up making impulsive decisions. Homer acts on instincts, emotion and often doesn't think things through to their logical conclusion.

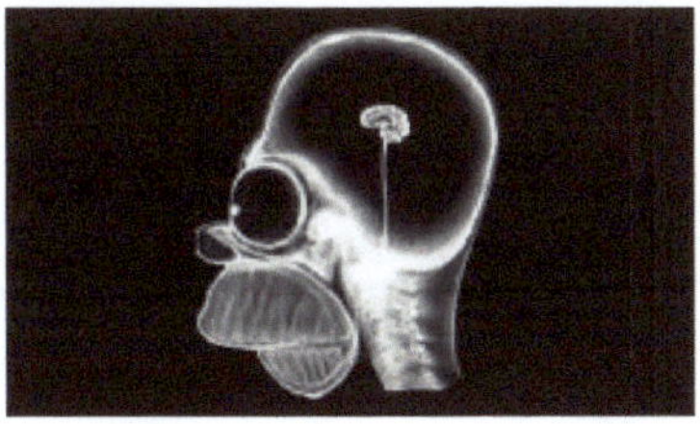

Credit: Cool Blog Sociale - 15 July 2008 – A joke image of Homer Simpson's head through X-ray" by SOCIALisBETTER is licensed under CC BY 2.0

In the book Thinking Fast and Thinking slow Kahneman called these two systems, System 1 (Fast Thinking) and System 2 (Slow Thinking).

Homer Simpson is like the system 1 part of the brain. The ancient emotional 'lizard' part of the brain and the oldest part of the brain. This is where fear and greed dominate. If it comes into conflict then it will fight, flight or freeze. Homer is very much the doer. He acts on impulse and emotion. This action if not done correctly can lead to doing the wrong thing from a long-term perspective. If you are in the supermarket and you are hungry then you are likely to end up buying lots of things that you were not intending to buy. Usually, high fat or high sugar, because this kind of high-value food was typically not available frequently for most of our evolutionary history. Therefore when we do have access to these types of foods we tend to gorge ourselves while we have the opportunity.

"Homer Simpson" by annulla is licensed under CC BY-SA 2.0

This is system 1 thinking. Afterwards, we can't work out why we ate this and have an inner conversation with our two selves 'why did we do this?' This inner dialogue is our two brains talking to each other.

Sheldon however seems - and probably is - smarter, he is the planner. Often thinking too much and often not taking action. He is trying to get all the information before making a logical and rational decision. This sounds like the right thing to do. However, markets don't work like this, there is too much information and there will never be a right time to buy as the market is constantly moving so you will never have perfect information.

"THE BIG BANG THEORY" by Chesi - Fotos CC is licensed under CC BY-SA 2.0

Sheldon is trying to calculate the perfect opportunity to enter the market when in reality there is no perfect moment. Sheldon gets caught up in 'analysis paralysis', where overthinking and over analysing means he becomes 'paralysed' and end up not deciding at all because he can't work out what the best decision should be. Meaning never entering the market, waiting for the perfect opportunity and the history of the stock market is that it will keep rising. Sheldon is constantly seeking the perfect answer but gets stuck, scared of making the wrong decision.

Markets are made up of lots of people making individual decisions and not all of these are rational decisions. As mentioned earlier, Benjamin Graham called this 'Mr Market', and explained that he has a split personality of either fear or greed, which means the price the market gives you on any one day, may not represent the fundamental value of a company. The markets often behave with a herd mentality.

These two people or systems are in a constant battle with each other. To be a good investor we need to understand how our brain is wired and how we have evolved over millions of years to make us terrible investors.

Emotional creatures not Lumbering Robots

How humans behave in regards to investing has become popular in recent years. It argued that many of the old economic models don't work simply because we are humans and we act irrationally. Human are not lumbering robots as Richard Dawkins suggested in his book The Selfish Gene, we are emotional creatures. We are not the rational actors that previous economic textbooks have portrayed us as. We are human and we have emotions, feelings and thoughts, all which impact our decision-making process. Humans are part of nature and not a human creation.

In his book Thinking Fast and Thinking Slow, it was argued that there are four main factors which affect our decisions when looking at behaviour economics. 1) Humans are often overconfident with our decisions. We think we are better investors than we are, we often exaggerate our skill and we often deny the role of change in our decisions. 2) Humans have biased judgement: This means we think we can control decisions, we think we can predict the future and we have hindsight bias meaning looking back at an event we think the outcome was obvious, even when the event was not obvious at the time 3) Humans suffer from Herding. Meaning we humans feel more comfortable moving with the crowd as we don't want to be left behind. We often follow the herd copying each other rather than making our own decision. 4) loss aversion, which means humans feel emotions two and half times more for pain of a loss of money than we feel emotions do for a gain of the same amount.

Money is a very emotional topic and it affects the way that our brains function. During unusual situations, for example, a stock market crash, the brain will release chemicals into our brain to set us into a fight or flight mode. This would have helped us for thousands of years as that danger was often a real-life bear in the woods rather than just a bear market. Your brain controls the way you think and the way you think controls you. The book 'The Chimp Paradox' by Professor Steve Peters explains it in much more details.

The three parts of the brain are:

1) The lizard brain. This is the survival-oriented part of the brain. This is your fight, flight or freeze area of the brain. This ancient part of the brain has evolved over millions of years to keep us out of danger and alive. During a stock market crash, our reptile panic mode can often come out to play. Being aware that this is happening is very powerful when investing.
2) The mammal brain. This is the functional worker part of the brain and sees the world as a set of problems and challenges to solve. Being on autopilot is a sign you are in mammal mode.
3) The human part of the brain. Here is your planning mode of the brain and seeing the world as a more connected place. If you are ever inspired or working towards meaningful goals, then you are in rational human mode or sometimes called entrepreneurial mode. When relaxed and safe it is much easier to think abstract thoughts, use our imagination and use our human powers of reason and rationalisation (this is why creating a life plan in chapter 4 is so important)

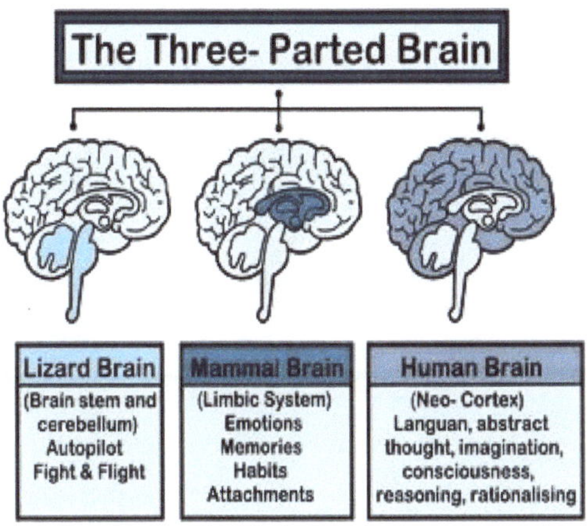

Being controlled by the lizard brain is not good for building long term wealth. If there is was a fire alarm, then the lizard part of the brain kicks into action. There is a hormone that gets released naturally in humans, part of the brain That means we will fight, flight or freeze. This reaction has evolved over millions of years to keep us safe and out of danger from the bear in the wood. It has a purpose and is useful in certain circumstances. In a market crash (a bear in the market), the same hormone is released and causes people to panic and sell their shares because they feel fear, and so their flight response kicks in. There is no turning this part of the brain off however we can understand it and automate our finances so we are not affected by this reaction. In a rising market greed increases. At these times, people think that they cannot lose, and the longer this goes on the more people forget about the last market crash.

Bubbles.

We don't know which parts of the brain are in control of us at any one time. This has been in effect throughout the history of the stock market. Bubbles form when the lizard brain part of the brain is in control. Even the smartest people are susceptible to this.

'I can calculate the motion of heavenly bodies, but not the madness of people.'

Isaac Newton 1642 – 1727

Robert Shiller said the internet bubble (1999-2000) can be explained by mass psychology, which he called it mass exuberance. A thing is only as valuable by what someone else will pay for it. If we don't learn the lessons of the past, we are doomed to repeat them. Greed has been an essential feature of every speculative boom in history. Participants ignore firm foundations of value.

A bubble starts when shares rise and people who own these get excited which causes more people to buy into the idea. Bubbles usually form when a new technology, trade route or market opens. This is often known as the greater fool theory as the price rises are only sustained by a new investor or a greater fool buying at a higher price. The best example of a bubble is the Tulip Bubble in 1636 – 1637.

New technology created new varieties of Tulip bulbs, more demand and not enough Tulip bulbs supply drove prices to astronomical levels, looking back this seems like madness. At its height, one Tulip bulb cost the same as a house in Amsterdam. People tell their friend about how easy it is to make money, due to jealousy, they buy into the bubble. The media and the press get on board with the story as they will sell more newspapers, causing more people to buy or more fools to join the party.

Remember the media and especially the tabloids do not make their money by giving investment advice (they can't give actual finance advice only report on the market). They make their money by selling advertising space to companies that want people to see these adverts. The media will stir up a frenzy to encourage more people to buy their newspaper and make more money from the advertising. They have no concern for your welfare.

The Seven Deadly Sins of Investing

1) Pride

Pride is deadly. Pride is thinking you know everything. It's going to stop you asking a silly question or asking for help. We are proud creatures and we often don't like to ask for advice or admit when we are wrong. Pride is an excessive belief in one's ability.

In all markets, there is no perfect information meaning that nobody can predict what other humans will choose to do. There are too many random events happening around the world, and that makes it impossible for someone to know all of the available information in each market. Think back to June 2016. If you had placed £10 on the three events of Brexit, Trump being elected and Leicester City winning the English Premiership football title, you would have won £10 million (according to the Independent newspaper). The odds of this prediction coming true was a 0.000033 chance of all three events taking place. This combination was thought so unimaginable that no one in the UK had a bet on them all.

Herbert Simon called this bounded rationality (winning a noble prize in 1978). Meaning we don't know what we don't know. Understanding that we can't know everything is a good step towards understanding how to invest. This is why financial education is so important and can stop you from becoming overconfident. Pride often comes before a fall. By trying to take too many risks or even worse not understanding the risk, you are causing financial pain for yourself and your family.

Money Tips: Lesson 1: Education is key. Knowing both yourself and the principles of investing will help you reduce your risk.

2) Envy

Today it's become normal to view other people fill our social media feeds showing us their new possessions like cars, TVs or swimming pools. Trying to impress others they don't really like by buying stuff they don't need. Envy is the desire for other traits, status, ability or situation.

I have been guilty of envy myself. I missed the boom in the London housing market. I was attempting to time the market and getting it spectacularly wrong. Average house prices in London have risen 518% since 1994 from £79,000 for an average house up to a price of £488,000 today (according to the office of national statistics). As a Millennial, it's hard not to feel envious of previous generations who take for granted having a home they can afford. It's important to follow your path and understand that there is an opportunity in every business cycle. Remembering Newton's third law of motion: for every action there is an equal and opposite reaction, meaning that a market rising by 500% is often not sustainable and every market that goes up can also come back down again (just look back to the housing rise and crash in the UK in the early 1990s or Japan in 1980s).

Having a life plan for the long term helps you to understand where you are heading for the future and how best to reach your goals so you can focus on how far you have come yourself rather than comparing your life to the lives of others.

Money Tips: Lesson 2. Have a life plan and know where you want to get to in both your life and your finances.

3) Sloth

Sloth is the avoidance of work and comes from not doing your research or not taking the time to learn to invest. Investing is a life skill and gets better by practice and learning from others. It's much easier to buy some time on someone else's tip or because they are buying it than understanding the fundamentals. Investing is more about understanding yourself than understanding different companies or the market. What are your aims and objectives? What do you want from the market? Having good daily habits with money, putting in the work and setting up correct investing systems can save you more work in the long term. It's also the discipline to spend less than you earn. Long term wealth can never build if you spend all your winning rather than reinvesting back into your business system.

Money Tip: Lesson 3: The hard road turns easy and the easy road turns hard. Putting the work in today will pay off tomorrow.

4) Greed

Greed is the desire for material gain. Everyone is a little bit greedy; we are only human after all. Lifestyle is different for everyone. We can choose to have a big lifestyle or a small lifestyle. When we think about it after health and family, lifestyle is all anyone wants in life. We need to understand our number, which means how much money we need to live on for the rest of our lives. If we want a big lifestyle then we will need a big number and if we choose a small lifestyle, we only need a small number. Once we understand this number this helps us accumulate it, manage it protect it and most of all spend it. This is proper financial planning

If we choose to spend more than what we earn rather than focusing on what is meaningful in life then this is where we get greedy. Greed can often come from wanting these things quickly. Investing is a long-term process and patience is important. Greed can mean a lack of patience, which can increase the amount of risk we take. Greed makes you overstretch yourself. Greed is wanting to have the golden eggs before the golden goose has had a chance to lay them (from the Aesop's children's fable 'The Goose that Laid the Golden Eggs'

Money Tip: Lesson 4: Patience and time is your friend in investment. Trying to rush the process is like rushing the oak tree out of the acorn. Anything of value takes time.

5) Gluttony

Gluttony is a desire to consume more than one requires.

Investing is a long-term process which involves buying assets (like businesses, property or by lending money) that will result in an income being paid to you. Speculating is a short-term process of trying to buy (or sell) something in the hope that someone else will pay more for it. Where speculating becomes dangerous is buying things that you cannot afford on credit or even worse, buying (or betting) on a leveraged position (also called buying on margin). This means you take a position of £1000 of exposure only having to put down £100 of your money. This leads to gluttony as this can lead you to spend more money than you have. Buying on margin can leverage your winnings as you are using borrowed money however if the position goes against you, you have to not only pay back your losses but also the losses that you have borrowed (usually from the broker). Things can spiral out of control quickly as you'll have to pay the borrowed money back with a high amount of interest and could encourage you to try to bet back your previous position. These leveraged or margins positions are at least partly to blame for the 1930s crash.

Money Tips: Lesson 5: If you don't have the money don't trade or bet with someone else's money.

6) Wrath

Wrath is extreme anger and there is a danger with this deadly sin. Wrath is an emotion and emotions can be dangerous when investing. There is a difference between getting emotional about what you can control and what you have no control over. We all have an individual sphere of influence and getting angry about what we can't control is futile. If you lose your job due to redundancy or because your industry no longer has the demand, then there is no point fighting since there is little chance that you can affect the outcome. Once you understand that you can't control external forces you can only control your reaction to it, and you can only choose your reaction to the stimulus. Having this choice is powerful.

Money Tips: Lesson 6: Know that there are opportunities in any market, and you can focus your energy discovering these opportunities.

7) Lust

Everyone loves a story as it appeals to the human part of our brain. There is a danger of falling in love with the story of an investment. This may be Steve Jobs coming back to Apple and saving the company or the potential of blockchain technology and Bitcoin. It's easy to get swept up in the emotion and we like to tell our friends about it. However, from an investing point of view, this can be dangerous. As discussed earlier in the chapter, we have evolved to be wired to be terrible investors. We often buy things that don't show any long-term value or that everyone else has bought into because of the same story and this has pushed the price of the shares up. Like always falling in love with the wrong person this can have negative effects on us. Being unemotional and unattached to our investments is important although it's much easier said than done. Putting money into investment funds or an index tracker where your money is pooled with other investors is a good way of stopping yourself falling in love with one share (and more importantly reducing company risk too).

Money Tips: Lesson 7. Invest in investment funds to stop yourself falling in love with one company (as well as reducing company risk).

Which of these deadly sins have you been guilty of?

<u>Money Tips</u>

We have evolved to be terrible investors. Follow the three laws of money:

- Pay yourself first automatically every month. Save up a three-month cash buffer, which covers for any emergencies.
- Once you have a three-month cash buffer. Transfer that automatic payment into a diversified portfolio every month. This means you get the benefit from pound cost averaging by starting to drip-feed money into the market every month automatically without fail. This means you buy less when the market is high and more when the market is low.
- Rebalance your portfolio every year to get back to your ideal asset allocation (discussed in chapter 10).

Chapter 9

Farm Finances How Much is Enough for your Basket?

'Imagine. You have enough money to last you the rest of your life.'
Paul. D. Armson. *Enough* 2016

Imagine you owned a farm, with enough food, resources and supplies to last you for the rest of your life. You were self-sufficient, self-reliant and independent. You didn't need to work for an income so you were free to choose how to spend your day. Your time was your own. If you could work for joy rather than work for necessity. Every morning you wake up felt like a weekend. You live your life on your own terms.

This farm had chickens, pigs, cows and you owned the farmhouse that you lived in. You had enough grain to feed the animals. You could happily eat the eggs or the cheese that they cows and chickens produced. If you need to you could kill the pig and eat the ham or you could sell the cow to market. You didn't worry about the ups and downs of the prices in the local market as it didn't matter to you as you have enough not just to survive but thrive. Whatever happened you would be alright. This is a big relief. This is being financially independent. This is having enough. This is being financially free.

Enough. Have you got enough? How much is enough for you and your family? You need to know your number. Your number is the amount of money you need for the rest of your life without having to work again. This means you will be financially independent or self-sufficient. Previous generations called this retirement.

Only a few hundred years ago the average humans would not last past their 35th birthday. We humans previously did not have to plan for old age. One thousand years ago we didn't need to think this far ahead. If we did live this long, then our investment was in our children or community that would take care of us. Today the world is a different place.

There is currently a retirement cliff edge fast approaching. People are not putting enough money to fund their lifestyles when they stop working. Many people are living lifestyles they can't afford even when they are getting paid let alone when they stop earning money.

In previous generations, it was your company that would support you in your retirement. You also had a safety net of the government that would top up your lifestyle with the state pension. Today the days of a final salary pension from your company are over and the government can't afford to support you. The fact is that nobody is coming to rescue you.

We need to take responsibility for our future and own ourselves first by being financially independent.

Being financially independent means that you are not dependent on anyone else. You are self-sufficient and you no longer rely on anyone else to support you. Being financially independent means that you don't owe anyone. This means that you are free. You are free because you are no longer dependent on anyone else. You do not owe anyone. You are free to choose how to spend your day. To wake up each morning and feel like it is the weekend. It's living your life on your terms.

You can know how much is enough by knowing your number.

What kind of lifestyle do you want? If you want a big lifestyle then you'll need a big number and if you want a small lifestyle then you'll need a small number. Imagine living until you are 90 years old. In the future, it will be common to live until 100.

Today we need to make grown-up decisions with our money and learn how to invest ourselves and understand our number - how much is enough.

<u>Be financially self-sufficient by making money your pet.</u>

Think of yourself as a farmer. Building up your farm over your lifetime When you want to stop working you need a big enough farm to live on for the rest of your life without needing to work. Once you stop working you can eat the farm produce that you have cultivated over your lifetime.

It's easy to blame everyone else, the government, the capitalist system, taxes. It is easy to blame everyone except yourself. You need to control your own economy. There are things you can control and there are things that you can't. It's much more effective to focus on what you can control. Accumulating every day by making the right choices. Today investing is a life skill that we can't put off any longer.

Think of yourself as your own business. Your own economy. We need to learn to create wealth and the only way to do this is to create value. Creating value takes time. Being responsible for the things that are affecting you. Being self-reliant with your money. If you worked at a job and didn't know where your budget was spent on you wouldn't last long in your job. Why expect the same with your own economy? You may get caught in the rain, but you can make the choice to bring an umbrella.

What is a tax shelter?

Imagine getting back to your farm and seeing some of the chicken's eggs had been devoured by a fox. This is what happens to your hard-earned savings if you don't put it in a tax shelter (which will be explained below)as the government will take a bite of your investments.

Now taxes are important don't get me wrong. They pay for schools, hospitals and trains to get you to work. However, another important element of taxes is that they encourage or discourage you from doing something. Think of cigarettes. We all know that they are bad for our health. They will kill you if you smoke for long enough, that's been scientifically proven. It costs a lot of money to treat smokers for lung diseases, which means that these beds are not being used to treat other people with other illnesses. What the government does is to put a tax on cigarettes to make smoking more expensive to encourage people to smoke less, meaning they will have fewer people to treat in hospitals. The same thing is true with investing. The UK government offers generous tax incentives in the form of an Individual Savings Account (ISA) or a pension to encourage us all to save and invest for the future.

A Fence around your Farm

A tax shelter is like the fence around your property. This stops the foxes from getting into your farm and government from taking a big bite out of your chickens or eating their eggs. This means your hard-earned money will be able to grow quicker and you will be able to spend more money on rearing more chickens for you to eat and to enjoy in the future safely. The government gives a certain amount of tax shelters, which are allowances given to you each year (or fences to continue the analogy) to give you the incentive to save more so they will have to spend less on looking people in their old age and more money on things like education, hospitals and transport, making sure that train you get to work runs on time or buying more trains so that you are less squashed on your morning commute.

The two main tax shelters that people in the UK should be using are ISAs and pensions. The main reason for saving into these is because of the tax breaks available. Saving into a pension or an ISA is the best way to avoid dividend tax and capital gains tax to help you grow your investments quicker in the future. The ISA allowance is currently £20,000 and a pension allowance is £40,000 a year.

Chicken ISAs (Individual Saving Account)

An ISA (Individual saving accounts) is a tax shelter that an individual in the UK has available. In the Farm Finances, this is represented by chickens. The more you feed the chickens (or the more money you add to your ISA) the bigger and fatter these chickens will grow and will become assets for the future. These chickens also hatch eggs which can grow into more chickens.

The ups and downs of the market prices are only half the story. When owning shares of a company you also receive a share of the profits (called a dividend). This is like a chicken laying an egg. You have the option of selling the eggs for money, eating the eggs (spending the money) or you can reinvest the eggs like incubating the eggs, which when hatched will produce more chickens for the future.

Your chickens and eggs can grow tax-free inside this ISA shelter. Think of this like a fence around your chickens that protects them from the foxes (the government) eating the chicken and their eggs (dividends) that you have saved.

There are five different types of ISA and the government has made it more complicated than it needs to be. Cash ISAs; Help to Buy ISAs; innovative finance ISAs; stocks & shares ISAs; and Lifetime ISAs. These are just tax wrappers and the different names just depend on what you are putting inside these tax shelters. The lifetime ISA is slightly different because the government will give you a bonus on top and there is a difference in terms of how much money you can put in.

The more you feed your chickens (the more you add to your ISA), the more your chickens will grow. The annual ISA allowance in 2020 is £20,000 and plans to be £20,000 in 2021 .

ISAs are more flexible than pensions because you can access the investments at any time. Unlike a pension which can only be accessed when you retire, which is currently 55 years old in the UK (although changing to 57 years old)

Grain is like Cash

On your farm, your grain stores is your saved money. You can choose to eat the grain (spend the seeds), plant the grain for future crops (invest the seeds) , store the grain (save into bank) or you can feed it to your animals (invest into the tax shelters) so they grow bigger and you can eat them later in life.
The more you work the more grain you can get.
The idea is to have enough grain to be able to live on for the rest of your life without having to work. Today interest rates are so low that keeping money in cash is not as productive as it used to be. It used to be normal to receive 5% interest rates from a bank. Today interest rates are nearer 0%. Inflation is like the rats eating away at your grain stores. This is why it's so important to invest for the future to get a better long-term return by feeding your chickens or pigs.

Farm Finances

Farmhouse
Having a family home is important. If you own your own house then this will mean that you don't need to pay rent on where you live. It also means that the landlord can't kick you out at a moments notice as they plan to sell your family home.

Property

A good thing about property as an asset class is that you can borrow money from a bank to buy your house without having the full amount saved up. This is known as a mortgage. You borrow money and pay back with interest for 25 or 30 years; you can live in that house today. This is called leverage. Think of this like a lever where you are using someone else's money that over time you pay back to the bank. For example: if you want to buy a £100k house you don't need to save up the full £100k. You can have £20k deposit and borrow the £80k as a mortgage. This is unlike shares of companies where if you wanted to buy a £100k investment you would need to save up the £100k yourself. This leverage works well when houses increase in price, however you need to be careful! When house prices fall you still need to pay back the money you borrowed. This could mean the amount you owe is more than the actual value of the property. This is known as negative equity.

Property has been a great bet over the last 30 years; however, this shouldn't be the only asset you purchase for your farm. Despite the common phrase 'you can't lose with property' this is not the case. Property in the 1990s in the UK fell significantly. Property is a market and is affected by demand and supply like other assets. Even if you have your farmhouse where you live you will still require assets that pay you an income when you stop working. You can't eat your house.

The Three Pension Pigs

So What is a Pension?

A pension is a piggy bank for grownups. Remember as a kid you collected your spare change in a ceramic piggy bank. A pension is a way to save for retirement. To pay you an income when you stop working. The government needs a way to encourage us to save towards old age to avoid over-reliance on the government. The government does this by encouraging us to save through offering generous tax incentives

The law in the UK around pensions has changed massively over the last few years due to pension freedom legislation in 2015. Many people don't realise or are confused with what a pension is or does.

To access your piggy bank money the only way to collect your savings was to smash open the piggy bank to redeem all your hard work. A pension works in a very similar way to a piggy bank. With a pension, you add money to the pot throughout your life and when you retire you can smash open your savings (or crystallise your pension to use the industry terminology).

The bonus is that not only to get the money you've invested; you will also receive the increased growth from the market. Where the pension gets exciting is the tax benefits you receive. You don't pay for capital gains tax, dividend tax or income tax on your money investing into a pension. You also get 'tax relief' from putting money into this investment vehicle. Tax relief means that you get back the income tax that you would have paid on any income that you received from your job. The amount of income tax you pay depends on how much you earn.

If you earn up to £37,500 then you are a basic rate tax payer and you will pay 20% income tax.

If you earn £50,000 then you are a higher rate tax payer and will pay 40%income tax on the amount between the basic and higher (£37,500 and £50,000).

If you earn over £50,000 then you are an additional rate tax payer and you pay 45% income tax on the amount above £150,000.

When you pay into a pension you get this income tax back as tax relief.

This means if you are a higher rate taxpayer if you add £100 you will receive £40 top-up from the government.

A pension is a piggy bank that you contribute to throughout your life. Your employer now legally must automatically enrol you into a pension scheme and match some of your contributions.

In the UK you must wait until aged 55 (and will now be older when a Millennial retires) before you can access your money from a private pension. This money that you received will be taxed as an income. Think about accessing your pension like slicing off a part of your pension (or the pig) and take an income each year like carving ham. You don't want to take the whole amount of the pension pot or you will be taxed heavily. The best way is to take small slices each year as an income so you can be tax-efficient so you get to keep more of your pension pig.

There are three types of pensions in the UK. Think of these like the three little pigs.

1) The first piggy bank is a state or Government Pension

You contribute from your earning income. This is called your national insurance and you need to contribute 35 full years to benefit from the full state pension. When you reach an age of 67 you will start to receive money from the government. A full state pension in the UK is currently £8000 a year.

2) A defined benefit pension (also called final salary pension).

This is where your employer will pay into your pension pot and at the end, your employer will pay you each month a guaranteed income for life. The amount you receive is calculated by considering several factors: how many years you have worked for that company, either your final salary or your average salary, and a contribution factor depending on the type of scheme you have. This type of pension is now very rare in the private sector and although it's still common in the public sector (like for teachers or doctors) it is now commonly calculated over an average of your career which makes it less attractive than in the past.

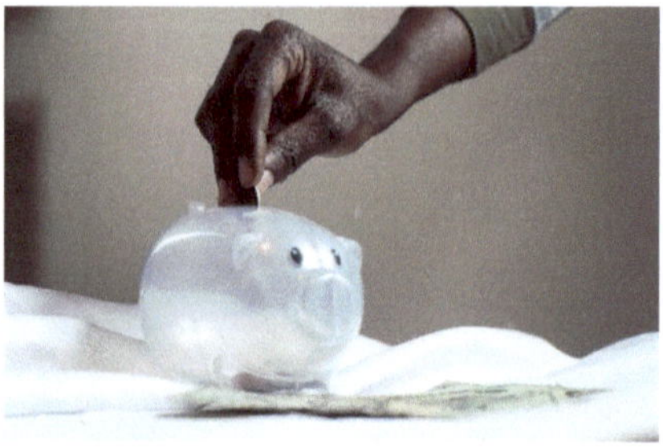

3) <u>Defined Contribution Pension.</u>

This is the most common type of pension today. You choose what you invest in inside the pension and depending on the performance of those investments what you put in is what you receive plus any growth. You invest in the pension pot throughout your life. You will receive tax relief to help increase the size of the contribution. This pot is invested in a combination of shares, property, cash, commodities and bonds, and the pot will grow throughout your life. This pot will grow tax-free.

The good news is that due to a government scheme called auto-enrolment your company by law has to set up a pension for you and must match some of your money. As a double bonus, you get your tax that you already paid on your income back to add to your pension pot. The downside is that you won't be able to access this piggy bank until you are 55 (in the UK). Think of this like feeding a pig that's going to grow into a large pig, which will provide an income for when you stop working.

Today it has never been more flexible nor have there been more opportunities. There has been a new law in the UK called Pension Freedom introduced in 2015 (most people don't need to understand this until they are nearing retirement). This has meant there is much more flexibility around pensions and means we can choose when to stop working.
We can have a staged retirement where we work part-time or work on a project that's more enjoyable or more meaningful. Still working for money and taking an income from our pot of retirement money.

Cash Cow

Today it has never been easier to start your own business due to improved technology.
A cash cow is having your own business. The internet and technology have meant that it is much simpler to set up and make money from a passion or a skill that you have.

A cash cow is a business that can pay you an income. It does take time to set up and grow a business before you get a return from the hard work you put into it. Think of it as a cow, it takes a lot of feeding and caring for before that cow produces milk that you can consume yourself or sell to the market.
Your cash cow generates profits in the form of milk (cash flow). If you are more entrepreneurial you can turn the cash flow into a higher value product like cheese. You also have the option to sell the cow to market (either as shares of the business or the whole business. or alternatively to grow the business by getting a bull and expanding

Farm Basket

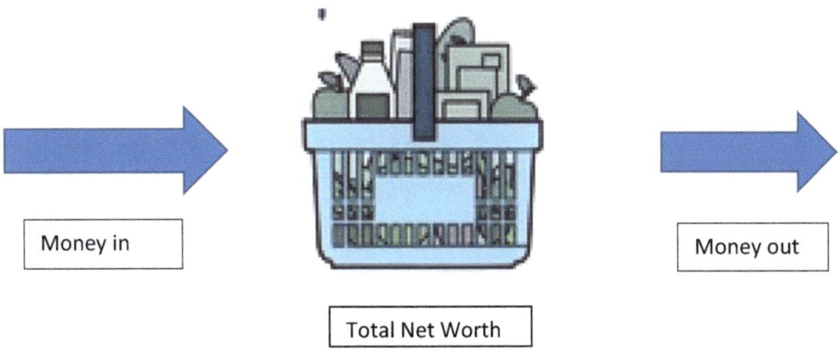

We all have a basket, which is our net worth (or the total amount of assets). To calculate your own basket add up the total amount of your assets like pensions, ISA investments, the price of your property, the valuation of your business and other money in cash or other investments. Take away any liabilities like credit card bills, loans or mortgages. The total amount is our net worth (or our basket).
This basket will show us how much money we have to live on for the rest of our lives. The assets we have in our farm basket is like a shopping basket of all the money available (or our total assets) to spend when we stop working.
The idea is to build up a big enough basket so that we can stop working before the current retirement age of 67. This is to be financially independent and retire early.

The basket has inflows and outflows. This means money comes in and money flows out depending on how much we are adding to our basket. The money flowing in is the income that we get paid. Our outflow is how much we spend.

When we stop working, we start to withdraw money from our assets (or basket) to pay ourselves an income to replace the income you currently receive from a job. These assets include our Pension Pig, our ISA Chickens, our Cash Cow, Our Grain money store.

The inflows of the basket are the income we receive. You can either take an income from the assets we own like dividends from shares that we own, rent from a buy to let property, interest from cash or coupons from bonds. We can also sell some assets and use this money to pay for our living expenses for when we stop working, perhaps even downsize our farmhouse and live in a smaller house or flat and use this extra money to pay for our expenses.

Our outflows are our current or future expenses, this is our daily spending like food, housing, entertainment, holidays etc.
We can choose to have an expensive lifestyle and require a large basket or have a frugal lifestyle and only need a small basket. The choice is yours.

The idea is to have enough assets from our farm to pay an income for when we stop working.
There will be three stages of expenditure. The first stage is the current lifestyle (how much your monthly expenses are), the second is the active retirement, where you may go on holiday or generally enjoy life as many people who have stopped working do. The final expenditure is for your later retirement, which may have higher medical fees or expenses for a retirement home or long-term care.

The basket aims to have enough assets to pay for when you stop working. The secret of retirement is to have multiple streams of income. This means that you are diversifying and reducing your risk.

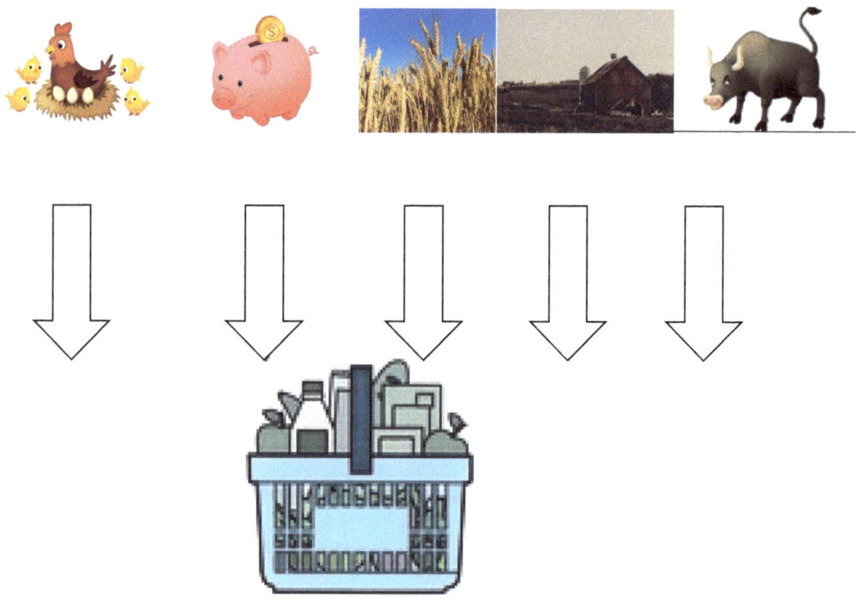

Your Basket is your net worth and is made up of your investments. Once you have built up enough assets to live on for the rest of your life then you can retire or work for joy rather than necessity.

The 4% Principle

Financial Planners today use the 4% principle to calculate how much money you need to pay an income for when you stop working. This means you can take 4% of the total net worth of the investment. If the total assets are getting 4% return on the investment then you can live off the assets by only taking the income on the capital. (assuming you get a at least a 4% return)

A sum of £650,000 can produce an income of £26,000 a year when you withdraw 4% each year from the main capital amount.

A sum of £1,000,000 can produce an income of £40,000 when you withdraw 4% each year from the main capital amount.

Our Own Little Farm

We need to think of ourselves as a business or farm. It doesn't matter what happens in the wider economy as you have created your economy. The idea is to become financially self-reliant. Treat money like a farm that you grow over your lifetime. So you don't need to work again. You only work for joy because you enjoy doing your work or because it helps a higher purpose or helps you become you are or who you want to be.

This is financial guidance and not specific financial advice. There are several good financial planning software programs to give you a more accurate picture of your retirement target number. In the Money Tipps workshops, we review and give access to some of the better tools to help you make better decisions with your money.

Here are three practical money tips:

1) Join your workplace pension scheme. This is as close to free money that you can ever get. You get a tax incentive and your employer also has to match your contributions up to a certain level. The downside to this is that you can't access your money until you retire (currently at a minimum age of 55) but this gives your money a chance to grow.

2) Clear your bad debt first before thinking about investing. There is no point gaining 8% on your investments if you are losing 20% on credit card debt payments. Use compound interest in your favour by clearing any debt that you may have from credit cards or loans.

3) Decide the spilt between pension and ISA. An ISA is also a tax wrapper however the incentives are not as good as a pension. You can access an ISA at any time of your life, and this can make an ISA more appealing if you are between 25-35 years old, as you may want more flexibility with your money. A rule of thumb model is the Sow, Grow, Dough Model. This is a simple and easy way to work out how to allocate your income how to allocate to an ISA or a Pension

Sow 10% into your Pension for the future, and Grow 10% into your ISA, leaving 80% Dough to spend on what you choose.

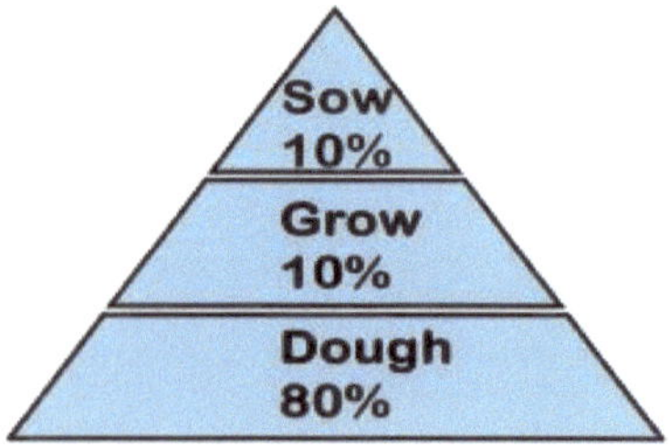
Sow
10%
Grow
10%
Dough
80%

Chapter 10

Re: Balance. How to live happily ever after without turning into a pumpkin.

'Economics needs a metaphorical career change: We need a change from engineer to gardener'

Kate Raworth, *Doughnut Economics*

We need to look to nature when investing. Think of rebalancing your investments like harvesting your garden each year. Taking the fruit that has grown and ripened over the year and removing any unproductive parts of your portfolio.

Re:Balancing your portfolio is acting like a gardener, who harvests the fruits in autumn and plants the seeds for the spring. Planting an apple tree for the future that will provide shelter from the rain in the winter, shade from the sun in summer and nourishment from the fruits in autumn. The leaves that fall from the branches every year may rot on the ground, however, this process provides better soil for other trees in the future to grow more trees.

Anything of value takes time to grow. You can't rush the oak tree out of the acorn any more than you can rush the income out of the asset. Nature's free-market takes time. We need to learn patience, courage and have a belief in better. If you want the fruits, you need the roots... This is having Millennial Money Mindset.

Rebalancing is moving your assets back into the formation that best suits you for your risk profile and the time frame of your investment. That may sound complicated and perhaps it is. It's the hardest step of the three laws of money accumulation to achieve, so it isn't easy but it is simple.

Poverty

Poverty means not having enough money to pay for the basic things in life. According to the Joseph Rowntree Foundation 'poverty means not being able to heat your home, pay your rent, or buy the essentials for your children. It means waking up every day facing insecurity, uncertainty, and impossible decisions about money'.

More than 16 million people in the UK have savings of less than £100 found a study by the Money Advice Service (MAS). In this situation, you are going to be living a life of constant stress and pain. Making sure you have enough money in the future to not only just pay for the basic things in life but to have enough money for a better quality of life. To be financially independent. To not rely on anyone else. Not a boss or having to pay a mortgage. In the past, they called this retirement. When you have enough money to live on for the rest of your life something or at least understand how your number and how much money you need for the rest of your life. Today this is called Financially Independent and Retire Early (FIRE).

Understand that humans are created for progress. We are constantly looking for ways to improve things. We will always have new problems to solve or a better way of doing something. Businesses who look to solve these problems and create value for others will grow over time. Taking from an area of low returns and placing it where it will make the greatest contribution. This is investing. Investing can be described as the arbitrage of knowledge. This means that we can see underlying value that the market doesn't yet fully appreciate - the value on offer or the price.

We need to Re:Balance

'A very simple investment technique called rebalancing can reduce investment risk and even increase investment returns. This technique simply involves bringing your assets back into the proportions suited to your age and risk profile'

Burton G. Malkiel, *A Random Walk Down Wall Street*

These well-known but little understood investment planning strategies can help both you and your business work smarter with your money. Giving you the mind space you desire to help you manage your money, so you don't have to worry, think, or even talk about money. You can instead concentrate on more important, productive aspects of your life. Maybe this is time with friends, family or simply having more 'me' time.

The aim is to have more time, freedom and control so you can enjoy life to its true potential.

Investing is simple but it is not easy. Humans are terrible investors. We have too many biases. We are emotional creatures, we suffer from loss aversion, we think we are better investors than we are. We don't know what we don't know as there is never perfect information, meaning we can never know everything.

We can counter this by setting up an investing system using the planning, rational and creative part of the brain rather than being reactive using the ancient reptile brain. This would allow us to automate our money so we no longer need to think, stress or worry about money again.

The very purpose of our lives should be towards happiness. We are all seeking something better in life. Be this more time with loved ones, more holidays and experiences, or whatever else. The point of better money management is to help you get the life you want, whilst feeling secure and in control and having peace of mind. What is peace of mind? It is a greater level of calmness in our minds. The greater our peace of mind, the greater our ability to enjoy a happy and joyful life. So, our very motion of life should be towards happiness.

Why follow the three laws of money?

There is a point where a saver turns into an investor. Investing can be painful. In addition to your day job you now must contend with budgets, taxes, and researching what to invest in. However, following the three laws of money means that this problem is solved.

1) Pay yourself first
2) Diversify
3) Rebalance

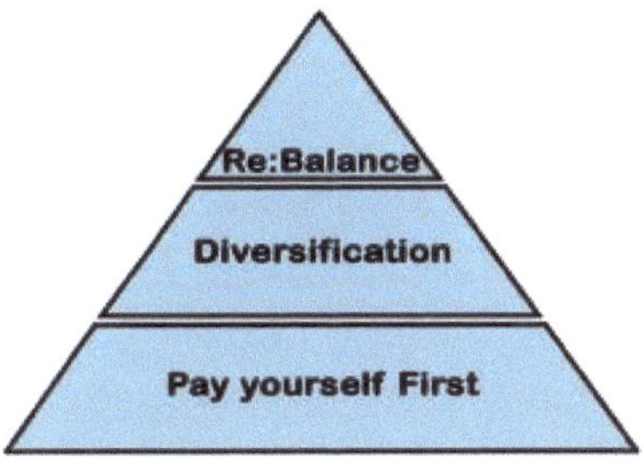

Why Rebalance. Be like Cinderella

We all wish that we have a fairy godmother who can reliably tell us when to buy assets low and sell them high. Rebalancing your portfolio is kind of like going to a party and forcing yourself to leave at the peak of the fun, just before the clock strikes midnight. It's a bit like a fairy godmother telling you to leave the party otherwise your investment vehicle will turn into a pumpkin just like what happened to Cinderella in the children's story.

Rebalancing goes against our human instincts. We want to stay at the party whilst the going is good. When the drinks are flowing everyone is happy and continue to party. To leave the party before the clock strikes midnight and find that the vehicle that is meant to get us to our happily ever after turns into a pumpkin. Rebalancing your portfolio once every year is the closest thing we have to this. We need to cultivate our pumpkin. We need to think like a gardener.

Cinderella: From Wikimedia Commons, the free media repository

As you leave the party you look around and all your friends are there, and everyone is having a good time. Why would you leave at the height of the party you ask yourself? That doesn't make sense. You decide to leave the party and you get home at a reasonable time, meaning you get a good nights sleep and can wake up the next day and can do something productive that morning. You call your friend who stayed at the party later than you. They explain that after you left the lights turn on and there was a rush for the exit. The party was over. There was a dash to leave as everyone tried to get a taxi at the same time. This increased the demand for taxis and increasing the price on the limited number of cabs available. After finally getting home they wake up late with a hangover and realized that for the extra time staying out late, they has spent a fortune compared which is not equivalent to the additional enjoyment (or return) he received.

The drinks are like the liquidity in the market. If there are cheap or free drinks on offer it's much more tempting to stay and enjoy yourself.

The markets are part of nature. They follow the laws of nature just like everything else in the Universe. The longer the party goes on for the bigger the hangover the next day. The market can't take continuously from nature any more than you can take apples from a tree continuously without any more growing on the tree. To counteract our nature, you need to set up a system that will automatically rebalance your portfolio. By rebalancing your portfolio will give you mind space that will benefit you no matter what happens in the markets you will be alright. This is a big relief!

Don't sell out. Rebalance! The most common investing mistake is to buy on the up, on the assumption it will continue to go up and sell when it goes down on the assumption it will continue. Don't sell out Rebalance. Do this once a year to check that your asset allocation (or your Football Team in chapter 5) is still in line with your goals and aspirations.

Rebalancing is the third law of money, and the concept is simple. If you have an asset allocation of 70% in shares of a business and 30% in bonds. Let's say the shares have done well and rose to 80% of your total portfolio and the bonds now makeup 20% of the total. Evidence suggests that it pays to rebalance by moving your assets back into the asset allocation that is right for you assuming that the risk profile and objectives of the person don't change.

A study by Forbes has shown that $10,000 invested in a way of a 60/40 split in the USA in 1985 and rebalanced annually, would have been worth $97,000 in 2010, whereas an unbalanced portfolio would only be worth $89,000. The ideal schedule to follow to rebalance would be once per year (or every six months if you want to be more in control of your portfolio) to keep it simple and to also reduce the costs of broker fees, taxes and investment charges.

Rebalancing is moving your assets back into the formation that is best for you. That may sound complicated but perhaps it is. It's the hardest step of the three laws of money to achieve.

Investing is a process, not an event. You hear about people getting rich instantly. Yes, this can happen, but these are the outliers and not the norm. Most wealth is created over time. Like a gardener patiently tending their crops following the steps in sequence can turn the raw seeds, earth, air, water and time into something completely difference FIRE (Financial Independent and Retire Early).

Rebalancing is like taking seeds from the apple and replanting them. It might not make sense at first but planning something that won't reap rewards for at least 5 years or even 10 or 20 years. Planting for the future with long term thinking is one of the most powerful things you can do with financial planning. Like humans, businesses also have a circle of life. We are all born, grow, get old and die. Businesses are the same. By rebalancing and renewing your portfolio each year you can gain from this balance. Rebalancing reduces investment risk and can increase investment returns. We all wish we had a fairy godmother who sits on our shoulder and reliably tells us to buy low and sell high. Rebalancing every year is the closest thing we have to that.

<u>The only certain thing is change</u>

Change is natural, which includes all the changes that happen in the stock market. Stock markets like all-natural cycles change and the only thing for certain is that change is inevitable. Balance is made up of imposing forces that are constantly changing. Instead of fighting against the current in a constant battle, we can go with the flow or the forces of nature.

This force describes how seemingly opposite or contrary forces may be complementary, interconnected, and interdependent in the natural world.

There is a co-existing of two opposing forces. Good versus evil, life versus death and risk versus reward. This gives the image of light destroying the dark even when they are both parts of the same system. The Yin and the Yang is represented in the *T*aijitu diagram (from ancient Chinese philosophy and shown above). The Yin represents the female energy and the yang the masculine energy (this doesn't relate to actual males and females but their energy). Removing one is as bad as removing both or the whole system. A population of only men on an island doesn't last very long. It is the interactions of opposite forces, which is how life is created.

The world is full of and made of differences and these opposites can live in harmony. We must embrace the differences and allow their differences to compliment you and make you more balanced. This dynamic story of growth and decay creates a cyclical nature of the markets, nature and the universe.

Nature doesn't complain of the winter or change, because it is part of nature. Without the light, there is no shadow, without the winter there is no summer. We understand that as one quality reaches its peak it naturally begins to transform into the other creating an endless cycle. This is seen through nature as crops or the stock market reaches its height in summer and dying back in winter, as a company is no longer profitable or providing value.

The seeds or money lives on in the spring.

Our own lives are cyclical we are born, live and we die. When you understand that life works in cycles it naturally makes you more optimistic. Nature is in harmony and in all ways balanced. Humans and the stock market come from nature too we must also be balanced.

Like sowing a seed, the pound coin in your back pocket grows into assets that will provide fruits. Different asset classes also take time to grow and different assets will grow at different speeds. An asset will eventually put money back into your pocket. It takes patience, courage and belief that these small seeds will grow into a mighty oak tree one day.

Emergence:

Emergence is seen everywhere in nature. Emergence means different, new and often unexpected properties which are created through a complex system. Emergence is the science of how complex parts can be organised into a simple whole and creates something that has completely new properties. Like mixing both Oxygen and Hydrogen and getting the property of wetness when water is formed (H2O).

If you have a tree seed that grows into a fully mature tree, this tree will produce more seeds (in more quantities than the original seed). Not only will these trees produce more seeds, but it will also create conditions that make it better for other trees to grow in. The emergence of the tree is the pleasure someone else gets from sitting under the shade of that tree on a summer's afternoon that was planted many years ago.

A human being is also an emergence. We are made up of different things like bones, organs and cells. All working together to form a self. We, humans, are naturally built to look for cause and effects. We want it to be simple. This is not how the world, money or the markets work.

> *'Success comes from a combination of things set up in just the right way. Money is the result of setting up and doing a specific combination of the right things in the right order. Money is an emergence it is not a simple cause and effect. Money is the result of creating value for others.'*

Eban Pagan, *Opportunities*. 2018

Emergence also happens with money. Putting a pound coin is together into a system that works together. That money will be greater than if you took each pound coin working on its own. This comes about because of interactions among the individual pound coins.

Any market (like the stock market) is an example of emergence on a grand scale. It precisely regulates the different prices of companies across the world, yet it has no leader. When no central planning is in place, no one thing controls the workings of the entire market. The money created that will provide an income for you to live a better life when retire is the emergent. Money is the result when you create massive value for someone else by either taking away pain or giving massive pleasure and setting up a system called a business to collect the money.

Money is not a cause and effect and we often can't understand this. Money is an emergent that occurs after giving value to the world. What is value? It is the satisfaction that someone gets using something. It is solving a meaningful problem. Value isn't a thing, it is a process. When valuing something, the bigger the problem, the value of solving it goes up. This is exactly why there is a better return when lending or owning growing companies or growing countries. The more value you create, the better the return, even if that means you are taking more risks.

Cash Flows

Money is not independent of nature. Money gets allocates resources to where it is the most productive. All things flow to where they will be utilised the most. Where they will add the most value. Good businesses attract investors because they create more value than the intrinsic price of the company. Like water flowing downhill, money also flows to where it is most useful. Cash flows. Money is liquid. You can't change the laws of nature. Nature follows certain laws, however, it is still unpredictable. No one can accurately predict if it will rain a year from today. There are too many variables and too much complexity. Just like we can't accurately predict whether the stock market will rise or fall a year from today. We need to learn what we can control and what you can't control and thrive no matter what happens. You can't control the tides, the wind or if it rains. You can, however, utilise nature through knowledge, understanding and intelligence. Nature is its own free market.

Supply and demand

Markets are infinite. Meaning that supply and demand will go on forever. Nothing in nature, the markets or in life happens in a straight line The river ebbs, flows and meaders in a constant battle between order and chaos, just like the price in markets. Following patterns of nature, although unpredictable, they form channels and deltas of information. Like a river the markets doesn't stop, even when the markets are closed, prices still move. (Interestingly the ratio between the average length of a river from source to mouth and as the 'crow flies' was calculated by Professor Hans Hendrik Stolum from Cambridge University as approximately 3.14, which is the value of pi. Pi (3.14) was discussed in chapter 3 and 7)

The market just like the river will remain even after we die many years from today. You are not battling the market, that will continue forever and therefore impossible to beat, you are battling yourself and that's the hardest part. Although we can't manage the markets, most importantly we can manage ourselves. We are finite. Over time the market will always win in the end. There is no perfect information as nobody knows everything at a given time. We don't know what we don't know and that's often the danger. This is why investing so difficult for many. It doesn't make sense because there is never the correct price or business to buy. We never stand in the same river twice just like a price can never be correctly measured. There is no perfect information and we don't know what we don't know. There is what we know and then there is what the world knows. Often business just like nature doesn't make logical sense.

Spinoza wrote in his book Ethics that there is two ways of looking at the world. From a limited point of view, under the aspect of time. The second way under the aspect of eternity or forever. Human nature and the limited days we have left to live means humans will always be divided between the two. A sensual life will pull us towards a time-bound partial view. Intelligence and reason give us access to another perspective, to participate in eternity, understanding that life will go on without us. The good news is that to beat the markets we don't need to be intelligent, hard-working or be that knowledgeable, we only need to do a few simple things in the right order to make all the difference.

Effective Market Hypothesis

The current thinking is that the market is efficient. Yes, it is but humans are not. The efficient market hypothesis is correct in the fact that simply tracking the market, is more likely to be successful than to pay a fund manager to manage your money after taking into account fees or just buying single shares of a company due to having counterparty risk. We must move to the effective market hypothesis. We must be effective investors by following the laws of nature using the three laws of money accumulation.

What is the Effective Market Hypothesis?

Effectiveness is doing the things that get you closer to your goals. Why you are investing is much more important than what you are investing in, how you're investing and more importantly how the stock market is performing daily. Investing that gets you closer to your goals is much more important than getting a good return and then spending your winnings on unimportant items.

We must do a few simple things in the right order to be more effective in investing. Effective investing can be learnt by following habits and even better can be automated by creating a system. The market is efficient as there will always be a battle between demand and supply. Don't do battle with the market, use the market as a garden. The soil supplies humans with the means to live. Nature becomes the original larder. The earth is the instrument of labour. Use the Farm Finances model to invest effectively.

Efficiency is doing a task in the most economical way possible (whether important or not). Investment returns are still important but not as important as getting the result of getting your goals in life. You could have enough money to fund your life after you stop working and then lose it all by taking more risks in the markets than you need to.

We need to move away from investing just for performance, to get the most efficient outcome and invest because of what we want from the market. Effective investing. Investing due to our own individual aims and objectives to invest on our own time horizon and in turn our own risk profile. We should not aim to get FIRE (Financially Independent and Retire Early). Fire can be a destructive force. We must aim for FISH (Financially Independent and Seeking Happiness), where we look to give value to the world by seeking for where we can make the greatest contribution. (this is discussed more in the Epilogue) Rather than looking to see where we can gain the most from the market by giving the least, we should look to see where we can give the most to the market and the world.

Re:Balance: The third law of Money Accumulation

It's not hard to make money in a broad range of assets. What is hard is to avoid the allure of throwing all your money after a new shiny object that everyone seems to be making their fortune on. It's human nature. Repetitive patterns in markets mixed with the psychology of the masses, and over long-time frames, there are waves of similarities. Trends and corrections lead to market cycles.

The best way to avoid heavy losses in the market - or getting swept up in the latest market craze - is to use the more evolved human part of the brain (called the Neo Cortex from the three-brain model). This part of the brain is responsible for abstract thought, imagination and reasoning. Setting up an automated system, whilst you are using this type of thinking is the best way to get Money Mindset. This means that you don't even need to think or worry about money again. This also prevents you from over trading (buying and selling too often) and making silly errors by investing whilst using the less evolved fight or flight part of the brain, which is not designed for building long term wealth.

Three successful and simple strategies are pound cost averaging, systematic rebalancing and using tax incentives to your advantage.

Pound cost averaging is setting your finances up in a way where you buy the same amount of a broad range of assets every month without fail. Buying during the bull market where prices are rising and during the bear market where prices are falling. Doing this reduces the risk of the ups and downs of the market. As you are buying the same amount each month. You buy fewer assets when prices are high and more assets when the price is low. This means that on average you will outperform the market.

A second technique to reduce your risk is systematically rebalancing. This means putting a system in place that will automatically move the assets in your portfolio that have increased in price and move them the assets that haven't risen or even fallen. Today it has never been easier or cheaper to invest beginning with a pound coin from your back pocket. Start using a multi-asset wealth account (Money Tipps reviews the latest products and gives you our honest opinion on each of them and their value for money). You can also use deep discount broker platforms or Robo advisers both offer a selection of portfolios templates of varying risk profiles, with assets from around the world of different shapes and sizes to build your own Football Formation Asset Allocation that is right for you, your future and your family.

Capital Gains Tax

A further benefit of rebalancing every year is that you can take advantage of tax allowances, given to everyone by the government to encourage us all to invest. By using an ISA or pension your money will be protected from capital gains tax. This also saves you the hassle of having to work this out yourself or paying an expensive accountant to do this for you.

Any gains outside a tax wrapper like an ISA or pension will mean gains in your portfolio and may be liable for a capital gains tax, reducing your overall basket of investments.

Rebalancing your portfolio is the hardest thing to do as it goes against our natural human behaviour. We want to stay at the party whilst the going is good however to counteract our nature you can set up a system that will automatically rebalance your portfolio.

Using these forces rather than have them work against you is the key to growing your overall portfolio. When everyone wants to leave the party at the same time this causes an imbalance the demand and supply of the market. This leads to more demand and less supply(the herd rushes to hail a limited number of cabs to get home). This is because everyone as a collective start panicking and thinks using the fight or flight part of their brain creating loss aversion. People fall back down Maslow's hierarchy of needs pyramid where safety, security and food are more important than the gains you have made and your rational long-term life plan using reasoning and logic.

Today it has never been easier to Re: Balance your portfolio. At a click of a button, you can set your investment portfolio to rebalance for you every year, without you even needing to think, stress or do anything. Many investment platforms can set this up for you at no extra charge. So, you can rebalance your portfolio to match your risk profile, asset allocation and age. It is like having a Fairy Godmother telling you the clock is about to strike midnight and who allows you to live happily ever after without turning into a Pumpkin.

These forces work against the growth of your portfolio. To be successful you need to have forces work for you.

The economist Hayek suggested that the economy should be more like gardeners tending their plants. To shift away from self-regulation or just leaving the economy without any help, to move towards realising that the economy needs stewardship to flourish. Gardeners don't just let nature take its course, they create conditions where plants and crops thrive. We need to decide what we want in our investing garden and set up conditions that will give our plants the best chance to grow. This needs to be done using evidence-based research that is successful in the past and applies that today. If you want the fruits, you need the roots.

Understand how money flows and moves naturally with its energy. Money is energy and we should not allow money to flow passively. Today we don't just want to be gardeners, we should create farmyard finances, using Pension Pigs, ISA chickens and Cash Cows. Investors like farmers tending their crops. A farmer is active and cultivates deliberately. They pick the best spot, the right time of year and the correct seeds. They pull up weeds, fertilise the soil and sow the seeds. They building fences (using tax shelters) to keep out the foxes. Think of yourself as a farmer actively tending your crops. Take advantage of the fact that water flows downhill and that the different seasons of the year provide different opportunities. You are not just the farmer, but you are also the results of the farmer's work. You become the fruit of your labour.

We do this by continuously forging a path every day through our individual choices, actions and relationships. We are not just who we are, we can actively make ourselves better investors all the time.

Knowing how much is enough for you gives you the mind space and security that you'll have the lifestyle you want now and for the rest of your life. Living in harmony whilst knowing your purpose and knowing what is enough brings happiness and happiness is the purpose of life. If you want the fruits, you need the roots. Miss enough precious moments and you'll miss a lifetime. Life is not a rehearsal. Rebalance.

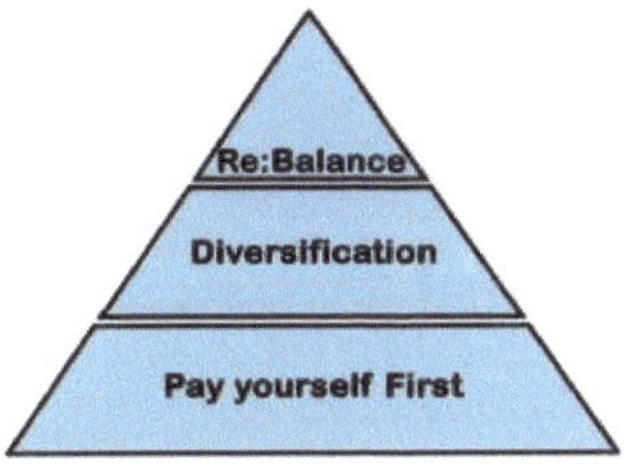

In the future Re:balancing can mean removing companies that do bad to the world and invest in companies that do good for the world. This encourages companies that solve meaningful problems and discourages companies that only chase profits at a cost to society, the world and the biosphere. We don't just need to Re: Balance our portfolio we need to Re: Balance the world. We discuss this in chapter 11 and ask again 'how much is enough?'

Chapter 11

Enough. How much is Enough?

What gets Measured gets Managed and the 7 Habits of a Highly Effective World.

'It always seems impossible until it's done.'

Nelson Mandela (1918 – 2013)

As humanity wakes up and looks into the mirror, after taking off our pandemic masks and seeing through our wrinkles and scars from the past, it will realise how far we have come as a species. In most of history, humans have had to worry about hunger, wars, disease or pests destroying our crops.

As we wake up in 2020 stretch our limbs, rubs our eyes and wash our hands. We open our diary to check what needs to be done and realise that most of our previous problems have been solved. Clean water, infrastructure, education, vaccinations, medicine and irrigation for crops have all made huge improvements that could only be dreamed about by our ancestors. Today we are more likely to die for obesity than starvation, more people die from old age than from war. We can lift our eyes to the horizon and wonder what to do with our day. What needs to be top of our agenda? What is going to demand our attention?

In the 12th century, King Canute tried to stop the power of the oceans. As King of England, he thought he could control nature. He was wrong. Humans have invented some amazing things, however as King Canute found out the hard way, it's impossible to defy nature.

Nature is unpredictable. You can do everything right at the moment and the results can go against you. You can choose how to set your sail, but you won't know for sure which way the wind will blow.

If you had a 10% chance of a fatal car accident, you'd take the necessary precautions. If you had all your net worth in one single share and that has a chance of falling 10%, you'd re-evaluate your asset allocation. So when we know that the world is warming and there is a 10% chance that this might lead to a catastrophe beyond anything we could image, why aren't we doing more about environmental destruction right now?

The Great Pacific Garbage patch is the largest landfill in the world. According to the book, *'What's Mine is Yours'* it is estimated to be twice the size of Texas and is 100 feet deep. This gigantic modern monument to our consumer society is in the Ocean dodged by sailors and shunned by fisherman, who call it a desert due to its lack of fish. These 3.5 million tonnes of rubbish are thought to contain 90% plastic, with everything from children's toys to toothbrushes and plastic bottles, which were likely used once and thrown away. 'It has been estimated that since 1980 humans have consumed one-third of the planet's resources – forest, fish, natural minerals, metals and other raw material'

Back to Nature

For all our technical inventions humans remain at the mercy to the elements. Nature is the principle that unifies all things. Everything in nature is reflected in ourselves.

The breath of every human life of every minute of every day relies on nature. However, an area the size of the country of Greece (5% of the earth's surface) is burned every year. The Amazon rainforest, the lungs of our planet are being burnt every day. The precious biodiversity of the old-growth forests is being cut down to be replaced by soy farms to feed cattle so we can eat a hamburger for dinner. There is so much that humans don't know about the millions of different species on the planet. The depth and complexity of the natural biosphere is incredible. It is in our interest to protect the biodiversity of the planet. We create many of our modern medicines from nature, as just one example, 47% of cancer drugs come from natural sources. We won't realise our full potential as a species unless we work with nature rather against it. We often forget that the most important and vital parts of Maslow's Hierarchy of Needs such as air, water and food, are reliant on nature.

We have been trying to move away from nature rather than towards nature. The world needs a portfolio of long-term investments of natural capital. A bio-diversified world is much less risky than relying on only a few species. We need better management of earth's natural resources.
Humanity relies on only four grasses for the majority of our global food sources. These four kinds of grass are wheat, rice, corn, and millet. If any of these crops fail, then so does the large chunk of our population that is fed by them.
One type of banana makes up 95% of the global output. A pest or disease could easily eradicate this banana species showing how fragile our human progress is.

There are important benefits of nature on human health and wellbeing. Evidence suggests that nature and the natural setting can reduce stress and improve wellbeing. In a study by Roger Ulrich showed that a hospital patient with a view of a natural environment had a reduced stay at hospital by a day, and required less pain medication and had fewer postsurgical complications than patients who instead could only see a brick wall during their stay.

Nature isn't just beautiful, it is practical. The natural environment provides essential services which save millions of pounds every year. Nature prevents floods, filters water and cleans the air. The increase of carbon dioxide into the earth's atmosphere caused by burning fossil fuels can be reduced by the humble tree.

Nature saves lives and communities in times of natural disasters. Engineers are increasingly turning to natural resources rather than concrete and machinery to prevent costly flooding. Acting sooner on environmental degradation makes it cheaper.

Rebalancing the Economy

Despite nature's great importance to nature, we have become disconnected.

We have become disconnected from nature. We have lost our inner truth or essence. For all the progress we have made we need to remember where we come from. 1000s of years ago, our ancestor would look up at the stars each night, seeing how insignificant human beings are in this universe. Light pollution from streetlamps and 24-hour convenience stores in cities across the globe have meant when we look up into the night sky we no longer see the vast galaxies and planets, which connects us with our place in the universe.

Cities have been disconnected from the countryside and many areas that we consider to be the countryside are now human constructions which have lost their alignment with the cycles of nature.

Ancient forests were cut down and burned to provide wood to light fires to keep humans warm during winter. Coal was used to fuel engines of industrial growth, oil for people to drive cars to work and help grow our food on the dinner table. Today natural gas from fossils from the past heats our water and our homes.

The amazing self-balancing act of nature is increasingly becoming unbalanced. We need to question the idea of unlimited growth because the more people who consume the earth's resources the less the capacity of the environment to withstand this change.

We often talk about a battle with nature forgetting that if there was a fight then we would be on the losing side. We often have an attitude towards nature that we don't see ourselves as part of nature but an outside force looking to dominate or control it. We have the illusion of unlimited power and this illusion is fed by our scientific and technological advances.

Humans are the children of nature, not their master. We have to conform our actions to certain natural laws. The system of nature which humans are a part of tends to be self-cleaning, self-adjusting, self-balancing, If we do not Rebalance our economy then mother nature will do it for us.

If we do not change our behaviour then humans will also be on the extinction list alongside the Tasmanian Tiger, Falklands Island wolf and of course the Dodo.

As a bee gathering nectar does not harm or disturb the colour or smell of the flower, so should business and individuals move through the world.

What gets measured gets managed

Human vices of greed and envy are systematically cultivated. Advertisers promote their products to teenagers intending to make it cool to consume. Our status in society's pecking order is still linked to what we wear rather than what we do, what we consume rather than what we have achieved. What we buy rather than who we are.

This consumption may increase GDP but not as people feel it. What were luxuries for our ancestors have become necessities today. GDP measures everything except what makes life meaningful.

'Earth provides enough to satisfy every human need but not for every person's greed'
Mahatma Gandhi (1869 –1948)

Our economy is focused on consumption rather than on the laws of nature. We need to understand the current continuous growth model is leading to environmental disaster and therefore economic catastrophe.

'You never know what is enough unless you know what is more than enough'

William Blake (1757 –1827)

Nature is in us, humans. Whether we realise or not. Nature is a part of us and not just its higher forms but all its wildness and all our grotesque habits. We need to work with nature, not against it.

Humans, nature and the universe all bear fruit, each in its season. All things are in a process of change, and all things are in the state of becoming. You are subject to constant alteration, and so is the world and the companies and business that provide goods and services.

Population collapse

Thomas Malthus' book in 1798 predicted a grim future for humans. He compared the difference between population growth and food production. Food production grew linearly, and the human population grew exponentially. Malthus feared that continuing population growth would lead to famine, disease, war and plagues. Luckily his predictions were wrong and human ingenuity, invention, better health care education and technology has now controlled the population growth using education, contraception and a movement towards gender equality. Food production has been increasing year on year, according to the book 'Factfullness' (which takes data from UN studies). Better technology and supply chains have eradicated hunger in most places in the world.

The human population has exploded in the last 1000 years (as shown by the graph below) after being stable for 10,000s of years. The world population is currently roughly 7 billion and due to the annual growth rate falling from 2.1 % a year to 0.1% a year, the global population is expected to rise to 10.9 billion before stabilising by the year 2100 (according to UN data). Humans have solved the population problem through contraceptives like the pill and better education.

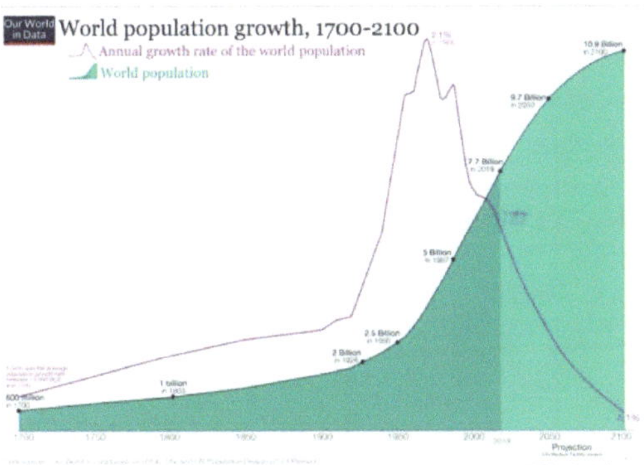

From Wikimedia Commons, the free media repository

Human consumption is the current problem. Our planet can't handle the current level of consumption. The huge amount of resources consumed by individuals in developed countries is no longer sustainable. Even if the 'developed' countries reduced consumption slightly the emerging countries including India, China, Brazil and African nations will soon catch up with our level of consumption. The more economically developed countries need to lead by example and show how a different future is possible.

'Wisdom demands a new orientation of science and technology towards the organic, the gentle, the non-violent, the elegant, the beautiful'

Schumacher (Small is Beautiful 1973)

It's not a question of choosing between modern growth and traditional stagnation. It's finding the right path to progress. The middle way between material thoughtlessness and traditional immobility.

We hold in our hands the tools that could be the solution to these problems. Moving away from a continuous growth model of Gross Domestic Product (GDP is explained below) to one that works with our fundamental nature and treats people like humans rather than just numbers.

We don't need mass production but production for the masses.
Rich people treasure peace more highly than poor people. Their wealth depends on making inordinately large demands on limited world resources and thus puts them on an unavoidable collision course with each other. When you have nothing, you have nothing to lose.
There are too many experts and gurus and not enough wisdom. There is a denial of wisdom. Wisdom demands a new orientation of science and technology towards the organic, the gentle, and the non-violent, the elegant and beautiful. Today we need a business model that works with nature. We need to evolve as a species and focus on progress and move away from a measure that was introduced to maximise production during wartime. Today we need to Re: Balance.

Growth Rate

What is useful? Should it be decided by the quarterly GDP figures or should it be what is useful to society? What is growth? Should growth be determined by how much is produced? Or should it be focused on the quality of life as we experience it? What values do we want to teach our children?

'What gets measured gets managed.'

Peter Drucker(1909 – 2005)

Let's measure something meaningful.

Imagine being in a car crash. This would be devastating for everyone involved, however, this would be a good thing according to our current measure of progress Gross Domestic Product (GDP). GDP tracks the value of goods and services. This car crash may cause injury or even death that's even before we mention the destruction to the victim's everyday lives, jobs and businesses. This crash, however, would be a positive thing for GDP because it would require a doctor to see to the patients, an ambulance driver, and two new cars would need to be bought which would be good for both the car and the steel industry due to this extra demand. GDP was introduced during the aftermath of the 1930s depression and then came about during World War 2 to increase the productivity of a country. GDP was an efficient way to make more stuff, however, today we need a measure that gives life more meaning.

GDP caused an arms race causing more destruction of the planet's natural resources. GDP measures consumption, meaning the more stuff that is made and then disposed of the better it is for GDP and the 'health' of the country.

GDP doesn't measure the things that matter. GDP rewards the person consuming on credit cards but punishes the careful saver and investor. It fails to measure the volunteer who helps to make someone's day at the old people's home or the grandparents who help with childcare.

GDP rewards consumption, however, the main problem with GDP is that it is measured by companies every 3 months (a quarter). Anything of value takes time to grow and this short measure doesn't allow for long term thinking that would benefit humanity.

What gets measured gets managed

GDP measures everything except what makes life worthwhile. We need a new measure where people matter. How do we measure this change? To move to a more meaningful indicator than our current choice. Kate Raworth in Doughnut economics uses a measure in the book that treats people as if they mattered. Treating the planet as a system of inputs and outputs taking nature into account in the economy and if managed correctly could create abundance for everyone, rather than scarcity.

There is an illustration of the doughnut below. At the bottom is the social foundation that meets the basics of human needs from Maslow's hierarchy. Meaning every human should have access to clean air, water, food, health and shelter.

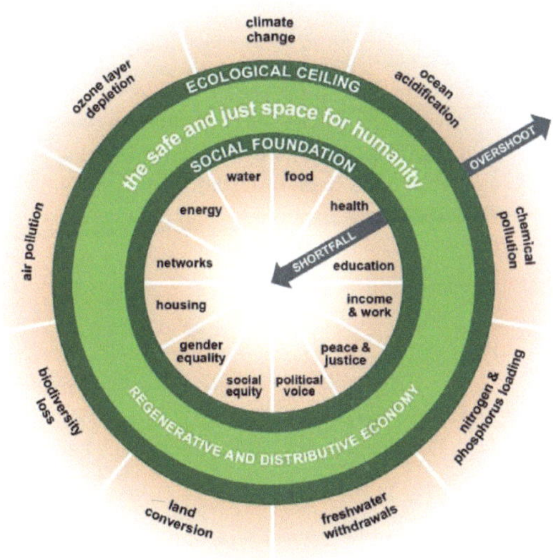

Author: DoughnutEconomics Kate Raworth

From Wikimedia Commons, the free media repository

There is a carrying capacity that the environment can support human life. This ecological ceiling is currently close to being breached which will result in devasting environmental disasters.

The regenerative and sustainable doughnut is the sweet spot in the middle where life can prosper, and progress happens. Like nature, businesses must focus on the whole life-cycle of their products.

We need to create businesses that consume less. A 10% growth rate means an economy will double every 7 years. We have an economy that needs to grow, whether we like it or not, it makes us thrive. We need to have an economy that makes us thrive, whether or not.it grows Is it possible to go slower by design, not disaster?

In this moment humans have in our hands the tools to turn nature into electricity. To be able to heat our homes and cook our food from the sun, fuel our transport with the wind and tides. A potentially limitless supply of energy. An abundance that our ancestors would have imagined in their wildest dreams.

The World Economic Forum reported in Carbon Brief that the third quarter of 2019, the UK's wind farms, solar panels, biomass and hydro plants generated more electricity than the combined output from power stations from coal, gas and oil. This is showing that a new energy system is possible based on clean renewable energy rather than fossil fuels which leads to climate change The potential of renewable energy has today shown that we can utilise the sun, the wind and the waves to satisfy our human hierarchy of needs. We need to put the use of fossil fuels on the extinctions list along with the dinosaurs and dodo.

We need to move our mindset to catch up with our reality.

We need to change our mindset to abundance and a growth mindset. We need to move to a regenerative economy, where everything is in balance. A wholistic economy, which is based on a conscious ecological model that balances the whole of the planet.

Today good business is good business. Irresponsible businesses are still in the old-world mindset and think only about the value they are providing to their shareholders. There is too much evidence today to have any excuses for the many waves of abuse that are happening in the management of land and the environment. Like viewing the evidence of a court case and deciding if someone is guilty or not. We can no longer ignore the truth as we see it today. We need to wake from our slumber and take a bold step forward.

This is a Millennial Money Mindset.

If we destroy the natural capital of the world that sustains us then the environment will deteriorate, rapidly reducing the carrying capacity of the world. If we kill the golden goose that has provided humanity with an abundance of golden eggs then there will be no companies, no profits and no planet if we continue at this rate. The mass extinction that is happening today will also include human beings on that list.

It is a tragedy of the commons that humans think on an individual basis and often not thinking at a global level. This happens more frequently when we are acting on the lower needs of Maslow's hierarchy. If we and our family are hungry then we do not care about the more complicated, higher needs from Maslow's hierarchy, all we need is to eat. When our stomachs are empty, we do not care about the beauty of architecture or a rainforest burning thousands of miles away. We think about how good the hamburger will taste rather than the land it uses, water needed, and the suffering of the animal it has caused getting this food to our tables.

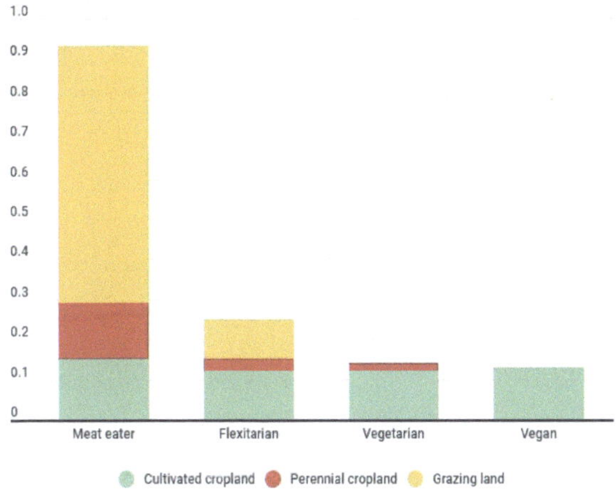

Hectares per year for varies diets.

Research published in the journal Science by J. Poore and T. Nemecek. Carried out at the University of Oxford on land use and greenhouse gases compared different food sources. The researchers found the amount of land is used for a meat-eating diet compared with a vegetarian and a vegan diet. Even reducing some meat consumption from a diet (a flexitarian) had a massive reduction in land required to provide food for a person

The study found that Beef production uses 36 times more land than crops for vegetables. Reducing people's consumption of beef could mean, global farmland use could be reduced by 75 per cent. This was estimated to free up the amount of land the size of China, the EU, Australia and the USA combined. Imagine if this land could be used to grow trees, re-wild the land, bringing it back into its original state as well as providing food, homes and communities for thousands of people. Creating abundance for everyone.

In the study at Oxford University and the Swiss agricultural research institute, Agroscope the Researchers Joseph Poore said 'High-impact beef producers create 105kg of CO2 equivalents (or over 2500 kilograms of greenhouse emission per year) and use 370m2 of land per 100 grams of protein. Low-impact beans, peas, and other plant-based proteins can create just 0.3kg of CO2 equivalents and use just 1m2 of land per 100 grams of protein.'

Understanding this evidence can have an impact on the choices we make for our weekly shop and the decision we make when ordering a meal at our local restaurant. Thinking globally, whilst acting locally can have a massive change on the planet.

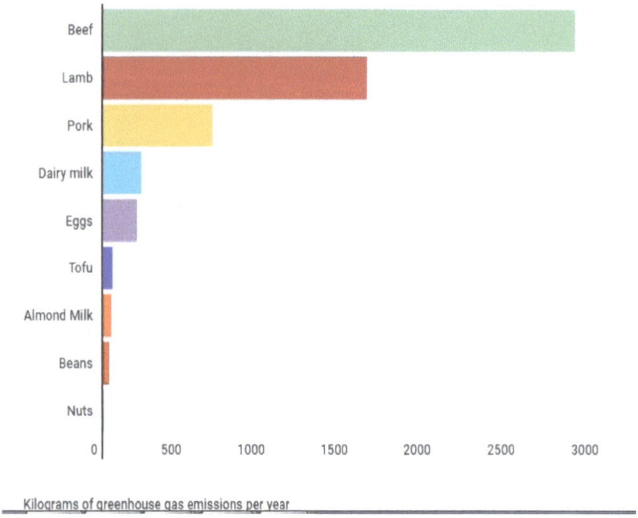

In 2019, 'developed' nations meat consumption reached an all-time high' According to the USA department of agriculture, 'The average American eats over 200 pounds of meat per year. That's equivalent to eating about 800 hamburgers and adding more emissions to the atmosphere per gram than any equivalent source of protein.'

Which milk is best?

As the graph below shows a simple change from dairy milk to non-dairy can reduce emissions, land use and water use significantly. This data is from the study conducted by Poore and Nemecek in 2018 and published in the journal Science.

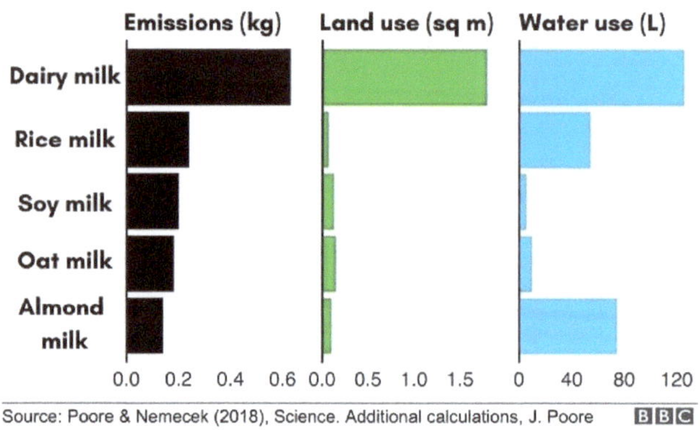

Credit @reducewastenow on Instagram

Humans need to change if humans are to not just survive but thrive in our new and changing environment. We need to evolve up the hierarchy of needs. We need to think on a macro level rather than a micro level. We must understand this environmental degradation is rapidly destroying our current civilisation.

The Snowflake and the World

We are connected to nature. We are the micro. The small snowflake and everything else is the macro, the city, the world, the universe.

The pound coin from our back pocket is the micro and the markets are the macro. We have a choice by choosing how to invest.

The good news is that social values have changed so much over the last few years that the tables have turned and, from this point onwards, responsible businesses will start to perform better over the long term. They'll be more innovative and learn faster because they're humbler and recognise that they need to take in and listen to regular feedback from all their stakeholders. They will attract a growing number of socially conscious workers, consumers and more importantly investors.

'There are fundamental improvements that are world-changing but are too slow, too fragmented, or too small one by one to ever qualify as news. I am talking about the secret silent miracle of human progress.'

Hans Rosling: Factfulness (2019)

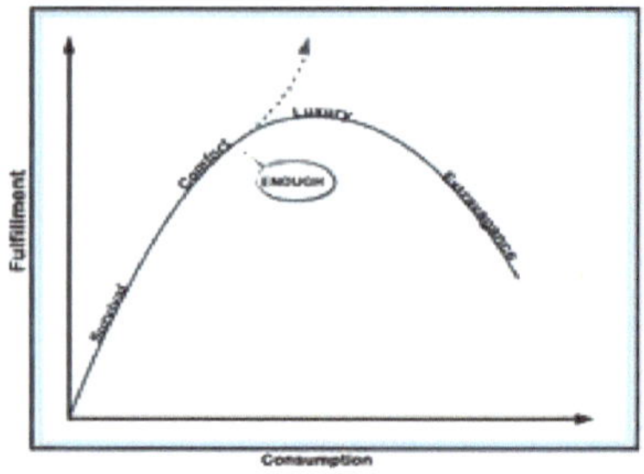

Is there enough money and resources to go around? What even is enough? Who can tell us when we have reached enough? Certainly not the economists and politicians who chase economic growth as the highest of all values and therefore believe that there will never be enough. We are in the process of stripping the world's resources and continued economic growth, which only produces more demand.

Imagine a pond, which has a limited carrying capacity. It only has enough food, water and air to hold a certain number of species.

Imagine a lily pad in this pond that doubles in size every day. How long until the entire pond is covered in plants?
Compound interest doesn't just work with money, but it demonstrates how quickly something can double. The lily pad illustration shows how growth can quickly get out of hand. Growing what seems like slowly and manageably can quickly cover the whole environment.
In only 8 days the pond becomes uninhabitable to not just the lily pads but also to other species in that pond. This shows the power of compound interest. Using GDP as a measure for growth is unsustainable and it is mathematically impossible to continue without destroying not just our planet but also our species.

This lily pad on the first few days can grow rapidly and the whole pond is not affected. On day four its halfway through the period of time but not half the pond is covered. The penultimate day that pond is half-covered.
This kind of growth is counterintuitive. It doesn't make sense to humans as we often think in terms of cause and effect. Until we have experienced compound growth ourselves, we can't fully understand a concept. If we don't understand something, then we will not act in the best interests of the whole planet.

Day 1

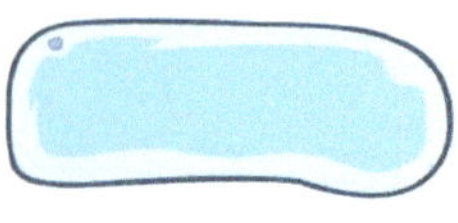

Day 2

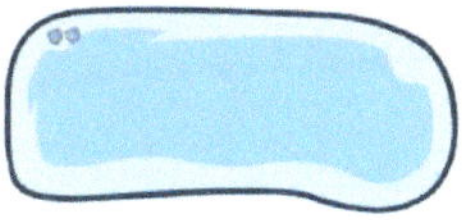

Day 3

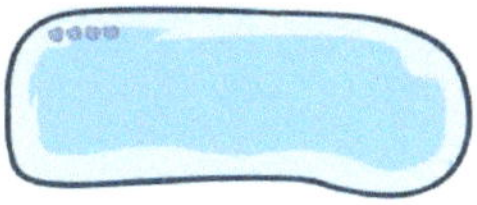

Day 4

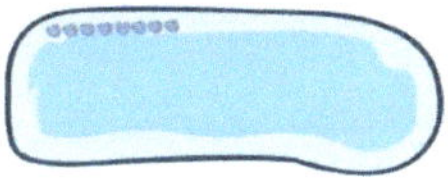

Day 5

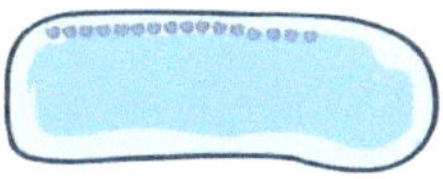

Day 6

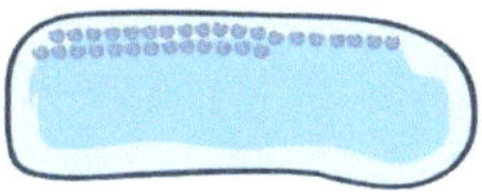

Day 7

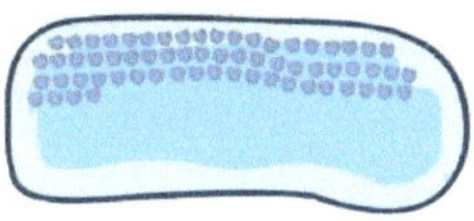

Day 8

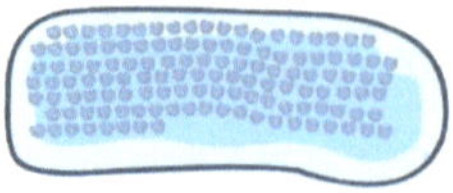

It is not just about doubling. It is about how much the current number has increased compared with the last number.

For example, if a country grows at 8% GDP using the rule of 72 (explained in chapter 3), this means that a county's GDP will double the amount it consumes every nine years. This will be measured as positive according to today's measure GDP.
72/8% growth rate= 9 years to double

Even if the world grew at 3% a year, quite a few economists would consider this a global recession. Anyone who believes in indefinite growth in anything physical, on a physically finite planet is either mad or an economist.
The continual grow model mathematically doesn't work. It is impossible to grow forever on a finite planet. We need to look at what progress means and what we want to aim for.

If we consume more resources at the same rate, then there will be no more world to pass to our children and grandchildren.
The world is too focused on short term visions of GDP. Governments are worried about having two quarters of the year that is in negative growth of GDP, as this is the technical definition of a recession. Continuing to follow GDP is a losing battle.

What is Progress?

Progress is a forward movement towards a destination. The problem is we have no destination to head towards. No end in mind that we should aim for.

We should be improving or getting better than the day before, and leaving the world in a better place than how you found it. We need to invest in infrastructure that will benefit both us or our children and also our children's children and beyond. We need to look at the great civilisations of the past and learn from them. The renaissance and the enlightenment periods of history which, due to expansion of knowledge, new ideas, and education combined, led to improvements to human collaboration, great architecture and an improvement on the quality of life for more people.

How do we know that we are moving forward? Hegel, the German Philosopher, believed that progress is ultimately furthered by the person who is out of step with the majority. Only this person, the genuine non-conformist, really experiences freedom. This person who questions the current understanding of progress or happiness. This unhappy consciousness is the source of progress.

'Machinery that gives us abundance has left us in want.

Our knowledge has become cynical.

Our cleverness hard and unkind. More than cleverness we need kindness and gentleness.

Without these qualities, life would be violent, and all will be lost.'

Charlie Chaplin, *The Great Dictator* (1940)

We need to head towards the United Nations Sustainable development goals. This is the 17 biggest problems that the world face today. The aim is to solve all these goals by the year 2030. This is a global blueprint for dignity, peace and prosperity for people and the planet, now and in the future. A blueprint to achieve a better and more sustainable future for all. (We should also add racial and ethnicity equality as an 18th UN goal).

We need to aim for these goals, rather than measuring companies on their GDP. GDP is a metric that is mathematically flawed. Let's measure what is meaningful. Let's measure how companies solve meaningful problems.

The 7 Habits of a Highly Effective World

Here is a model which builds on Steven Covey's 7 habits of highly effective people and places the concepts into the extinction rebellion symbol of the hourglass. There are 7 habits in this model and they move through three stages of the model, which are: 1) dependence, 2) independence and 3) interdependence.

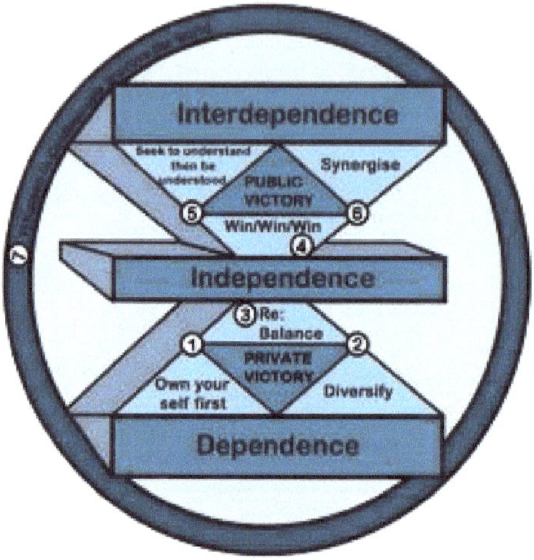

Getting financially independent using the three rules of money. Own yourself first, diversify and Re:Balance.

1)We need to own ourselves first.

We all need to, first of all, take responsibility for our actions. Whether we know it or not our actions have consequences.

We need to own ourselves first. Be the change you want to see in the world.
We need to stop linking consumption with status. We should be made to feel important for who we are and what we have achieved rather than the stuff we have bought.

Companies must leave no trace. Taking nothing away but problems. Companies need to take ownership of the lifecycle of their products.
We also need to be proactive rather than reactive. Be an owner, not a consumer. Either you are producing, or you are consuming. Are you adding value? Buying shares in companies means you become an owner. Helping business to expand and more jobs to be created. Too many people are focused on how much return they can get from the market. How much they can take whilst give the least. This is unsustainable. When you lend money to a company or government or when you pay money for a share in

a company you are giving money that will be better used. That will help more people or solve more problems. We have become disconnected from this fact.

Aiming to be net-zero. To give more than you take. To produce more than you consume. To give only memories and leave only footprints in the sand.

Being responsible and investing in companies that produce progress, not just profits.

2 Diversify

Diversification of not just of financial assets but of biodiversity assets or natural capital. Relying on one or two species for food is a disaster waiting to happen. Having a wide variety of species will only benefit humans. The lack of biodiversity is worrying. We need to rebalance not just with our money but the world, aiming for a more biodiverse world.

We also need to have a diversity of people too. We need to have a diversity of gender, race and religion. The more diversified a population of ideas, beliefs and people, the stronger it will become

3 Re: Balance

Rebalance not just our portfolios but the world. Rebalance to bring back the natural balance of land use. E.O. Wilson recommends that the earth returns to forest and wilderness. He recommends 50% of the earth's surface to be Rebalanced to be returned to its natural environment. Returning the land to forests and natural landscapes rather than farmland for food would solve many of the environmental problems.

4 Think win/win/win

Businesses need not just make a profit; they need to solve meaningful problems and they need to contribute to the enhancement of the world.

Not just a win for the company making a profit or win/win for the company and the customer. But win/win/win. Win for business and win for the customer, and also win for the planet.

5 Seek first to understand then be understood

We need to look at the evidence. Like a court case looking at all the evidence and making an objective, rational decision with the facts in front of you. Evidence-based research, which has been peer-reviewed (meaning it has been sense checked by others who have knowledge, experience and understanding in that area) is important in getting to the truth. However, science can't become arrogant. Scientists also don't know what they don't know and are humans after all. Remember that the greatest minds once thought the earth was flat.

6 Synergise

The challenge is to apply the principles of creative cooperation, which we learn from nature to our social interactions and our investments. The essence of synergy is to value each other's differences. To respect them and build on our strengths to compensate for our weaknesses.

7 Kaizen (Continuous Improvement)

Kaizen is a Japanese concept which means change for better. It aims to continuously improve the way that processes are carried out. Every day getting better. Asking ourselves not what the right way is but what is the best way today, and continuously looking for a better way tomorrow. The Kaizen circle is the emblem of the universe as well as representing the mundane egg. Evolving over times filling ecological niches. Kaizen is continuous improvement.

Cyclical Evolution

It's not just our species that needs to change but our companies need to evolve. Becoming an owner of companies means you have the decision on what we want our companies to become. As a shareholder of a company, you become an owner. This means you have the legal right to vote and choose what companies we create. We can vote on the goals and targets of companies and the leaders of that company. This is evolution. It is not necessarily the fittest or fastest that survives but the species that adapt the quickest.

Creative destruction

Evolution is the never-ending flow of creative destruction out of itself. All creation, through continuous moving never arrives at any state other than that of ceaseless flow. Herbert Spensor's book First Principles said that '*evolution as an ever-increasing complexity with equilibrium as its highest possible state, having a deep understanding of nature and its laws. No one can live intelligently without fundamental knowledge of nature.*'

> *'The death of earth is the birth of water, the death of water is air, the death of earth is fire and back around.*
>
> *We should pass through tiny fragments of time with nature and leave it gladly, as an olive might fall when ripe, blessing the earth which bore it'*
>
> Marcus Aurelius *Meditations* 175 AD

The best metaphor for future companies and a sustainable economy is the kitesurfer. Think of how a kitesurfer rides her surfboard across the rolling waves whilst catching the wind in her sail, continuingly adjusting, bending dipping and twisting. There needs to be both markets driven by the customer, the conditions of the economic winds, as well as the positive impact we are making in the world by powering forward using renewable forces.

Technology has changed everything. The internet has meant that things have changed so quickly. Since the year 2000, there has been a huge wave of change happening. This has been getting bigger and faster due to what is called divergence. This is where several different technologies develop at the same time and create unexpected results or emergence. These ideas change whole industries. Will you be stuck clinging to the old rules, or will you be riding this new wave?

You can't choose the weather, but you can choose how to set your sail.

Today we are at a crossroad as we move out of the industrial age and into the knowledge economy, you can feel the wind of change on your cheek. Will you embrace this change? You still have time to respond and be proactive. You know the tides are changing. You can adapt and can thrive in any conditions if you follow the three laws of money.

We need to have companies that solve meaningful problems for the customer, not just making a profit, whilst not causing more problems to the planet. The best guide to this is the 17 UN world goals.

"The biggest risk is not taking any risk. In a world that's changing really quickly, the only strategy to fail is not taking risks"

Mark Zuckerberg Facebook Founder

The Invisible hand of the markets.

'To see the world in a grain of sand, and to see heaven in a wildflower, hold infinity in the palm of your hand and eternity in an hour'

William Blake (1757 – 827)

Harmony is a state recognised as the prerequisite of beauty. A compound is termed beautiful only when its parts are in harmonious combination. The world is beautiful because it acts in harmony with nature and nature is harmonious. It is interdependent.

Nature is an inexhaustible storehouse of riches that won't run out. Knowing this you can have an abundance mindset or a growth mindset rather than a fixed mindset. Nature is formed for the advancement of life. It's a good time to be alive. Believe in yourself and good things do start happening. A seed planted in the ground springs into action and in the act of living produces hundreds of more seeds. At the same, a pound coin invested into the stock market over its lifetime can multiply itself. It is forever becoming more.

'Don't worry about a thing, cause every little thing is gonna be alright'

Bob Marley (1945 –1981)

Businesses have evolved. Daniel Priestly uses a powerful metaphor of the age of hands, age of head and age of hearts. For thousands of years, humans were in the 'age of hands' where humans became brilliant tool makers, which could move things that could shape our world to our will. We thrived because of our hands, working the farmland or crafting tools to make life easier. This was until the industrial revolution, where the machinery we built could out-compete our dexterity. This was the 'age of heads'. One machine in a factory could outcompete 100 people and one engine were faster than the quickest horse.

Today we are moving to the 'age of hearts' This means that businesses that solve meaningful problems will outcompete companies looking just to make a profit. Technology today is moving us towards protopia, meaning a state of becoming rather than a destination. Things are better today than yesterday.

The internet has changed everything. Today business has evolved. Previously the company sold the commodities or products they had to customers. Today the customer is in charge. Once we realise this it will be a change in mindset similar to when Copernicus realised that the earth went around the sun rather than the common thinking at the time of the sun moving around the earth. Today companies must go around customers to solve their problems. Today businesses (like the Tinman from Chapter 3) need a heart.

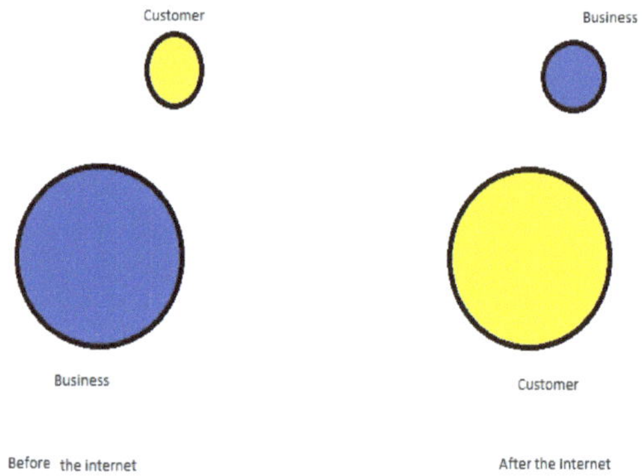

'The balance of power is shifting towards consumers and away from companies. In the old world, you devoted 30 per cent of your time to building a great service and 70 per cent of your time shouting about it. In the new world that inverts.'

Jeff Bezos Amazon Founder

Money mindset is about shifting your self-image from someone who adapts to things and consumes to someone who creates things too. It's not how much you can get from the market but how much you can give to the market. Many short-term traders are looking to see how much they can take from the market. The point of any market is a tool to make things better or to make money by giving value. Any successful trader or investor makes money by giving value to the market, and by seeing something that the market doesn't fully appreciate.

Our fulfilment and happiness are based on how much we can give, not on how much we take. We as humans need growth, whether that's emotional, spiritual or intellectual. We also need to contribute, we need to go beyond ourselves, give care and serve others. And that's another way to look at an investor.

There are order and predictability in nature. Look at the smallest seashell or a flower petal and up to the swirling of a hurricane to the vast Milky Way galaxy, they share a similar pattern.

The micro and the macro.

You and the world. Every action has an equal and opposite reaction. A tiny ripple in a pond moves outwards and affects everything in the pond.

We make decisions daily that have an impact on the whole world.

We need to ask ourselves: What is progress? We need to focus on our problem-solving abilities. What values do we want our children to have? What is useful? It is not for the markets to decide but society.

Every decision you choose to make is like a universal law and the actions you take influence everything else in the universe. The pound coin in your back pocket is connected to everything else in the markets around the world. Self-transcendence is about rising from our individual needs and relating them to what is greater than ourselves, whether this is raising healthy child, growing a community garden patch or improving a social policy. To have one person breathe easier because you have lived. This is when we know we have succeeded.

You have the choice to invest the pound coin from your back pocket into a company to help it grow and solve more people's problems. You have the choice what type of company you invest in. A company that does good or a company that causes harm. Any revolution starts with the people rather than the industry

Looking up at the sky at night you realise that you are one part of the greater whole, one part of something greater than yourself, maybe that is your community, the natural world, or the universe. The millennial snowflake and the stars.

Pension funds

Capital (meaning the supply of money) is now in the hands of ordinary people. This means ownership of companies that produce a profit is changing hands. Moving from companies who would look after your pension to pay you an income in retirement. To the everyday person who is now in control of their future income in the form of assets. These assets have been accumulated through investing through your pension and ISA investments.

This shift in ownership can have a massive impact on which companies receive money for future investments. Never before have there been such enormous pools of money held by ordinary people who pool their money together called institutional investors, meaning similar to pension funds. There is currently £3 trillion in UK Pensions and 18 million people are currently saving into a pension (according to Make My Money Matter non-profit organisation).

These pools of money dwarf anything the great capitalists of the past controlled. Pension funds are the savings of today's employees. Their main purpose must be to protect the financial future of the present employees. With life expectancies almost double that of the 19th century a huge threat for the ordinary person is living longer than their money. This money needs to be invested wisely to ensure people can live a good life when they stop working.

This means the ordinary worker now controls the capital. These investors control huge pools of money that are the future pensioners (this means you). You now own hundreds of companies around the world. Just by working and your employer contributing to your pension you have now become a business owner. You are in charge. When owning shares of a business you can even vote on key decisions for the direction of the company or who will lead the company into the future.

When children read about the Millennials in history books hundreds of years from today. What will be written about us? We are at a crossroads in history, we can all feel it. Change is happening more rapidly than at perhaps any other time in history. Will we be the generation that let paradise and abundance slip through our fingers, being too distracted scrolling through our phones to appreciate what we have and how far we have come. Or will this be the start of a revolution of change, prosperity and happiness? A new renaissance created by a financial awakening, a new wholistic economy that balances the whole of the planet and benefits the many rather than the few. Ensuring that our species and millions of other species across the globe survive and thrive for 1000s more years.

The three laws of money

1) Owning yourself first. Taking responsibility and being proactive. Pay yourself first and build a £1000 emergency fund.
2) Diversify. Split your money between land/business and reserves (cash, bonds and insurance). Then follow the Football Formation Asset Allocation.
3) Re: Balance. The micro and the macro. The snowflake and the stars.

Knowledge isn't enough, you have to apply the principles and execute your ideas of what you have learnt. It isn't an art or science; it's a practice and applying daily habits. You should own yourself first, diversify and rebalance.

'You can't take away someone's story without giving them a new one'

George Monbiot Out of the Wreckage (2017)

When we develop the right story and learn how to tell it, it can help navigate us towards our unique happiness. A story that learns from the past, places us in the present and guides our future.

Our purpose is often similar. We often don't know what we want from life or where we are heading. We often can see the path although we can often feel or sense it, or some clues are left that we need to work out. It begins with the smallest things in our daily lives, from which we change everything. If we begin there, then everything is up to us, like a sapling that has been bending and bowing gracefully with the winds, pliable and soft. It stands up again when the storm has passed. Its very weakness is what has allowed it to flourish and prevail.

Humanity looks into the mirror today and sees a combination of stone age emotion, medieval self-importance and today's access to technology give us what our ancestor would consider god-like abilities, where we can communicate instantly with anyone on the planet, we can fly to any part of the world in hours and heal the sick with modern-day medicine. We should not reject technology but use it as a tool to improve our lives and create a world of abundance. To help mould and shape our environment for the better. To not be independent from nature but to be interdependent with nature.

We need to work out our purpose, which is discussed next and how you can use the Japanese concept of Ikegai to find your unique purpose.

Is the person you see in the mirror the person you want to see reflected at you? If not, you need to grow your roots because if you want the fruits you need the roots. The roots are your money mindset.

Epilogue: What's your Why? How to Find Your Purpose.

Nothing is stronger than an idea whose time has come

Victor Hugo (1802 – 1885)

The knife reflection caught my eye as the steel blade headed towards my body. I felt my eyes get heavier as I slowly drifted to sleep. The news of a cancerous mole on my lower back shocked me more than the news of my redundancy that same week. This left me reflecting on my life and how little I had achieved. I imagined my funeral and who would attend and what people would say about me.

This changed my mindset.

Feeling the blood rushing from my face, seeing my image reflecting at me from the window I noticed my skin get noticeably paler. Hearing in a 'restructuring' meeting I was told I was to be made redundant after working for this company for twelve years.

Being a gas trader forged in the high-pressure environment of the trading floor. My biggest daily trading gain was £940,000 when a pipeline from Norway froze over during a bitterly cold Saturday morning in February. I was in the office at 7 am choosing to be at my desk rather than at home in my warm bed. I managed to source gas from France to meet the gas demand for people warming their homes as Britain woke up that morning to turn on their heating.

Working on the trading floor with eight computer screens around me felt like I was in a microwave oven, slowly frying my brain leaving it will little nutrition. Did I want to work twelve-hour days for the rest of my life, spending weekends in the office rather than at home? That decision was made for me hearing news about my redundancy. Those words still ring in my ears today.

My redundancy allowed me to choose what I wanted to do with my life. Analysing my strengths, people's problems that need solving and my passions. I looked at where I could make the greatest contribution. One of my greatest strength and joys was managing and investing my own money. A Financial Advisor seemed a perfect fit. I passed numerous written and practical exams; I gained a regulatory licence to give financial advice from the Financial Conduct Authority (FCA). I decided to roll the dice and start my own Financial Planning practice, giving financial advice to my clients.

The people I advised varied greatly, everyone from investing their £15 million bitcoin winnings, rockstars who just signed their second album deal and to Sunday league football dads who wanted to invest their £50 weekly savings for their first child's future.

Time is our most important asset.

Great investors don't just know when to buy the latest stock; it's more about managing yourself, knowing your objectives and your attitude to risk. This gives you the mental and mind space to focus on the important things in life; your friends, family or having more 'me' time.

How many days did I have left to live? I didn't know for sure. No one does. If I lived a good and long life perhaps, I would live to 90 years old. I calculated how many days left to live if I lived a full life. I had 18,980 days until I would be 90 years old. In 57 years, that's 684 months of expenses that I would need until I would be financially free.

Time often expands to fill a task that we want to achieve. (This is known as Parkinson's law.) Parkinson's law states that work will expand to fill the time you give to it. Meaning the longer you give something to achieve the longer it will take you. This concept works with your life too. Do you want to have to work every week until you are 67 (The current state pension age) Or do you want to have enough assets to pay you an income to give you the freedom to choose how to spend each day?

How many of these did I want to be working and how many did I want to be living?

My goal had been to have enough assets to pay myself an income, so I could choose how to spend my time. To me, this was being free.

How many days until I was free? Free to live the life I choose.

Imagine you live to 90 years old. How many years is that for you? Calculate how many days you have left to live.

90 years old – your age today ----------- X 365 (days) =--------- days left to live if you live a good life

Calculate how many months of expenses that would be?

How much do you spend each month?

How many months of expenses do you need to be financially independent?

<u>Think about Time Differently</u>

When we think about time, we often think about the clock on the wall. We can understand how the clock ticks and what makes the clock tick. The more important question is why does the clock tick? Do we exist in time or does time exist in us?

> *'I stop suddenly and do nothing, nothing happens. I am thinking about nothing. I listen to the passing of time.'*
>
> Carlo Rovelli The Order of Time (2017)

Start thinking about your last day not as a punishment but as an inevitable law of nature. We all die but how many of us really live? This mindset removed my fear of death, I had always unconsciously feared death, however, if you are afraid of dying then you will never achieve anything of greatness. Knowing how much time we have left to live pushes us to do more with our lives, appreciating and making the most of each day. We must understand that we all will die at some point. Knowing these are the rules of the game from our conception will have the mindset that nothing will take you by surprise.

Time often feels like it contracts and expands, by this I mean I remember long, careless summers playing as children seem to last a lifetime, whereas as we get older a year can feel like it passes in a blink of an eye. We are born with so much time, that we often don't appreciate it and use it wisely. We are not given a short life, but we squander it doing wasteful things. We often spend our time occupied by pursuing other people's money or complaining about our own money. Many people have no fixed goal or aim for their life's course. It is only a small part of life that we live. We are often frugal with our personal property or our money but when it comes to wasting time, we give our time away, the one thing we should be frugal with. We watch mind-numbing television or work at a job that we hate just to pay for a few moments of peace in overpriced city property.

I saw myself working in that corporate job, living the same day over and over for the next 25 years. You don't need to be old to die, working in that corporate job I was dying a little every day because I wasn't living.

We often think that time is linear like it is a straight line from birth to death. This is often not our experience in reality. When we think about time, the past, present and future are all jumbled up in our heads. Two important moments in time though they may be years apart link themselves immediately in our minds. Think about your birthdays of the past and how we can link each year instantly in our mind even though they are years apart. The past and the future are just an illusion. We can imagine a future that will never be, or we can think about a different outcome happening from the past. The actions we take in this moment can affect the life we will be living in the future.

Imagine your 60-year-old self. How do you want you be living? What do you want to see in the mirror reflecting at yourself? Who do you want to become when you look into that person's eyes.

Today we can choose to start to invest or we can choose not to. That decision creates two different outcomes, two different lives we will live, two different people we will be. The future could be very different.

'There is no fate but what we make'

Sarah Connor, *the Terminator (1984)*

There is no such thing as time management. Time is not ours to control, time will continue no matter what actions we take. We are all given a certain amount of time in our lives. We can only manage what we do with our time. We get to choose what to decide what to do with the time we have. The past and future are an illusion. All we have is this present moment. We need to focus on doing what is fulfilling, meaningful and purposeful.

Time is a precious commodity. No matter how much we can pay, there will always be a limited supply.

'All we have to decide is what to do with the time that is given to us"

Gandalf, *The Fellowship of the Ring* (1954)

Imagine if we measured time differently. By how many days we have left to live rather than how many birthdays have passed since we were born. Knowing I had a finite time left to live made me appreciate the moments. Every breath I took a gift, as I imagined the grains of sand fall through the hourglass, every grain of sand falling meant another day gone forever.

Not knowing where your time goes is like the sand falling through an hourglass without a bottom. No matter how much you pour in nothing settles and it escapes through the holes and the cracks. The present time is so short, so much so that most people are unaware of it. Time is irreplaceable. We can substitute one resource for another, wheat for corn for example. We can exchange money for human labour. But there is no substitute for time. If we want to know how short life is then work out how much of your life is your own.

Our lives are divided into three parts. The past, the present and future. Of these the present is short, the future doubtful and only the past is certain. In the present, we only have a moment at a time. All we have is this moment and we have a choice of how we can spend this moment, to ask ourselves if doing this thing in this moment will bring me happiness?

When it would come to the end of my life, I would realise that my life was preoccupied with doing nothing or doing work that other people wanted me to do. As a child, I would dream about what I wanted to become. I had promised higher and greater things for myself. I realised how short my life was because none of it was my own.

'Did I live?

Did I love?

Did I matter?'

Brandon Burchard, The Millionaire Messenger (2011)

Working that corporate job I was living my life on autopilot, proceeding through the day doing what came naturally to me. In a sense, I was unconscious of my behaviour. This type is routine activity is low impact on the human brain, this type of thinking doesn't require as much energy, thought or planning. Today we need conscious attention. We need to wake from autopilot and think with imagination, abstract thought and more importantly consciousness, using the more evolved human part of the brain. We need to make intelligent decisions about our behaviour, that will benefit us and the world long term..

I felt alienated from the work I was producing. Answering emails, pointless meetings and making money for the company that employed me. I couldn't connect what I was doing with the wider world. My labour was not an act of personal creation or personality. It was just ticking the same checklist every day. I was working just to survive and pay the bills rather than utilising any unique talents or creativity. I realised that I didn't own my time. I couldn't choose what to do with myself, and therefore, I wasn't free.

I was like an ant going back and forth each day. Working, but not achieving anything meaningful. I was living in busy idleness. Confusing business with busy-ness. Working every day without a purpose. Each morning standing on that escalator on my way to work. I was moving but not getting anywhere.

How was I going to spend the 18,980 days I have left to live?

Unlike ants, human beings can form an idea. We can make a conscious choice of what to do in each moment. We can make a decision and a conscious choice to live in the present and take actions that will affect our future self. We are responsible for every action, and every action has an equal and opposite reaction. We can choose to act or choose not to act, this is still deciding on what we will be. Everything is becoming.

'Because it's a bittersweet symphony this life
Trying to make ends meet, you're a slave to the money then you die.'

The Verve 1997

Money Mindset

Stepping out of the hospital that day my head feeling groggy from the pain killers, although the light seemed a little brighter than I had remembered it. It had felt as if I had woken up from a very vivid dream.

I reached inside my jeans pocket and felt a scrunched-up paper. I pulled it out of my pocket and slowly unravelled the old tatty piece of paper. It was the goal that I had written many years ago and what seems like a lifetime ago. I read the words in my head.

'I will be a millionaire by the time I am 35. '

Why £1m? It was not about the money but the person it would make me become to achieve this goal. It was the freedom that money could bring. It was the time that money would give me and the ability it would give me to choose how to spend my time. We have all been given one life, we must work for our freedom, so we can pursue our happiness. It was time I wanted, not the money. Time to live my life, doing what matters to me most. To have the choice to work for joy rather than necessity. This to me was happiness.

£1m sounds like a lot of money today but if you work out future expenses with inflation it isn't. It was the amount that would be enough to live comfortably for the rest of my life. If you invest £1m and get 4% returns you will get an income of £40,000 each year without needing to work at a job that you hate.

That day I was 36, and my target had been missed by quite some margin. I was not rich. I had failed in the goal my 18-year-old self-had set for me - to be Financially Independent and Retire Early (FIRE) by having £1m by the age of 35.

After my redundancy I decided to rebalance my portfolio, this was the third and final law of money. This meant splitting my money between businesses (shares), some money in reserves (bonds and cash) and finally to invest into property.

Rather than waiting to afford an overpriced London property, I used money that I received from my redundancy I bought a small flat in Bristol, which needed a lot of work. This was the final piece of the jigsaw. I had split my money between land, business and reserves. I no longer stressed or worried about money. The ups and downs of the markets which caused countless sleepless nights became irrelevant. No matter what happened in the markets I would be alright.

I had discovered money mindset.

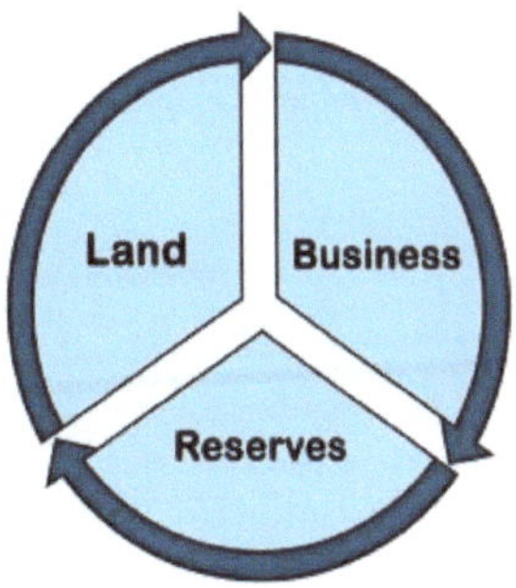

I may not have been free financially, but I was free mentally. Whereas before I would worry about spending too much, losing my money on the stock market, checking the news each morning to see if any big news story would affect any of the companies I had bought. Spending hours of time stressing and worrying about money.

Following the three laws of money accumulation meant I had mind space. I could think about the things that were important to me. I felt like I had hope and belief that was on track financially and heading towards a better life.

I had followed the three laws of money accumulation. I paid myself every month automatically into a diversified portfolio. When I first set this up, I thought there was no way I could afford this money to leave my account each month. However, after a while, I hardly noticed the money leaving my bank. I put 10% into a pension and 10% into an ISA. I got used to living on 80% of my earnings.

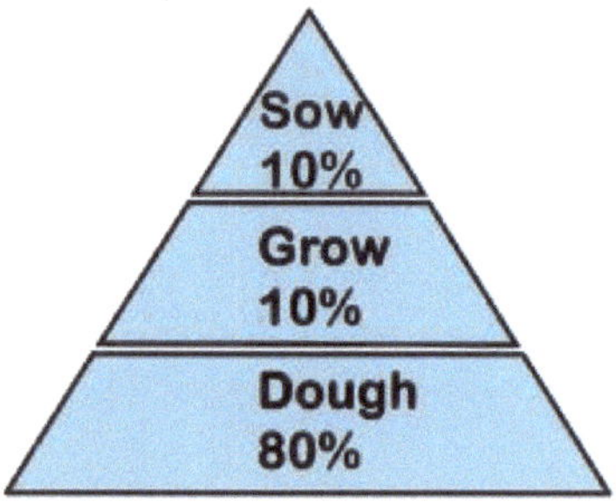

10% in pensions to sow for the future
10% to grow in ISAs
80% of your dough to spend on what you like

Standing outside the hospital, I realised it was not about 'retiring early'. What would I do with myself each day if I did have enough money not to work each day? Life was more about giving back, doing something meaningful, having a purpose and moving towards that goal daily.

In that moment I changed from wanting to be Financially Independent and Retire Early (FIRE) to wanting to be Financially Independent Seeking Happiness (FISH).

I realised that the purpose of life was to seek happiness.

Happiness = Purpose + Progress

To reach this goal of a happy and fulfilling life, then your mindset is key. Once you understand money mindset then you experience a greater level of calm and can enjoy a happy and joyful life. You realise that material possession is not what makes us happy and it is more about a circle of friends and family whom we trust and relate to emotionally. As well as finding a purpose that suits our strengths and passions we should aim to make a meaningful contribution to the world.

The goal of money mindset is improved happiness.

Perhaps it is a paradox that we should move towards happiness. That by doing this we lose the loves, hates and passions that take place spontaneously. We often think that happiness should be as unpredictable as thunder and lightning and as momentary as a rainbow.

Happiness depends on your sense of the world. The world of a happy person is different from the world of an unhappy person. They experience the world differently. The happy person is happy that your actions can affect things with your thoughts. If you act upon your plan you can take steps to improve things this can lead to happiness.

'Trying to capture happiness is the same as giving up on the beauty of wildflowers by the side of the road in favour of a formal garden. This is a romantic idea and shouldn't be discarded as romance is made for dreams and dreams are an essential ingredient of happiness.'

Edward De Bono, The Happiness Purpose

Today the wildflowers by the road will only grow if we take action by making an effort to grow them. We must ask ourselves in each moment, will this bring me happiness?

We are the authors of our own creation – a lead actor in our own film.

Having good money mindset means that you are not affected by the ups and downs of the markets. The markets are just a tool that you can use to create the life you want.

What is more exciting is that you get to be part of the money mindset movement. I have taken the baton from the greats from the past and I hope that you will take the baton from me and move forward in your investment journey.

'The world is my world, and the way I live determines its structure.'

Ludwig Wittgenstein (1889 –1951)

Ask yourselves 'Did I used this day as best as I could? Did today's actions bring me closer to my happiness? Humans have a seed of perfection that if nurtured can grow into the best version of ourselves, with our unique skills, talents and experiences. We need to understand ourselves and where our unique jigsaw piece fits in with the rest of the universe.

'Once the basic needs are met, the message is clear: We don't need more money, we don't need greater success or fame, or more stuff to consume – Right now, at this very moment, we have a mind, which is all the basic equipment we need to achieve complete happiness.'

The Dalai Lama, *The Art of Happiness*, 1998

Will this bring happiness? We need to move from suffering - where there is pain from things that are out of our control - to be responsible. This means we can proactively respond to something that affects us.

Focusing on what we are grateful for. This is owning yourself first.

The truth.

The truth is perhaps as important. We need to be true to ourselves. Being authentically you.

Ask yourself where can you make the greatest contribution? I was working in a job that was not making the best use of my skills and experiences. I was not being true to myself.

Henrik Ibsen, the Norwegian playwright calls the comforting story that we tell ourselves 'the vital lie'. This is the lie we all tell ourselves, which hides a painful truth of who we are.

By revealing the truth, you shine away from that one thing onto something else. Like shining a torch at the subject in a dark room, the subject lights up but the rest of the room then becomes dark.

The truth can come from knowledge. Knowledge comes from education and experience. The truth is the focus. Knowing what is important to you. What are your aims and objectives? Imagine the best version of yourself. What would that look like? Who would you be? Who do you want to become? Then shine your focus and energy on becoming that person.

To gain knowledge we need both experience and education.

Experience + Education = Wisdom

The highest form of knowledge is wisdom. Wisdom is where you can see yourself and something bigger than yourself. We don't just need to know ourselves, we need to BE ourselves. This is being authentic. It's coming to terms with the external world and still being ourselves. The ability to see yourself and the world. To not just know thyself but to be thyself.

You need to discover your purpose. The area where your unique talents can make a difference in the world. In Maslow's hierarchy of needs, this is becoming the self-actualised person. Maslow said this is to become everything that you are capable of becoming.

You can take action in this moment that will change the course of your life. Each decision can last decades either positively or negatively.

What is your purpose?

Something wasn't right in my gut. After my redundancy, I had retrained and was qualified as a Financial Adviser, running my financial planning practise, with my portfolio of clients. I wasn't happy with the work I was doing. I was comfortable but I had a feeling of emptiness.

I remember vividly as a client, with £15ms of assets I had been working with for months, finally signed the paperwork with his Montblanc fountain pen. I should have been delighted. But before the ink even dried on the contract, I had this weird feeling in my stomach that wasn't quite right. Helping rich people pay fewer taxes didn't seem the right thing to do. I started imagining how many schoolbooks could be bought or hospital beds could be provided with the £10,000s I would be saving the client paying in tax. I was taking that money away from libraries, hospital and schools.

I didn't feel right taking that money from people when all they needed was better education. I was not just taking their money, I was taking their freedom. Expensive fees would eat the foundations of their hopes and aspirations for the future like a termite eating the foundations of their dream home.

I was missing the fourth step in finding your Ikikai - a Japanese concept meaning the reason for being. It didn't fit with my purpose in life and I knew that in that moment that I could never be truly happy doing this for the rest of my life. I decided from that day to change from saving taxes for a rich few to helping as many people as possible with their money. I left my role as a Financial Adviser to set up my own money coaching company called Money Tipps to educate, inspire and coach people to invest for a happier life. I would empower people to make their own investment decision saving them £10,000s over a lifetime from paying an expensive adviser to give them specific financial advice

Ikigai gives you the reason you get up in the morning or the thing that you live for. Ikigai means the source of value in one's life or the things that make life worthwhile. It comes from a Japanese word meaning life and the results or fruits of our life.

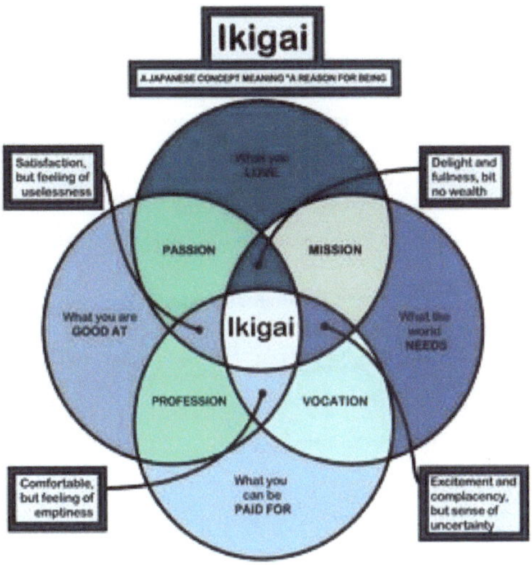

To work out your Ikigai you take what you're good at, what you can be paid for, what you love, and finally what the world needs. This will give you your Ikigai. What was your reason for getting up this Monday morning?

Do you know your Ikigai or purpose?

1) What are your strengths? Do you have specialised knowledge or skills? What are we good at? What skills do we have? Where have you many hours of deliberate practise or experience? What comes easily to you that is difficult for others?

2) Where is there a demand for services or a product? What problems do people need solving? Where will someone pay you for your time or services? Where are people experience pain or suffering? Where can you give someone massive pleasure or take away pain?

3) What are you passionate about. What subject do you light up when talking about it? What you would you enjoy talking about on a Saturday night or if you had a Saturday morning to yourself with nothing planned, what would you love to spend your time doing?

4) What does the world need? What one of the 17 UN goals could you solve? What's your 'big game'? Looking at the 17 United Nations goals is a good way to see 17 big problems that need solving today. Can you contribute to solving them?

Money Tipps is committed to providing good quality education, which is one of the UN 17 Goals.

When we look back at our lives on our death bed many years from today, have we lived for something?

Have we achieved a goal and lived a purposeful life? Whether it is improving a community garden patch, raising a child, or changing a social condition, it's important that we feel that we have made a difference. We have a decision in each moment to ask ourselves. Will this bring me happiness?

Your Purpose

What I was missing was that I felt like I wasn't contributing or giving back to the world. I asked myself: 'Where could I make the greatest contribution?'

How could I find my purpose and track my progress in achieving this goal?

I looked at my strengths and experience, where there was a demand or problems I could solve and what I enjoyed talking about on a Saturday night. Plus, what the world needed. What could I offer the world?

In that moment I had my Epiphany. I would share my Football Formation Asset Allocation with the world. This was my concept which I used to explain the complex Modern Portfolio theory (for which Harry Markowitz won a Nobel Prize in 1990) to my clients. The concept could explain the world of investing simply.

I created a card game, which made asset allocation and investing simple, fun and achievable. 90 minutes on the pitch can compare to 90 years of your life.

We all have a limited amount of time on the pitch of life.

Your purpose is the feeling you get when what you are doing is bigger than yourself. Where you are needed and that there is something better ahead to work for. Where you are good at what you do, and you can help others. Where you are your best self?

I could make the greatest contribution by improving financial education. I decided to start a money coaching company called Money Tipps (Tax, Investments, Property, Pensions, Savings). Money Tipps educates, inspires and coaches people to make their own money decisions. To be empowered to make their own decision saving them £1000s over their lifetime compared with expensive financial advice fees. This was my Ikigai.

Where can you make the greatest contribution? Where can you do your best work? Where can you solve other people's problem?

'At the start of your day, say I am ready for a day's work. As if I was going out to do what I was born to do.

The purpose for what I was brought into the world.

Was I created to wrap myself in blankets and keep warm? Were you born for all feeling and no action? Can you see the plants, birds, spiders and bees all doing their own work, each helping in their own way to order the world?

Marcus Aurelius (121 – 180 AD), *Meditations*

Self-Transcendence

To gain happiness we need to move up the hierarchy of needs. Think of it like climbing a ladder, progressing from our lower needs to a more evolved higher needs as each need is solved and then next more complex need emerges.

Maslow's hierarchy of needs has changed the way we think about human needs and wants from the basic needs up to higher needs. Maslow wrote about a final need, although it was not published in his original book This need was at the top of his triangle, above self-actualisation. He called it self-transcendence. This means seeing ourselves connected to something bigger than us.

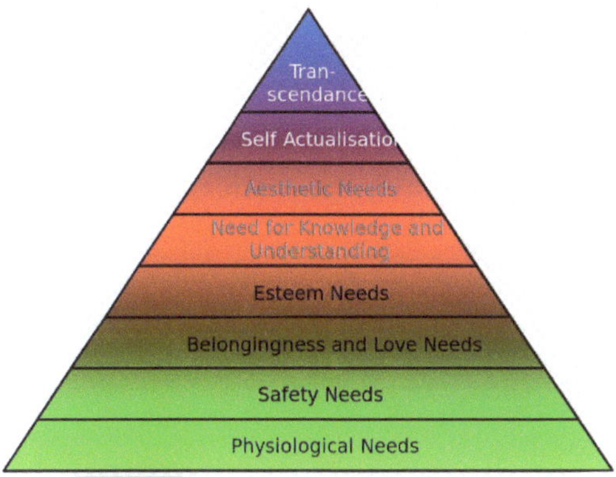

From Wikimedia Commons, the free media repository

Self-transcendence is considering yourself an integral part of something bigger than you. This may be a community, a city, or the cosmos. Once we meet our lower needs on Maslow's triangle a new, more complex need emerges.

As the evolution of species, there is also an evolution up the hierarchy of needs in our lifetime, moving up the pyramid, and can easily slip down if any of the lower needs are not met. This means that the tiny millennial snowflake is connected to everything else in the world. We are the micro and the universe is the macro.

We are all human beings. We are all being in this world and relate to everything just by the fact that we are all experiencing this world together. We all have our own unique experiences and take on the world. We all have a unique potential, like the acorn seed that could grow into the oak tree if given the correct conditions. We all have an essence that we could potentially be if we act and take our opportunities. Being authentic and bringing something new into the world. No one can be exactly like you. We all have individual experiences, personalities and education. We are all unique snowflakes that can have an impact on the world. We are all like a unique jigsaw piece that fits into the puzzle of the universe.

'Everybody's a genius. But if you judge a fish by its ability to climb a tree, it will live its whole life believing it is stupid'

Albert Einstein (1879 - 1955)

Why give away the Millennial Money Mindset formula? Something that has taken me years to craft. Why give away the 10-step investment journey and make it available to the general public for the price of a book. For people to copy and use themselves? I have charged £10,000s to clients in the past for this knowledge.

Many people advised me against writing this book. The financial advice company I worked for refused to allow me to release it. I was banned from publishing this book if I wanted to keep my job. I thought so many people could benefit from this knowledge. The company wanted to keep these strategies to themselves as they would make more profits. There are some experiences along my journey that have had a profound impact on me. I faced the possibility of dying a few years ago or at least realised that we are all here for a limited time. When you come to terms with your mortality it changes your perspective on things. It makes you think of your contribution, your legacy and your impact on the planet.

Don't get me wrong. I hope this book helps grow my business.

I have a bigger goal that goes beyond myself. A goal that is so big and out of the box that I am almost embarrassed to write it down for people to read it. It may seem impossible now. My vision is that the Millennial Money Mindset will change the lives of people across the world. I want to change the way investing is done throughout the world and possibly forever.

My vision is simple. To help people make better money decisions so they live happier lives

This is the reason for publishing this book. I started writing this book as I everything I would tell the 25-year-old version of myself. To share this knowledge with others to save them time, money, energy and stress and worry. However, I changed along the journey. I have grown my money mindset. I have changed from wanting to be Financially Independent Retire Early (FIRE). It changed to wanted to be Financially Independent and Seeking Happiness (FISH). We all want something better; we all want to be happy. This is the purpose of life.

<u>Our greatest resource is education</u>

Modern life is more complex than our ancestors could ever imagine, this means everybody needs to be highly educated. The point of education is the transfer of ideas of value, which will improve what we do with our lives. More education can only produce more wisdom.

'The most perfect education is to strengthen the body and form the heart. To enable the individual to gain habits of virtue as will render them independent'

Mary Wollstonecraft, *A Vindication of the Rights of Woman* (1792)

Education should be the key to everything. We need more than just training, or just information or just a diversion. What we are looking for is ideas to help them understand themselves and the world a little better. A sense of participation and purpose.

Investing is seen to be risky mainly because so few of the so-called investors know what they are doing. They may have the education but not the experience or perhaps the experience but not the knowledge.

Humans must experience something before we truly understand it. Imagine an apple. How would you describe it to someone who had never heard of such a fruit, let alone eaten one? Maybe before eating an apple we see a picture of this fruit. Do you fully understand it without picking up the apple and feeling skin, and then tasting it? How do you describe the taste of this apple to someone who has never tasted such a fruit? It is like trying to understand sex before losing your virginity or knowing how to be a parent before having children. Once you experience something new then things make sense at a higher level, we understand more, we know more, we become more.

Investing is commonly believed to be enormously risky and indeed it is if you are investing in untested markets like cryptocurrencies, biogenetics or perhaps if you only buy one company. Theoretically and mathematically investing should be the least risky thing you do. In a world that is changing faster than ever, the riskiest thing is not taking any risks.

To be a good investor we need methodology and follow well-known rules, rather than investing on perception and mood. Investing must be based on fundamental mathematics, evidence-based research, the scientific method and the laws of nature.

Investing in 'high risk' areas doesn't need to be high risk. It does need to be systematic; it needs to be managed and above all, it needs to be purposeful.

Today everyone needs to be an investor. Investing is a behaviour that can be taught and learnt, rather than a personality trait. Investing is a mindset.

Money Tipps gives away all the secrets that the Financial Services industry want to keep for themselves to make a greater profit. Money Tipps gives away all these secrets by providing good quality education because we believe in a better world. We believe that knowledge and education should not be for the privileged few that can afford the £100,000s in financial advice fees.

Money Tipps believe in a world where people don't stress about money, Money Tipps believe in a happier world, where people have enough assets to pay themselves an income that can last a lifetime, where you can focus on your purpose, what you were born to get up in the morning to do, where your talents, skills and experience can contribute and make a difference to others and the rest of the world.

To have Millennial Money Mindset by Following the three laws of money accumulation

1) Pay yourself first

2) Diversify

3) Re:Balance.

The Millennial

Come gather round, people wherever you roam
Admit that the waters around you have grown

You better start swimming or you'll sink like a stone.

Don't speak too soon as the wheel is still in spin.

For the loser now will later win.

The present now will later be past.

The order is rapidly fading.

The first one now will later be last.

The Times are changing.

Bob Dylan The Nobel Prize in Literature 2016

The rules have changed.

The rules have changed. And so must you.

The millennial often ridiculed for being a snowflake, melting at any sign of trouble. The baby boomer generation tells Millennials to stop buying lattes and avocado on toast to afford a home in London, not realising how unaffordable an average home is comparing to when they were young.

Maybe millennials are like a snowflake. Snowflakes are complex, beautiful and everyone is different. Each snowflake is different, unique and yet tantalisingly similar. Each having their own unique genius like an individual jigsaw piece that fits into the puzzle that is the universe. Snowflakes have a deeper beauty that contains in an idea that all the similarities and structure can explain the laws of nature. The universal laws can explain the complexity from a snowflake to the stars. From the micro millennial snowflake to the macro universe. Everyone and everything is connected. All is one and one is all. Like the pound coin in your back pocket is a tiny part of a huge system, you are a small part of the universe. Your individual decisions have an impact on the whole. How you decide to spend your pound coin is part of a million other decisions on money. Investing into a company for good, will have a consequence just like spending or investing in a company that does bad. We need to own ourselves first and take responsibility for our actions. We need to be proactive rather than reactive. Taking actions to improve our lives and the lives of others. From the micro to the macro. The small to the big. The snowflake to the stars.

'Each snowflake has the same building blocks, the same beautiful symmetrical forces of nature at their heart, the way they form are all different. No two snowflakes are alike as no paths through time are alike. So it is with snowflakes, stars, planets and people. Looking at a snowflake you see an underlying world, a deeper structure of nature itself. The universe is a snowflake. '

Brian Cox Forces of Nature

One individual snowflake make melt under heat or pressure yet two or more snowflakes together start to form a snowball. The snowball starts to accumulate over time growing quicker and quicker the more snowflake working together. Each snowflake may represent a moment in time yet together, a snowball can create a movement.

Being a Millennial does not have to mean you were born between 1980 and 2000s. Having a Millennial Money Mindset does not matter about your age. You can be 9-99 years old. A Millennial Money Mindset is an attitude. The Dictionary definition of a Millennial means it is relating to a period of a thousand years. We need to think to the next 1000 years and imagine about the world people will be living in in the year 3000. Societies flow and meander, progress and regress. We are still in the foothills of human development as practically every scientific and social discipline is revising the scope of evolution.

No snowflake ever falls in the wrong place

Zen proverb

Money

Millennial Money Mindset means being an owner. You are in charge! We are all investors today. If you have a pound coin in your pocket, then you are an investor, if you are employed in the UK, then you are automatically enrolled into a pension. This means you are an owner of hundreds of companies around the world. You need to take ownership of your own money in your pocket. To create your own little business. A small factory that we can craft and call our own. Every pound coin invested is like a worker for your factory. We need to become a creator and not a consumer. A producer of our own means of production and what we produce must be valuable to others. To create your own employment by servicing and giving something better to the world. Strive to become a master in your chosen endeavour. To create yourself out of nothing. Do more than you are paid for. To create something that will outlast you.

Every time you get paid then a part of that money is yours to keep. Every pound coin you keep is like a worker for you, who works tirelessly for you morning, noon and night.

Remember life is good. Enjoy it while you can. Live according to your income. Spend less than you earn and put money away as soon as you get paid.

Fortunes that comes quickly also will go quickly, anything of value takes time to grow. Money in your wallet feels gratifying yet loses money over time through inflation. Make your money multiply. Think long term at where you can make the greatest contribution. Money can increase rapidly when invested. Profit from the laws of money. Learn from people who have been successful before. Investing in land (the roof over your head), businesses (companies in the stock market) and keeping a third in reserves (bonds, cash of different currency including cryptocurrency and having, insurance to protect you from harm,).

Mindset. The rules have changed.

So, what is Money Mindset?

Money mindset is an attitude. Attitudes are the mirrors of the mind; they reflect our thinking. Your outer world is a reflection of your inner world. Your mindset becomes your reality and what you think about you become. Become the change, you want to see in the world and the world starts to change around you.

Just like nature, it may take time. Anything of value takes time to grow. You can't rush the oak tree out of the acorn. Nature has patience that good things will come, it's the courage to take action, it is a belief that things can be better. If you want the fruits you need the roots.

As above so below, as below so above.

We become what we think about most of the time. When we have a growth mindset of constant improvement, we can achieve more than previously believed. That we believe we can evolve or get better by forging a path every day, that gets us closer to our purpose or our essence of who we are and all that we can be.

Capacity (or how much we think we can achieve) is a state of mind, when you believe you can do more, your mind thinks creatively and shows you the way. Look at things not as they are, but as they could be. Visualisation adds value to everything. Good money mindset visualises what can be done in the future and is not stuck in the present or scared of the past.

There are two ways of looking at the world, a fixed mindset or a growth mindset. A fixed mindset, or limited point of view, means that we are born the way we are and there is no way of changing. A growth mindset describes the opposite, a mindset within which we can learn, grow and change. It is an attitude of nothing resting, everything moving everything vibrating and everything being in motion. Things can be better; we can improve, and we can contribute to other's growth. Through experience and education, we can learn new things and improve our lives.

The rules have changed. With these different times, we need different minds. These are chaotic and turbulent times. There is a rhyme to both reason and unreason. There is always a rhythm. Like a tide, everything flows in and out, there is sinking and arising. Everything changes and nothing remains still, like the flowing river you can't step into that same river twice. With all life, things are born, grow and then die, only to be reborn.

In this chaos lurks order and in deeper order lurks more chaos. Great ideas are forged in chaotic times. These ideas come from the right mindset. Max Weber the sociologist believed the rise of capitalism in the 17th century was due not to the technology but to a change in the spirit or a new attitude rather than the new technology, machinery or how people worked. For a change to our current system and a post-capitalism movement to take place where businesses focus on purpose and happiness rather than just profits, we need a new attitude or mindset. We need to create a conscious ecological model that balances the whole of the planet.

We often think that labour or work is exclusive to humans. When we look to a spider building its web it could easily resemble the work carried out by a weaver, and when we watch a bee and their work in the construction of their hive it could shame many human architects today. What distinguishes the worst architect from the bees and the spiders is that even the worst weaver or architects create the image in their mind first. We, humans, are conscious and can decide in this moment on the choice of action to take.

We decide on how we affect the universe in every moment we live.

Let's work for a new world, a better world. A decent world that allows people to do work they love, that gives youth a future and old age security.

Today you need to be responsible for the decision and choices you make every moment and every day. Responsible for your own actions and the consequences of your actions. Your actions have an equal and opposite reaction. Today we have more information and knowledge than ever before. Today we need to imagine a better future.

The rules have changed. Today you need to be proactive and make the tough decision about your future self. The normal consciousness with which we experience life does not give us a reliable picture of the world. This normal consciousness is like a kind of sleep. It creates an illusion of separation, going through the day on autopilot. Half asleep and out of control of yourself rather than being alive and feeling connected. We need to wake from our slumber. Wake up to the fact of the injustice of businesses that are only in business for profit and not purpose. Wake up to our loss of connection with nature and the environmental catastrophe we are facing. Wake up to the inequality many people face on a day to day basis. Wake up from the disconnect between Wall Street and main street from the City of London and the towns and villages across the United Kingdom. Understand that if humans don't change our ways that nature will continue, and it will be human beings that will be extinct.

The internet has changed everything. Rub our eyes as we wake up and see into the future. The worldwide web means what happens anywhere happens everywhere. This concentration of knowledge has meant that everything is connected to everything else. Today the internet has meant we can access information as easily as turning on a tap. Knowledge from the experts present and past. We need to use our imagination to create our future, a better future. Using technology to see further than we ever thought possible. Imagine putting on a pair of goggles for the first time and looking underwater and seeing a new world of possibilities.

To have an economy that is more like an ecology of nature rather than the efficiency of machinery, without losing our connection from nature. Not a utopia where everything is perfect, this is impossible as the only permanent thing is change. We should aim for a protopia where every day is a little better than the day before. Continuously improving today for a better tomorrow. Nature never hurries, little by little and atom by atom the work is completed. Today everything is becoming. We must imagine a better world.

The rules have changed. The money we spend influences the world we live in. The money we save and invest also influences the world. Pension funds are the savings of today's employees. These pension funds control huge pools of capital. This capital can be invested in companies that do good or companies that do bad. Since the pension freedom act in 2015 in the UK, you can choose how to access and invest your pension. You the people have the power to decide where these vast sums of capital are invested. You the people have the power to decide on a better future. We must use this power. We must invest for good rather than for bad. We must move away from the forever growth model and the age of mass consumption and move towards an economy like an ecology, a regenerative economy where everything is in balance. To learn from nature, to evolve and to rebalance.

It is about creating the future rather than consuming the past. To understand that everything is connected in ecological harmony. We should focus on the economic climate of long term growth rather than the economic weather and the daily fluctuations of the share price. The GDP measure that only tracks progress every quarter is not effective. The forever growth model is not sustainable, understand that the self and the economy is both distinct and a blended part of a larger compassionate whole. We need a holistic economy. An economy that creates rather than an economy that consumes itself.

Investing needs a metaphorical career change: We need a change from engineer to a gardener. We have lost our connection with nature. When we walk through a forest and hear no birds, we feel that something is missing. When we walk through a forest and hear the birds and see the butterflies flying above, we feel fuller and more alive.

The rules have changed. We have a choice to live in harmony, with a greater whole whilst knowing your purpose. Knowing what is enough can bring happiness, and happiness is the purpose of life. Once our basic needs are met the evidence is clear. We don't need more money, or more material possessions or fame. We have a mind and right now in this moment, we have all the equipment to achieve happiness. Rene Descartes began the Renaissance period when writing his famous phase 'I think therefore I am'. The French philosopher had it backwards. We are conscious human beings with a mind and therefore we think.

I am and therefore I think

To be alive is to be present in this moment. To be conscious of one's own self is the root of all things. Today we need to think with the more evolved part of the brain that makes us human beings. This change in mindset may begin a new renaissance period. A new way of thinking. A new great awakening not seen since the enlightenment period of the 17th Century. A new age of hope, courage, and belief.

When we can access fresh drinking water, when there is no hunger in our stomachs and when we have somewhere warm and safe to sleep, then we have the freedom to think. Human nature changes as the conditions of existence change. If we are worrying where the next meal is coming from, or how to pay the bill that just landed on the doormat then there is low mental bandwidth meaning a low ability to think. Meaning a low ability to make good decisions, to stick with our plans and resist temptations.

Better conditions mean we have time for better abstract thought, reasoning, and imagination. Time to think about how to solve the world's complex problem for the future. We can invest our time into work that fulfils and nourishes us, that taps into our individual genius and help solve other people's problems. The power to think is what creates humanity.

We cannot control the events in our lives, but we can control what those events mean. We can choose where to focus our thoughts. What we think we become. To tame the wild beast that is our subconscious mind, the ancient survival autopilot fight or flight mode, that fear and stress creates. Take control of your thoughts no matter what. Like a rider who must tame the horse, whose back they sit upon. Working together with the animal that sleeps within you can create something more powerful than you could dream possible. Working together with nature, to become interdependent with nature rather than independent from nature.

Descartes thought that the mind and body was separate. 'I am' he said, 'only a thinking thing, that is a mind, intellect or reason.'

However, we are more than that, we have a mind, a heart and we can breathe. We take a breath of air only because of the presence of trees in the world. We are interconnected with the rest of the world

The mind and body is not separate but a connected whole. All is one and one is all.

I can think, I can breathe, I can grow

Everything is becoming and changing. Nothing is permanent but change. We are all connected to everything else. Nothing stands still, we are born, grow and then die.

A forever happy life is impossible. Once we reach one need, a higher more complex need emerges, this is the beauty of life. The highest we can achieve is not a happy life but a heroic life. Become the hero. The hero's quest is one where you are not satisfied by a life of perpetual comfort and pleasure. A life that strives for each day to be meaningful, challenging, and exciting.

The meaning of life is to be alive. To think, to breath and to grow. The time to be alive is now

The Millennial has had more knockdowns than any other generation can remember. A jab in the face from the financial crash that we didn't cause, a right hook from an unfair political system, a punch in the gut from a housing market that has locked many out of owning our own home and in 2020 a global pandemic that has created uncertainty and instability for millions of people around the world.

But when we were close to defeat, we rise to our feet. As we look up from scrolling on our phones and look out into the cosmos to imagine a better world. We wake up and feel the earth beneath our feet on a planet travelling 67,000 miles per hour, we realise that human nature is not static, nor is it finite. It is abundant. Forever growing and forever providing. We can create new systems when we change our mindset and rules for living. To become conscious of oneself. We can wake from our financial slumber to create money enlightenment. In this financial awakening, we can have the courage to use our own understanding to make decisions for ourselves. The courage to use our own mind without needing to pay for financial advice. We must dare to know!

The rules have changed. The misery that is upon us is just the passing of time. The bitterness of men who are scared of future progress. Today it is you the individual who has the power. You the individual who has the tools in your hand to change how the world is run. You the individual have the pound coin from your back pocket, to change how companies are managed.

The rules have changed. Today it is the individual who can control and own these companies. We should live by each other's happiness, not their suffering. This life can be free and beautiful, a wonderful adventure. You can start the hero's quest of investing today. A hero is someone who gives their life to something bigger than themselves. You can be the hero of your own quest, the lead character in your own film. Reach inside your pocket and feel the pound coin between your fingers. This pound coin is a tiny part of a huge system, you are a small part of the universe. Each individual decision you make has an impact on the larger whole. You have the power to impact the world each pound coin you hold in your hand and every time you spend, save or invest.

Humans have lost our connection with nature. Nature is the principle that unites us all to all things. Nature out there is the same as nature within, everything in nature is reflected in ourselves. It is something to be worked on and improved. We have constructed the world and therefore we can change it. We must create wisely. We should not want to be exactly like nature, spontaneous, and constantly struggling. We must build on what is natural to make it better. To evolve and be the best human beings can be. We can harness the mind to improve ourselves. The mind is an asset able to create human morality, imagination, and innovation. We are the cause and the creator of our external world. The world outside reflects the world within. We become what we think about.

To each of us, there comes a moment in our lives, where we are figuratively tapped on the shoulder and asked to do something special, something unique to us and something fitted to their talents. What a tragedy if that moment, which could have been our finest hour, we find ourselves without the courage or belief that great things can happen to us too.

You must make this decision, you must use the pound coin from your pocket, you must invest.

Life is not a rehearsal. Miss enough precious moments and you'll miss a lifetime.

We need to change our mindset. We need to own ourselves first. We need Millennial Money Mindset

If you want the fruits you need the roots.

The good news is that you have already started to contribute, by purchasing this book. Money Tipps plant a tree for every book we publish and five trees for every money coaching package purchased.

We want to contribute to forests both in the United Kingdom and around the world. Our overarching mission is to help more people become financially independent and seeking happiness.

If you take one thing away from this book, then take one piece of action to help you make better decisions with your money.

If you found this book educational, or if it has helped you in any way, then please tell at least one person about this book or about Money Tipps as it helps us spread our message and helps our mission of providing good quality education.

If you have reached this far you have broken through the inertia of moving towards where you want to be financially. To continue this momentum, you need to take the next step. One way is to participate in a learning experience called Football Formation Asset Allocation. It contains a card game, online course, a life plan template, a cash flow forecast and workbook, where you track your goals, savings and investments. You will also receive a ticket to a live face to face masterclass, where you will be in an environment with like-minded people aiming for a better life. You will be with people who have a similar experience, struggles and challenges. This will mean you will learn much faster by being surrounded by your peers.

It's a five-step method to get money mindset, involving building your portfolio around a football team. I appreciate that you are busy, the aim is to teach you how to invest so you only need to spend 90 minutes a year managing your investment team (like a football game). Here is one of the players from your investing team the goalkeeper, which is the insurance (below):

MONEY TIPPS

Insurance

Goalkeeper

Growth	***1***
Risk	***3***
Access	***1***
Intelligence	***7***
Strength	***3***
Defence	***94***
Attack	***17***

The last line of defence is your goal keeper. Insurance protects you against the risk of bad things happening. Life insurance will pay your loved ones if you die. This could be used to buy a house or to pay for living expenses for your family. We all hope that nothing bad happens to us or our loved ones. Life is unexpected and life insurance gives your peace of mind that the worst things can happen and you will still be alright.

Money Mindset: The Five Step method.

01) OWN YOURSELF FIRST. BY BEING RESPONSIBLE, PROACTIVE AND PAYING YOURSELF EVERY MONTH AUTOMATICALLY

2) HAVE A CASH BUFFER (£1000 UP TO 3 MONTHS OF EXPENSES) TO COVER ANY EMERGENCIES

3) CREATE A LIFE PLAN AND WRITE DOWN YOUR FIVE YEAR GOAL

4) DIVERSIFY YOUR INVESTING AROUND THE FOOTBALL FORMATION ASSET ALLOCATION

5) REBALANCE YOUR PORTFOLIO ONCE A YEAR

This book is dedicated to my son Nathan; thanks for the hours of board game testing.

'A lovely Sunny day so I'll meet you at the Library gates.

Keats and Yates are on your side

While Wilde is on yours

So, we go inside, and we bravely read the books, all those lives where are they now?

With loves and hates and passions just like mine. They were born and then they lived and then they died. It seems so unfair and I wonder why?

You say that the sun rises, and you claim these words as your own, but I've read well, and I heard them said 100 times may be less may be more.

If you must write prose and poems
The words you use should be your own'

(Credit to) Steven Patrick Morrissey (1986)

If I have seen further, then it is by standing on the shoulders of giants. Or if I have seen clearer then it is by wearing glasses using the technology invented by others. If I have discovered truth this was by building on previous discoveries.

Special thanks to the UK library service where I have spent countless hours studying and researching thousands of books over the years. Thanks also to Brixton Library, West Norwood Library and Primrose Hill Library.

Referencing is an almost impossible task in 2020. We have access to millions of web pages written by thousands of people. I have been inspired and learn from hundreds of authors and speakers all who improved my work through their knowledge and wisdom. My goal was to help people make better decisions with their money and ultimately help as many people as possible. I have taken ideas from many different sources and I have done my best to include any sources which contributed to my work. If you feel that your book or webpage should be on this list, then please let me know and I will attribute your work. I intend to add to the vast body of work on Financial Literature and I can only hope that my contribution has made a difference to at least one person's life.

If anyone would like a more detailed breakdown and reviews of the books in Millennial Money Mindset: If You Want the Fruits you Need the Roots then please visit my YouTube channel Millennial Money Mindset or my Instagram page Millennial Money Mindset where I comment and review these books in more details and how they helped my work.

If you have found value in this book then please tell a friend about Millennial Money Mindset: If you want the fruits you need the roots. This movement can only be possible with the help of you.

Thank you so much for your time in reading this book. I hope that Millennial Money Mindset has improved your life in some way

References

Prologue

Office of national statistics

Bank of England .co.uk

Robert T. Kiyosaki, 1997, Rich Dad Poor Dad: What The Rich Teach Their Kids About Money That the Poor and Middle Class Do Not! Plata Publishing

LinkedIn Article '2019 is Crucial For Entrepreneurs' by Daniel Priestley

Rich Jenkins Independent newspaper article 28 May 2018 https://www.independent.co.uk/news/health/stress-causes-uk-money-worries-skin-health-a8372676.html

Peter Drucker 1 Nov. 1994 Publisher: Routledge Post-Capitalist Society
Peter Lynch 21 Aug. 2000 One Up On Wall Street: How To Use What You Already Know To Make Money In The Market Simon & Schuster

Thomas L. Friedman, 2007, The World is Flat: The Globalized World in the Twenty-first Century. Penguin

Lynda Gratton & Andrew Scott, 2016, The 100-Year Life Hardcover. Bloomsbury Information

George Monbiot, 2017, Out of the Wreckage: A New Politics for an Age of Crisis. Verso Books

Chapter 1

Derek Darby, Jane Vessey, Chrish Gilchrist, 2014, Investing Principles and Risk Ro2. The Chartered Insurance Institute

Adam Smith, 1776, Wealth of Nations. Publisher W. Strahan and T. Cadell, London

Adam Smith, 1759, The Theory of Moral Sentiments. Printed for Andrew Millar, in the Strand; and Alexander Kincaid and J. Bell, in Edinburgh

Joseph Stiglitz, 2012 The price of inequality by W.W. Norton & Company

David Bach, 2016, The Automatic Millionaire. Currency

Marcus Aurelius, 180 AD Meditations. Unknown

Lao Tzu, 4th century BC, Tao Te Ching. Publisher unknown

Issac Newton, 1687 Mathematical Principles of Natural Philosophy. Benjamin Motte publisher

George S. Clason, **1926** The Richest Man In Babylon. Penguin Books

Wallace D. Wattles, 1910 The Science of Getting Rich with How to Get What You Want. Elizabeth Towne Company

James Clear, 2018, Atomic Habits: An Easy & Proven Way to Build Good Habits & Break Bad Ones. Random House Business

Tony Robbins, 2017, Unshakable Your Financial Freedom Playbook. Simon & Schuster

M. J. DeMarco, 2011, The Millionaire Fastlane: Crack the Code to Wealth and Live Rich for a Lifetime. Viperion Publishing

Hermes Trismestigustus, 100 CE, The Corpus Hermeticum. Publisher unknown

Daniel Priestley, 2013, Entrepreneur Revolution: How to Develop Your Entrepreneurial Mindset and Start a Business that Works. Capstone;

Timothy Ferriss, 2009, The 4-Hour Workweek: Escape 9-5, Live Anywhere, and Join the New

Rich. Harmony

Escalator research https://www.bbc.co.uk/news/uk-england-london-39206856

Chapter 2

Steven Covey, 2004, The 7 Habits of Highly Effective People: Powerful Lessons in Personal Change. The Free Press

James Allen, 1903 As a Man Thinketh. CreateSpace Independent Publishing

T. Harv Eker, 2009, Secrets of the Millionaire Mind: Mastering the Inner Game of Wealth. HarperCollins

Tony Robbins, 2014, Money Master the Game 7 Simple Steps to Financial Freedom. Simon & Schuster
Napoleon Hill, 1937, Think and Grow Rich. The Ralston Society

Professor Michael Puett and Christine Gross-Loh, 2016, The Path. Penguin

Abraham H. Maslow, 1954, Motivation and Personality. Pearson

Dale Carnegie, 1936, How to Win Friends & Influence People. Simon & Schuster

Peter F. Drucker, 2008, Managing Oneself. Harvard Business Review

Sam Conniff, 2018, Be More Pirate: Or How to Take On the World and Win. Penguin

David J Schwartz, 2006, The Magic Of Thinking Big Paperback. Simon & Schuster

George Kinder, 1999, The Seven Stages of Money Maturity: Understanding the Spirit and Value of Money. Dell Publishing Co Inc.,U.S.

Peter F. Drucker, 1966, The Effective Executive. Routledge

The Dalai Lama , Howard C. Cutler, 1999 The Art of Happiness: A Handbook for Living. Hodder Paperbacks

Edward De Bono, 1990, The Happiness Purpose. Penguin

Research on lifetime earnings by Casumo .com , who commissioned the study in 2017

University of Michigan in 2013 by Stevenson and Wolfers on self reported happiness

Dotcom Secrets by Russel Brunson.

Chapter 3

Neal Lawson wrote in the book 'All consuming'

Frank Baum, 1900 The Wonderful Wizard of Oz. George M. Hill Company

The Wizard of Oz, 1939 Directed by Victor Fleming

George Monbiot, 2017, Out of the Wreckage: A New Politics for an Age of Crisis. Verso Books
Joseph Campbell, 1949 The Hero with A Thousand Faces. New World Library

Manley P. Hall, 1928, Secret Teachings of All Ages. Jeremy P Tarcher Publisher

Ralph Nelson Elliott, 1946, Nature's Law: The Secret of the Universe. Snowballpublishing

The Matrix , 1999 directed and written by the Wachowski's

Alice, Schroeder, 2009, The Snowball: Warren Buffett and the Business of Life. Bloomsbury Publishing

Robert Kiyosaki, 2000 The Rich Guide to Investing, What the Rich Invest in That the Poor and Middle Class Do Not! Warner Books

Daniel Priestley, 2017, 24 Assets: Create a digital, scalable, valuable and fun business that will thrive in a fast changing world. Rethink Press

Rav Ashi and Ravina II* 4th century, Talmund *(according to Wikipedia The Talmud is a compilation of sources and commentaries, compiled over a period of a few centuries. It is not a single written 'book' with a particular author although Rav Ashi and Ravina II have been given credit for their work).

Average house prices in London have risen 518% since 1994 from £79,000 for an average house up to a price of £488,000 today, According to the Office of national statistics

Guy Shrubsole 2019, Who Owns England?: How We Lost Our Green and Pleasant Land, and How to Take It Back. William Collins Publishers

Thomas J. Stanley and William D. Danko, 2010, The Millionaire Next Door: The Surprising Secrets of America's Wealthy. Taylor Trade Publishing

Study on self-reported happiness University of Michigan in 2013 by Stevenson and Wolfers

Russell Brand, 2014 Revolution. Century Publishing

Karl Marx, 1867, Das Kapital. Verlag von Otto Meisner

Goodwin, Nelson, Harris, 2009, Macro Economics in Context. M.E. Sharpe

Jim Rohn and Chris Widener, 2005, Twelve Pillars. Jim Rohn International

Russel Brunson, 2015, Dotcom Secrets. Morgan James Publishing

Helen Savage, Maria Shortland, 2017, R04 Pensions and Retirement Planning. Chartered Insurance Institute.

Chapter 4

M. J. DeMarco, 2011, The Millionaire Fastlane: Crack the Code to Wealth and Live Rich for a Lifetime! Viperion Publishing;

Brian Tracy, 2010, Goals!: How to Get Everything You Want -Faster Than You Ever Thought Possible. Berrett-Koehler Publishers

Edward C. Banfield, 1970 The Unheavenly City: The Nature And Future of Our Urban Crisis. Boston: Little, Brown and Company,

Peter F. Drucker, 1966, The Effective Executive. Routledge

George Kinder, 1999, The Seven Stages of Money Maturity: Understanding the Spirit and Value of Money. Dell Publishing Co Inc.,U.S.

Derek Darby, Jane Vessey, Chrish Gilchrist, 2014, Investing Principles and Risk Ro2. The Chartered Insurance Institute

Tim Ferriss, 2007, The 4-Hour Workweek: Escape 9-5, Live Anywhere, and Join the New Rich. Crown Business

Daniel Priestley, 2017, 24 Assets: Create a digital, scalable, valuable and fun business that will thrive in a fast changing world. Rethink Press

Simon, Herbert A., 1947, Administrative Behavior: A Study of Decision-Making Processes in Administrative Organization, first edition, New York: Macmillan.

Issac Newton, 1687 Mathematical Principles of Natural Philosophy. Benjamin Motte publisher

Chapter 5

Harry Markowitz, PORTFOLIO SELECTION, 1952, The Journal of Finance. Wiley Online Library.

Eugene F. Fama And Kenneth R. French , 2010 Size, Value, and Momentum in International Stock Returns. Fama-Miller Working Paper. Elservier

William Bernstein, 2000, The Intelligent Asset Allocator: How to Build Your Portfolio to Maximize Returns and Minimize. McGraw-Hill Education

James Tobin, 1980, Asset accumulation and economic activity : reflections on contemporary

macroeconomic theory. Basil Blackwell

Robert Kiyosaki, 1997, Rich Dad Poor Dad: What the Rich Teach Their Kids About Money That the Poor and Middle Class Do Not! Plata Publishing

Derek Darby, Jane Vessey, Chrish Gilchrist, 2014, Investing Principles and Risk Ro2. The Chartered Insurance Institute

Helen Savage, Maria Shortland, 2017, R04 Pensions and Retirement Planning. Chartered Insurance Institute.

Andy Couchman and Ron Wheatcroft, 2016, R05 Financial Protection. Chartered Insurance Institute

Carol College, Sonia Gable, David Harrowven, Tessa Roberts, 2016, R03 Personal Taxation. Chartered Insurance Institute

Tessa Roberts, Duncan Minty, 2016 R01 Financial Services, Regulations and Ethics. Chartered Insurance Institute

Ray Dalio, 2017, Principles: Life and Work. Simon & Schuster

_Adam Smith, 1776, Wealth of Nations. **Publisher** W. Strahan and T. Cadell, London

Chapter 6

Issac Newton, 1687 Mathematical Principles of Natural Philosophy. Benjamin Motte publisher

Leonardo of Pisa (Fibonacci), 1202, Liber Abaci. Publisher unknown

Nikolai D. Kondratieff, 1926, The Long Waves in Economic Life. Martino Fine Books

Charles Darwin, 1859, The Origin of the Species. publisher John Murray

Schumpeter, *1945,* Business Cycles, A Theoretical, Historical, and Statistical Analysis of the Capitalist Process. McGraw Hill Book Company

Schumpeter, 1942, Capitalism, Socialism and Democracy. Harper & Brothers

Steven Covey, 2004, The 7 Habits of Highly Effective People: Powerful Lessons in Personal Change. The Free Press

Three Initiates ,1908, The Kybalion: Hermetic Philosophy. Tarcherperigee

Simon, Herbert A., 1947, Administrative Behavior: A Study of Decision-Making Processes in Administrative Organization, first edition, New York: Macmillan.

From Wikimedia Commons, the free media repository

https://commons.wikimedia.org/wiki/File:Kondratieff_Wave.svg

Thomas Sowell, 2003, Basic Economics A Citizen's guide to the Economy. Basic Book

Neva Goodwin, Julie Nelson, Jonathan Harris, Brian Roach, James Devine, 2008 Macroeconomics in Context. Routledge

Paul Mason, 2015. Post Capitalism: A Guide to Our Future. Allen Lane

Tony Robbins, 2017, Unshakable. Simon & Schuster

Mark Douglas, 2000, Trading in the Zone. Nyif
Business cycles, wikipedia

https://en.wikipedia.org/wiki/Business_cycle

Kate Raworth, 2017, Doughnut Economics: Seven Ways to Think Like a 21st-Century Economist. Random House Business

Ralph Nelson Elliott, 1946 Nature's law: The secret of the universe (Elliott Wave). snowballpublishing.

LEONARDO DA VINCI EXHIBITION IN LONDON, 2019 LEONARDO DA VINCI: A LIFE IN DRAWING

Simon Sinek, 2009, Start With Why: How Great Leaders Inspire Everyone To Take Action. Penguin

Peter Drucker 1 Nov. 1994 Publisher: Routledge Post-Capitalist Society

The Four Seasons Poems, 2008, Edited by J.D McClatchy. Alfred A. Knopf

Ed Downs, 2000, 7 Chart Patterns That Consistently Make Money. Marketplace Books

Hyman Minsky, 2008, Stabilizing an Unstable Economy. McGraw Hill

Daniel Priestley, 2017, 24 Assets: Create a digital, scalable, valuable and fun business that will thrive in a fast changing world. Rethink Press (Dent Books)

Chapter 7

Derek Darby, Jane Vessey, Chrish Gilchrist, 2014, Investing Principles and Risk Ro2. The Chartered Insurance Institute

Julian Bray, 2015
, Economics of sea transport and international trade. Institute of Chartered Shipbrokers

George Kinder, 2000, The Seven Stages of Money Maturity: Understanding the Spirit and Value of Money in Your Life. Dell Publishing Co Inc

Vilfredo Pareto, 1935, The Mind and Society, Vol. 1: Trattato Di Sociologia Generale. Forgotten Books

Pete Matthew , 2018, The Meaningful Money Handbook: Everything you need to KNOW and everything you need to DO to secure your financial future. Harriman House.

Richard Koch, 2007, The 80/20 Principle: The Secret of Achieving More with Less. Nicholas Brealey Publishing Ltd

Chapter 8

Benjamin Graham, 1949, The Intelligent Investor, Harper

Daniel Kahneman, 2012. Thinking, Fast and Slow. Vintage

Richard H Thaler, 2009 Nudge: Improving Decisions About Health, Wealth and Happiness. Penguin

Steve Peters, 2012The Chimp Paradox: The Acclaimed Mind Management Programme to Help You Achieve Success, Confidence and Happiness. Ebury Digital

Daniel Priestly, 2013 , Entrepreneurial Revolution, Capstone

Robbie Burns, 2005, The Naked Trader: How anyone can make money trading shares. Harriman House

Chapter 9

Paul D Armson , 2016, Enough?: How Much Money Do You Need For The Rest of Your Life? CreateSpace Independent Publishing

Michael Puett and Christine Gross-Loh, 2016, The Path: A New Way to Think About Everything. Penguin

Jim Rohn, 2017, The Ultimate Jim Rohn Library. Nightingale-Conant

Danby Bloch, Carol College, Sonia Gable, David Harrowven, Tessa Roberts, 2016, R03 Personal Finance study text. Diploma in Regulated Financial Planning. Chartered Institute of Insurance.

Helen Savage, Maria Shortland, 2017, R04 Pensions and Retirement Planning. Diploma in Regulated Financial Planning. Chartered Institute of Insurance.

Derek Darby, Jane Vessey, Chrish Gilchrist, 2014, Investing Principles and Risk Ro2. The Chartered Insurance Institute

Chapter 10

Kate Raworth, 2017, Doughnut Economics: Seven Ways to Think Like a 21st-Century Economist. Random House Business

Burton G Malkiel, 1973, A Random Walk Down Wall Street : The Time-Tested Strategy for Successful Investing. W. W. Norton & Company

Hyman Minsky, 2008, Stabilizing an Unstable Economy. McGraw Hill.

Joseph Stiglitz, 2013, The Price of Inequality. Penguin Books

Money Advice Service blog written by Andy Webb

https://www.moneyadviceservice.org.uk/blog/millions-at-risk-with-savings-of-100-or-less

Jonathan Davis, 2017, The Investment Trust handbook 2018. Harriman House (evidence on rebalancing by Forbes)

Adam Smith, 1759, The Theory of Moral Sentiments. Printed for Andrew Millar, in the Strand; and Alexander Kincaid and J. Bell, in Edinburgh

Lao Tzu, 4th century BC, Tao Te Ching. Publisher unknown

Mary Wollstonecraft, 1792 A Vindication of the Rights of Woman. Penguin Books

Derek Darby, Jane Vessey, Chrish Gilchrist, 2014, Investing Principles and Risk Ro2. The Chartered Insurance Institute

Rav Ashi and Ravina II* 4th century, Talmund *(according to Wikipedia The Talmud is a compilation of sources and commentaries, compiled over a period of a few centuries. It is not a single written 'book' with a particular author although Rav Ashi and Ravina II have been given credit for their work).

Steven Covey, 2004, The 7 Habits of Highly Effective People: Powerful Lessons in Personal Change. The Free Press

Steven Johnson, 2001, Emergence The connected lives of ants, brains, cities and software. Penguin Books

E.F Schumacher, 1974, Small Is Beautiful. A study of economics as if people mattered. Abacus

Eben Pagan, 2019 Opportunity: How to Win in Business and Create a Life You Love. Hay House.

Joseph Rowntree Foundation definition on poverty

https://www.jrf.org.uk/our-work/what-is-poverty

Friedrich Hayak

https://en.wikipedia.org/wiki/Friedrich_Hayek

Tony Robbins, 2017, Unshakable Your Financial Freedom Playbook. Simon & Schuster

Simon Singh, 2011, Fermat's Last Theorem. Harper Perennial.

Chapter 11

Yuval Noah Harari, 2015, Sapiens: A Brief History of Humankind. Vintage

Yuval Noah Harari, 2017, Homo Deus: A Brief History of Tomorrow. Vintage

King Canute and the tide

https://en.wikipedia.org/wiki/King_Canute_and_the_tide

Naomi Klein, 2014, This changes everything. Publisher Simon & Schuster

Gernot Wagner and Martin Weitzman, 2015, Climate Shock: The Economic Consequences of a Hotter Planet

Max Roser, Population growth

https://commons.wikimedia.org/wiki/File:World_population_growth,_1700-2100,_2019_revision.png

Roger S Ulrich, 1984, View Through a Window May Influence Recovery from Surgery. Science 224(4647):420-1. PubMed

Rachel Botsman, Roo Rogers, 2010, What's Mine Is Yours: The Rise of Collaborative Consumption. HarperCollins

E O Wilson, 2007, The Creation: An Appeal to Save Life on Earth. W. W. Norton & Company

Schumacher, 1973, Small is Beautiful: A Study of Economics as if People Mattered. Blond & Briggs Ltd

Steve Hilton , 2016 More Human: Designing a World Where People Come First. PublicAffairs

Thomas Robert Malthus, 1798, An Essay on the Principle of Population. W. W. Norton & Company

Hans Rosling;Ola Rosling;Anna Rosling Rönnlund , 2018, Factfulness: Ten Reasons We're Wrong About The World - And Why Things Are Better Than You Think. Sceptre

Kate Raworth, 2017, Doughnut Economics: Seven Ways to Think Like a 21st-Century Economist. Random House Business

https://commons.wikimedia.org/wiki/Category:Doughnut_(economic_model)#/media/File:Doughnut_(economic_model).jpg

Kate Raworth Doughnut Economics

Peter F. Drucker, 1994, Post-Capitalist Society. Routledge

Ikegai concept

https://en.wikipedia.org/wiki/Ikigai

World Economic Forum, 2019, Carbon Brief

Abraham H. Maslow, 1954, Motivation and Personality. Pearson

Research published in the journal Science by J. Poore and T. Nemecek. Carried out at University of Oxford

In 2019, 'developed' nations meat consumption reached an all-time high' According to the USA department of agriculture,

Georg Wilhelm Friedrich Hegel, 1807, the Phenomenology of Spirit. Oxford University Press

Charlie Chaplin, 1940, The Great Dictator,

United Nations Sustainability Goals

https://www.un.org/sustainabledevelopment/sustainable-development-goals/

Steven Covey, 2004, The 7 Habits of Highly Effective People: Powerful Lessons in Personal Change. The Free Press

Daniel Priestley, 2017, 24 Assets: Create a digital, scalable, valuable and fun business that will thrive in a fast changing world. Rethink Press

Extinction rebellion emblem inspiration for the 7 habits of a better world

https://en.wikipedia.org/wiki/Extinction_symbol

Kaizen definition

https://en.wikipedia.org/wiki/Kaizen

Charles Darwin, 1859, On the Origin of the Species. Empire Books

Herbert Spencer, 1860, First Principles. Adamant Media Corporation

Marcus Aurelius, 161–180 CE Meditations. Penguin Classics

Daniel Priestley, 2013, Entrepreneur Revolution: How to develop your entrepreneurial mindset and start a business that works. Capstone

Make My Money Matter non-profit organisation

https://makemymoneymatter.co.uk/

Epilogue

Carol Dweck , 2012, Mindset: How You Can Fulfil Your Potential. Robinson

George Clason, 1926, The Richest Man in Babylon. BN Publishing

Carlo Rovelli, 2018,The Order of Time. Allen Lane

Seneca, 50 AD, On the Shortness of Life. Penguin

Martin Heidegger, 1927, Being and Time. Wiley-Blackwell

Then and now, YouTube channel

Timothy Ferriss , 2007 The 4-Hour Workweek: Escape 9-5, Live Anywhere, and Join the New Rich. Harmony.

Edward De Bono, 1990, The Happiness Purpose. Penguin

Abraham H. Maslow, 1954, Motivation and Personality. Pearson

Brendon Burchard, 2011, The Millionaire Messenger: Make a Difference and a Fortune Sharing Your Advice. Simon & Schuster

Ryan Levesque , 2015, Ask: The Counterintuitive Online Method to Discover Exactly What Your

Customers Want to Buy...Create a Mass of Raving Fans...and Take Any Business to the Next Level.

Dunham Books

The Dalai Lama , Howard C. Cutler, 1999 The Art of Happiness: A Handbook for Living. Hodder Paperbacks

Karl Marx, 1867, Das Kapital. Verlag von Otto Meisner

Hermes Trismestigustus, 100 CE, The Corpus Hermeticum. Publisher unknown

Ikegai concept

https://en.wikipedia.org/wiki/Ikigai

Mary Wollstonecraft, 1792 A Vindication of the Rights of Woman. Penguin Books

Peter Drucker, 1966, The Effective Executive: The Definitive Guide to Getting the Right Things Done. HarperCollins Publishers

A list of books that were influential to my writing, which I may or may not included in the chapter breakdown

The Theory of Moral Sentiments by Adam Smith

FCA Guides R01 – R06 Financial Planning Textbooks

The 7 Habits of Highly effective people by Steven Covey

An Essay on the Principle of Population by Thomas Malthus

Start with Why by Simon Sinek

Capital by Karl Marx

The Great Big Success Quote Book by Cameron Clark

Emergence by Steven Johnson

The Snowball Warren Buffet and the Business of Life by Alice Schroder

How to Win Friends and Influence People by Dale Carnegie

The Four Seasons Poems by Alfred Knopf

No Logo by Naomi Klein

The E-Myth by Michael Gerber

How to Get Rich by Felix Dennis

The Big Short by Michael Lewis

The Effective Executive by Peter Drucker

World Order by Henry Kissinger

One up on Wall Street by Peter Lynch

On the Shortness of Life by Seneca

The Black Swan by Nassim Nicholas Taleb

Postcapitalism: A Guide to our Future by Paul Mason

The Intelligent Investor by Benjamin Graham

The Science of Getting Rich by Wallace D. Wattles

The Undercover Economist by Tim Harford

The Under Cover Economist Strikes Back by Tim Harford

The Seven Stages of Money Maturity by George Kinder

Dotcom Secrets by Russel Brunson.

The Kybalion Hermetic Philosophy by Three Initiates

The Four-Hour Work Week by Timothy Ferriss

The Magic of Thinking Big by David Schwartz

Key Person of Influence by Daniel Priestley

Innovation and Entrepreneurship by Peter Drucker

The Hard Thing About Hard Things by Ben Horowitz

The Investment Trust Handbook 2018 by Jonathan Davis

The Naked Trader by Robbie Burns

Value Based Financial Planning by Bill Bachrach

Twelve Pillars by John Rohn and Chris Widener

Factfulness by Hans Rosling

The Meaningful Money Handbook by Pete Matthews

Emotional Intelligence by Daniel Goleman

Small is Beautiful by E.F Schmacher

Kakebo The Japanese Art of Saving Money by Hani Motoko

More Human by Steve Hilton

Climate Shock by Gernot Wagner and Martin Weitzman

24 Assets by Daniel Priestley

Lean in by Sheryl Sandberg

The PowerHouse by Steve Levine

Doughnut Economics by Kate Raworth

The 100 year life by Lynda Gratton and Andrew Scott

Expert Secrets by Russell Brunson

Branding Small Businesses for Dummies by Raymond Aaron

Rethinking the Economics of Land and Housing by Josh Ryan-Collins, Toby Lloyd and Laurie Macfarlane

The Secret Teaching of All Ages by Manly P. Hall

A Random Walk Down Wall Street by Burton. G Malkiel

Opportunity by Eban Pagan

Nature's Law by R.N Elliot

Real Estate Riches by Dolf De Roos

Rich Dad's Retire Young Retire Early by Robert Kiyosaki

The Money Diet by Martin Lewis

Phishing for Phools by George Akerlof and Robert Shiller

Irrational Exuberance by Robert Shiller

The Wealthy Investor by Bernice Cohen

All that Is Solid by Danny Dorling

Elon Musk by Ashlee Vance

The Joy of Tax by Richard Murphy

David and Goliath by Malcolm Gladwell

Outliers by Malcolm Gladwell

Tipping Point by Malcolm Gladwell

Selecting Shares that Perform by Koch Gough

The Zulu Principle by Jim Slater

The Rich Guide to Investing by Robert Kiyosaki

Prophecy by Robert Kiyosaki

Financial Freedom by Grant Sabatier

The Happiness Purpose by Edward DeBono

To Sell is Human by Daniel Pink

Drive by Daniel Pink

The Secrets to Winning Office Politics by Marie McIntyre

Interpreneur by Simon Coulson

Trading in the Zone by Mark Douglous

The Lean Start up by Eric Ries

Beyond the 4% Rule: The Science of Retirement by Abaham Okusanya

What's Mine is yours by Rachel Botsman and Roo Rogers

Enough by Paul D Armson

Managing Oneself by Peter Drucker

The Principles of Scientific Management by Frederick Winslow Taylor

Philosophiæ Naturalis Principia Mathematica by Issac Newton

A Vindication of the Rights of Woman by Mary Wollstonecraft

Quantum Mechanics by Jim Al-Khalili

Nudge by Richard Thaler

The Blind Watchman by Richard Dawkins

The Selfish Gene by Richard Dawkins

The God Delusion by Richard Dawkns

The Great Crash 1929 John Kenneth Galbraith

Revolution by Russell Brand

The Origin of the Species by Charles Darwin

The Art of Happiness by The Dalai Lama and Howard Cutler

Blue Ocean Strategy by Chan Kim and Renee Mauborgne

The Ultimate Jim Rohn Collection by Jim Rohn

Deep Work by Cal Newport

Mindset by Carol Dwerck

The Creation by E.O Wilson

The Drucker Lectures by Peter Drucker

Think and Grow Rich by Napoleon Hill

Your Secret Wealth by Jay Abraham

The 10X Rule by Grant Cardone

Who Owns England? By Guy Shrubsole

Ikigai: The Japanese Secret by Hector Garcia and Francesc

Real Magik: Ancient Wisdom by Dean Radin

12 Rules for Life by Jordon Peterson

Money: Know more make More by Rob Moore

High Performance Habits by Brendon Burchard

Ask: The Counterintuative online Formula by Ryan Levesque

The Dip by Seth Godin

This is Marketing by Seth Godin

Tribes by Seth Godin

Guns, Germs and Steel by Jared Diamond

The One Thing by Gary Keller

Contagious by Jonah Berger

Sell or Be Sold by Grant Cardone

Unscripted: Life Liberty and the Pursuit of Entrepreneurship by MJ DeMarco

The Millionaire Fastlane by MJ DeMarco

Oversubscribed by Daniel Priestly

Crushing it by Gary Vaynerchuk

Jab, Jab Right Hook by Gary Vaynerchuk

Atomic Habits by James Clear

The Chimp Paradox by Steve Peters

The Intelligent Asset Allocation by William Bernstein

Principles by Ray Dalio

Talk like Ted by Carmine Gallio

The Order of Time Carlo Rovelli

Critique of Pure Reason by Immanuel Kant

Being and Time Heidegger

Unshakable by Tony Robbins

Homo Deus By Yuval Noah Harari

Sapiens by Yuval Noah Harari

Tao Te Ching by Lao Tzu

Out of the Wreckage by George Monbiot

The Paradox of Choice by Barry Schwartz

Rise of the Robots by Martin Ford

Rational Optimist by Matt Ridley

Why Nations Fail by Daron Acemoglu

Rooftop Revolution by Kevin Pierce

Be More Pirate Sam Conniff

Asset Accumulation and Economic Activity by James Tobin

All-consuming by Neal Lawson

The Wonderful Wizard of Oz by L. Frank Baum,

The Hero with a thousand Faces Joseph Campbell

Talmud Religious Text

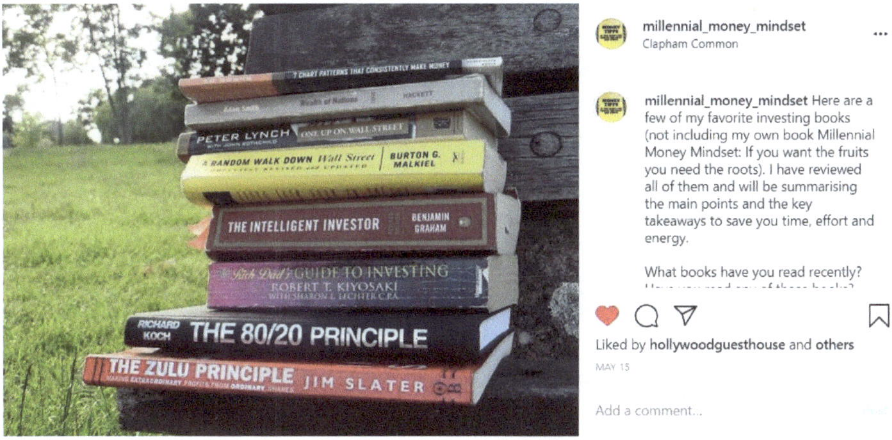

Economists I researched their work from Wikipedia

Eugene F. Fama

William F. Sharpe

Harry Markowitz

James Tobin

Herbert A. Simon

Milton Friedman

Friedrich Hayek

Simon Kuznets

Paul Samuelson

Paul Krugman

Elinor Ostrom

Robert J. Shiller

YouTube Channels

The School of Life YouTube Channel

Then and Now YouTube channel

Academy of Ideas YouTube channel

CPSIA information can be obtained
at www.ICGtesting.com
Printed in the USA
LVHW071759150921
697892LV00001B/17

9781916054554